TAKE
BACK
THE
GAME

TAKE BACK THE GAME

HOW MONEY AND MANIA ARE RUINING KIDS' SPORTS— AND WHY IT MATTERS

LINDA FLANAGAN

PORTFOLIO | PENGUIN

PORTFOLIO / PENGUIN
An imprint of Penguin Random House LLC
penguinrandomhouse.com

Most Portfolio books are available at a discount when purchased in quantity for sales promotions or corporate use. Special editions, which include personalized covers, excerpts, and corporate imprints, can be created when purchased in large quantities. For more information, please call (212) 572-2232 or e-mail specialmarkets@penguinrandomhouse .com. Your local bookstore can also assist with discounted bulk purchases using the Penguin Random House corporate Business-to-Business program. For assistance in locating a participating retailer, e-mail B2B@penguinrandomhouse.com.

Library of Congress Cataloging-in-Publication Data
Names: Flanagan, Linda (Journalist), author.
Title: Take back the game : how money and mania are ruining kids' sports-and
    why it matters / Linda Flanagan.
Description: [New York] : Portfolio/Penguin [2022] |
    Includes bibliographical references and index. |
Identifiers: LCCN 2022014464 (print) | LCCN 2022014465 (ebook) |
    ISBN 9780593329047 (hardcover) | ISBN 9780593329054 (ebook)
Subjects: LCSH: Sports for children—Economic aspects—United States. |
    Sports for children—Social aspects—United States.
Classification: LCC GV709.2 .F538 2022 (print) |
    LCC GV709.2 (ebook) | DDC 796.083—dc23/eng/20220506
LC record available at https://lccn.loc.gov/2022014464
LC ebook record available at https://lccn.loc.gov/2022014465

Printed in the United States of America
1st Printing

BOOK DESIGN BY FINE DESIGN

To my mother and first coach,

Carol Head, whose strength and

warmth taught me how to be

CONTENTS

Author's Note   xi

Introduction   xiii

Part I

**How the Game Changed When
We Weren't Looking**   1

Chapter 1

Money   3

Chapter 2

The Stakes (and Status)   27

Chapter 3

College   44

Part II

The Six Paradoxes of Youth Sports Today   *61*

Chapter 4

The Myth of Character Building   *65*

Chapter 5

The Parent Trap   *79*

Chapter 6

Body Slam   *92*

Chapter 7

Lonely at the Top   *107*

Chapter 8

The Trouble with Coaches   *122*

Chapter 9

The Connection Conundrum   *136*

Part III

Taking Back the Game   *159*

Chapter 10

What Parents Can Do   *161*

Chapter 11

How Coaches Can Help   *187*

Chapter 12

Reform Opportunities Post-Pandemic:
Bold Models and Ideas that Work   *211*

Conclusion   *237*

Acknowledgments   *243*

Notes   *247*

Index   *273*

AUTHOR'S NOTE

To protect the privacy of the girls I coached, I have deliberately changed their names and altered identifying details about them and their families. I have done the same with specific individuals who requested anonymity, as well as the scads of boys and girls who cycled through our family home or populated my son's teams. I've kept their unwitting parents out of it, too. It might be helpful to bear in mind that most anyone referred to by first name alone is a pseudonym. If I included a first and last name, that person has agreed to be publicly identified. I also use the pronouns he/him and she/her interchangeably.

My goal throughout has been to tell the truth: about becoming an athlete myself; about rearing a young jock in a sports-obsessed community; and about bringing along another generation of runners in an unfamiliar world. I've also strived to be clear in showing how the youth sports ecosystem has affected families, communities, and individuals, for better and worse.

INTRODUCTION

The kid was on fire. He crisscrossed between opponents, dribbled left-handed, and snatched balls away from unsuspecting players. One minute he was knifing through a gang of defenders clumped awkwardly around the opposing basket and reaching up for a lefty layup; the next he was sending laser passes crosscourt to a teammate with good hands. Other boys seemed trapped in amber, while this kid danced circles around them.

"Go, Paul!" I yelled cheerfully. Paul, I should say, is my son, and I was thrilled to see him lighting up the court.

It was a Saturday morning in January, and my husband and I were perched on wooden bleachers in an elementary school gym watching our youngest child dominate another youth basketball game. The gym was stuffy and smelled vaguely of paste and dust, and Paul was drenched in sweat. Always an enthusiastic player, he dazzled that morning, darting around at warp speed and playing all roles on the team: racking up points, stealing lazy passes, grabbing rebounds, rallying his teammates.

"That kid must have older siblings at home to play with," a man sitting behind us growled to his wife.

When the game ended, Paul loped over to us on the bleachers. Other kids heading toward their own parents called out to him, "Great game, Paul!" One of his teammates gave him a sturdy pat on the back along with the congratulations. "Hey, nice game," a man said. As we all walked out of the gym together, adults and kids glanced over at us. I draped my arm around Paul's narrow damp shoulder and lifted my chin. My husband, Bob, did the same. Swooning with pride, we marched out to the car in the school parking lot and glanced around for others eager to congratulate us. (*Us?*)

For the next hour or so at home, we huddled around the kitchen table and rehashed the game, recounting Paul's star turns and quizzing him on what he was thinking at the time. While we were at it, I prepared a thick peanut butter and honey sandwich, no crusts, and handed him a tall glass of chocolate milk. Meanwhile, our two older kids, neither of whom would be caught dead watching their little brother play basketball, were splayed out on the soft brown couch in the family room, still in their pajamas, drunk on *Full House*. Except for the disenchanted siblings, that postgame powwow was an intoxicating, self-congratulatory lovefest.

Something had come over me as I observed my child shine on the court. It would come over me again, later, when Paul excelled on the baseball and soccer fields, too. It was pride, irrational happiness, self-satisfaction (*self?*), joy—a surprising, if unspoken, elevation of standing in the community.

Even then, I knew it was weird—a tiny bit shameful (and possibly extremely lame). I recalled how my parents had engaged with my four siblings and me when I was growing up. While they had encouraged our athletic pursuits, carting us to practice and attending games when they could, they hadn't attached their psyches to our performance; their work, friendships, and other adult responsibilities took precedence. Our games were mindless diversions and an afterthought to their fuller and more complicated lives. But their indifference didn't feel like a deficit of love. Rather, it signaled that my games were my endeavor and that their affection for me—for all my siblings—was independent of what we achieved in sports.

Something had changed. I couldn't figure out why Paul's athleticism seemed to matter so much to me, and why kids' sports animated everyone in my orbit. But I felt that pull from his earliest days. And by the look of the fields around town, all of them cluttered with children dressed in uniforms and ready to play, other parents felt that pull, too.

These motherly intuitions about sports' inflated role were confirmed after I became a high school cross-country coach. When I stepped outside the gym that first morning, energized and wide-eyed about sharing my sport with the teenage girls gathered around me, I had no clue what was to come. It took about three weeks for the combustible nature of youth sports to reveal itself. All around me, parents and coaches began to squabble—over practice schedules, playing time, and who did or didn't make the team. The athletic director, God bless him, appeared to spend the first half of his day talking mothers and fathers off the ledge, and the second half advising coaches on how to break bad news to unhappy kids. In short order, my own inbox began to fill with requests from runners (or their parents) pleading for special dispensation: *Can I train on grass instead of pavement? May I leave practice early tomorrow for math tutoring?* The sports themselves, with all the complicated gifts they can bring, rarely entered the conversation.

Running has long been a font of pleasure for me, and not merely for the daily dose of dopamine it sends sloshing through my brain. It's the friendship and camaraderie nurtured over hard runs, sometimes in the foulest conditions, that have made the sport so meaningful to me.

When my children were young, I used to meet a posse of fellow women runners every Tuesday at eight thirty to tackle a workout collectively. One especially memorable morning, when we took a left out of the parking lot and headed toward Woodland Avenue, rainwater was already burbling out of potholes on Butler Parkway from the previous night's storm. It still hadn't let up, and the chilly air and drenching rain made the outdoors raw and miserable. It was the kind of day that made even mall walking unappealing, because the trek from the parking lot to the front doors would be enough to soak you. But there we were, a gang of eight middle-aged women runners of varying experience and ability, heading for the hill we'd vowed to run up, again and again, as part of our training for upcoming races.

We clung to the left side of the road and splashed our way over to the base of the hill, about two miles from where we began. Dead leaves had dammed the sewers, forcing the rain into angry rivers that swamped our shoes. Before long, the cheap cotton gloves I'd thrown on at the last minute were saturated, and my fingers started to stiffen. The rain and wind turned up the volume outside, stifling normal conversation.

"How many sixty-second hills are we supposed to do today?" Anne shouted to me on the way over.

A car swerved around us and honked disapproval. When we started the first of our hill repeats, several drivers speeding down the road seemed to gawk at our insouciance. What the hell were we thinking? We headed up the hill in groups of two, pumping our arms, gasping for oxygen at the steepest part halfway up, and striving to cover more ground in this burst than the one before.

"Looking good," Anne Marie yelled to runners slaloming up as she worked her way down.

Archie and Marianne clapped twice when Anne and I slopped past them.

"You got this," I called out in return.

Apart from my run years ago during a minor hurricane, or my very short (and foolish) training run in negative-forty-degree weather during college, the conditions on the day of these hill repeats were some of the bleakest I'd experienced. But when the workout was over, after I'd fled to the hot shower and dried my hair and reclaimed my normal body temperature, the warm bliss of human connection crowded out any

memories of the bitter, driving rain. I'd never felt closer to those women—
to Anne, Monica, Archie, Linda, Dawne, Anne Marie, and Marianne—
than I did after that inhospitable run against the elements and our own
bodies. Even today, twenty years later, I remember the profound satisfaction that came with triumphing over the unforgiving slope of Woodland
Avenue during a low-grade monsoon, all of us bound together by purpose and mutual affection.

Sports can do this for you.

But the changes that were occurring in youth sports—and by that,
I mean organized athletics for children of all ages, through high
school—were undermining their purpose. While no one was looking,
when we grown-ups were busy building our own lives and tending our
own families, kids' sports took a turn. These shifts became apparent to
me while watching my son play, and became unavoidable the longer I
coached.

"Most people are oblivious to the dramatic changes that have taken
place in youth sports during the last twenty years," Jay Coakley told
me. Coakley is widely considered the country's preeminent sociologist
of sports; though retired, he continues to write, deliver speeches, and
work behind the scenes to improve the culture of youth sports. "The
stakes have changed so dramatically, but most people are ignoring them,"
he said.

What changed?

The first is commercialism, a function of businesses large and small
that spotted an opportunity for profit in youth sports and sold it to eager and worried parents who wanted to give their kids an edge. Realizing that Mom and Dad would spare no expense when it came to their
children's athletic prospects, private companies and entrepreneurs began to invest heavily in youth sports. Since the 1970s, when public investment in community sports dwindled, and private companies filled
the gap, kids' athletics have grown into a multibillion-dollar industry.
Author Michael Lewis, who wrote the definitive account of Wall Street

culture in *Liar's Poker*, has compared the business of youth sports to "the market for addictive drugs": unregulated, full of desperate actors, and fueled by money.

Another beneath-the-surface transformation in youth sports is related to large, imperceptible cultural shifts that also began in the mid-1970s and altered the way parents engage with their children. Economic decline, climbing divorce rates, and exaggerated fears of stranger danger, among other sweeping changes, prompted middle-class parents to fixate on their children in ways previous generations had not. It's now the default posture of modern parents—and I don't exempt myself here—to hover and fret over our offspring and strive to give them every advantage.

"Today it is the unimpeachable conviction of the middle class," wrote Jennifer Senior in *All Joy and No Fun*, "that children be perfected and refined in order to ready them for the world ahead."

This mindset has prompted the swelling of structured activities for kids, including, especially, organized sports, which have the advantage of conferring prestige on child and parent alike. Little by little, a child's visible success became a proxy for the parents', prodding the latter to cultivate their sons' and daughters' skills even more furiously. In this way, children's sports have ballooned in importance to adults, which explains why so many parents today think nothing of giving over weekends and vacations to their kids' games—something older generations, including my parents', view with bafflement and alarm.

A further major change rattling the youth sports ecosystem comes from colleges and universities. As admission to elite institutions has become more competitive, parents and kids have turned to sports as a way to gain entry to schools. Colleges and universities have encouraged this strategy by offering enormous advantages in admissions to recruited athletes. Indeed, according to Rick Eckstein, sports sociologist and author of *How College Athletics Are Hurting Girls' Sports*, recruited players with lesser academic qualifications are admitted at four times the rate of similarly qualified applicants without an athletic résumé. This reality has fueled the perceived need for kids to play sports: as a hedge against the swelling cost of college tuition and a possible way into more competitive schools.

I describe youth sports as an ecosystem because it's an interconnected world where various actors work together, and where one constituency's actions can flow through and transform others—and the system itself. Thus, the youth sports industry inviting families to buy more equipment and join more teams whips up anxious parents who want to boost their kids' life prospects, while the machinations at competitive and expensive colleges, with their mysterious admissions practices, keep the system spinning. Don't allow the word "system" to fool you: there's no one on top of it all, pulling the levers.

Somewhere along the way, kids' sports stopped being for kids.

Hold on! you might think. *I want my kids in the game because exercise and team sports deliver virtues and advantages; they build character, promote well-being, and foster social connection. (And for God's sake, it keeps them busy.)*

It's my belief that many of these merits have been thwarted, warped, or corrupted.

Thanks to the extravagant investments in kids' sports, parents' Olympian commitment to their children's recreation, and the exalted role of athletics in higher education, much of what we love about youth sports—and why we want our children to play—has been eroded. The ideals we claim to cherish, the values we hope our kids will realize through sports, often turn out to be comforting fictions. It's a paradox; several paradoxes, in fact. These contradictions illustrate the way that our assumptions and expectations about the integrity of sports are foiled at every step—usually by money, anxiety, and ambition.

Most of us have politely ignored or misperceived the larger forces at work that have changed youth sports and corrupted their purpose. We're too close to the action, too frantic about winning and keeping up and fitting in, to see what's really happening on the playing fields, courts, and tracks.

There's a line I love from the author Marilynne Robinson. In *Gilead*, she wrote, "When things are taking their ordinary course, it is hard to remember what matters." Every parent should have these words tattooed on her wrist as a regular reminder that the picayune dramas of family life, especially those involving sports, can subvert and undermine what we care about most. I don't know about you, but what matters to me is not my children's knack for dribbling or flair with a bat. What matters to me is what kind of people they are: kind or cruel? Generous or self-centered? Lazy or industrious? Had Robinson's words been embossed on my skin, perhaps I'd have viewed my nine-year-old's basketball skill more with humble equanimity than with bloated pride.

If you're perusing this book while waiting for your eight-year-old's club soccer practice to end, and possibly feeling a little bit queasy about what's going on here, please read on. There are ways to counteract the larger forces at work that normalize travel sports for elementary school kids. Parents and coaches aren't powerless. They—we—have a duty to correct some of the distortions that have crept in. With any luck, this book will help you restore your grip and hold on to what counts.

But the systemic problems in sports can't be wholly repaired from the bottom up. Low-income families in sports-starved regions need something more drastic: collective action and major reform in the ways this country provides sports to kids.

Now, courtesy of COVID, we have a rare opportunity to make that happen. For despite all its miseries and disruptions, the pandemic has made two things clear. First, kids need sports and exercise. The collapse of team play during the worst of the pandemic devastated thousands of children who had relied on sports for fitness and mental health, underscoring why we encourage athletics in the first place. Second, the wild variation in youth sports options around the country, with some children crossing borders to sneak into tournaments and others remaining isolated in their basements, uncovered how screwed up and disjointed our system is. COVID has laid bare the inequities and failings of our current model.

"The opportunity is now, and the window will close," asserted leaders from the Aspen Institute's Sports & Society program in their 2021 *State of Play* report. We need to grab hold of this moment and build a new model for kids' sports.

For too long, money and mania have warped what we love about our children's athletics: the fun; the friendships; the growth that comes from competing, either alone or with others. All of us adults circling on the sidelines need to step back, take a few thousand deep breaths, and reclaim our senses. We need to return youth sports to the kids who play. Offer more to those who want them. And then politely get out of the way.

It's time to take back the game.

PART I

HOW THE GAME CHANGED WHEN WE WEREN'T LOOKING

CHAPTER 1

Money

Despite the loud rain pummeling my car's windshield, sweet sleep descended on me as I sunk into the driver's seat, now reclined at a forty-five-degree angle. It was a Sunday evening, about 7:00 p.m., and there I was in Saddle River, or some other New Jersey town about an hour from home, waiting for my son's soccer game to end. Parents had fled to their cars to avoid the deluge, and the game was interrupted periodically by thunder. Paul snapped the back door open and hopped in.

"Rain delay," he said, waking me. "If it doesn't stop soon, they're going to call it."

He was eleven, still verging on scrawny, and his shiny maroon uniform glistened with water. Mud clogged his cleats, and soon my car began to smell like earth and rain. The team had played for about twenty minutes, and that was after a late start. Paul began to shiver while we waited, so I started the car to get the heat going. It was now approaching 8:00 p.m., and the spring rain had turned the field into a slurry of muck and grass.

This was a travel soccer match with the look and feel of something important. Officials had been hired to referee the game and police the players: regulation socks only, uniform tops always tucked in. By now, all the coaches and referees stuck on the field were huddled in a tight circle and eyeballing the clouds. In another ten minutes they surrendered: game off.

Paul and I got home that night about nine fifteen or nine thirty. He'd barely played, but we'd spent close to four hours out of the house. For dinner that night, the rest of my family had scrounged up something or other—maybe Kraft mac and cheese and half a bag of baby carrots, an extravaganza of orange—and Paul would have to settle for Bagel Bites. It was late, with a full week of school ahead. And I'd missed watching *The Simpsons* with my husband and our two other kids.

That night I wondered, and not for the first time, if children were being served by all this—if the totality of the sacrifices made by so many for sports made any sense at all. The puffery of the soccer league itself, with its bylaws and travel mandates and insistence on formality over fun—what was that about? My son's soccer experience bore no relation to the game I had played growing up. What had been relaxed but spirited for me—we tore around in old sneakers and shorts at a clumpy park nearby—was now formal and serious, an athletic event managed by adults featuring properly dressed kids on a manicured field. Apart from the passage of time, something big had changed the game.

Open your eyes and there it is: money. Big money has transformed youth sports. The presence of it, the promise of it, the perversions it generates, are visible to those who dwell in this universe. Business has always played some part in kids' sports; what's changed in recent decades is the nature and extent of it. In 2019, the youth sports industry was valued at an estimated $19.2 billion, according to WinterGreen Research—an increase of more than 90 percent since 2010. By way of contrast, the NFL's estimated value in 2019 was $15 billion. Susan Eustis, who headed the team at WinterGreen that carried out the study, was surprised by this finding. "Who would have thought that youth sports are a bigger industry than the NFL?"

The ten most valuable sports brands will be familiar to all. There's Nike, Adidas, Under Armour, Reebok, and Puma—ubiquitous equipment makers that not only sponsor athletes and teams but also sell sneakers and shorts to mere mortals who exercise, including kids. ESPN, the YES Network, and Sky Sports—the media conglomerates that broadcast athletic competitions far and wide—are also on the list. Rounding out the top ten are UFC, the mixed martial arts promotion company, and Gatorade. Though their markets go way beyond kids, all of these brands pitch to children and profit off kids' enthusiasm and lobbying skills with their parents. Even UFC, which allows fighters to go after each other with punches and kicks to the limbs (but holds the line on gouging), offers training programs for children to "combat the negative impact of screen time with the positive influence of fitness," according to a UFC Gym website. The Sports and Fitness Industry Association reported in 2020 that sales of equipment, athletic shoes, and clothes was up by 3.9 percent in 2019, outpacing growth in the GDP.

Another huge player in the youth sports economy is sports tourism. Hotels, airlines, tournament owners, and amusement parks like Disney, which launched the sports travel juggernaut with its Wide World of Sports complex in Orlando, have profited off families' willingness to get on the road and watch their kids compete. In 2016, visitors to sporting events—most of them for kids—spent $10.5 billion, an increase of 26 percent since 2012, said Mass Mutual. Closer to home, club teams and private coaches and specialized fitness trainers are showing up on every corner, seducing families with the promise that this extra investment in time and money will take their child "to the next level," wherever that is.

More recently, established technology companies and hungry start-ups also are finding ways to make money off youth sports. Does your team need a referee or umpire, ASAP? Check out the Silbo app, and they'll find you one. How about an athletic trainer? Download Go4-Ellis, and choose from a list of thousands who are looking for daily work. If your team is plagued by concussions, consider HitCheck, an app that allows for "sideline assessments" of players to help monitor their symptoms. AmperVue seamlessly aggregates game highlights. Playeasy pairs event organizers, teams, and leagues with facility owners, to smooth out wrinkles when booking sites for tournaments.

I don't mean to suggest that any one of these apps is evil or defective, or that hotel chains, shoe companies, and pop-up gyms are saturated with malevolent characters who are conspiring to ruin kids' sports. I do mean to suggest that all are for-profit entities with one purpose at their core: to make money. Mark Hyman, director of the Shirley Povich Center for Sports Journalism at the University of Maryland and a student of youth sports, put it like this: "There has never been a better time to start a business selling sports to children and their parents."

And sports sociologist Jay Coakley warns, "Any time the livelihood of adults depends upon kids doing certain things in sports, there is potential for abuse."

Unorganized Sports

I remember sports being different when I was a kid. You likely do, too. So does a man named Danny O'Sullivan. When you first meet him, it's a challenge not to gawk. Danny is impossibly tall, ridiculously lanky, a skyscraper of a man who must clonk his head on doorframes and ceilings several times a day. He's the guy you spot from a distance and murmur about to your friends—"Look how tall that man is!"—before realizing that *of course* they've already noticed. If his extraordinary height, six foot eleven, is a nuisance, Danny doesn't show it. He smiles a lot, and his hazel eyes brighten whenever he talks. He likes being tall, he tells me, and rarely thinks about it.

At fifty-two, his hair is streaked with gray. From the neck up, he reminds me of pre-*Ozark* Jason Bateman; they've got the same moppish hair and disarming smile. Though we're talking in a noisy café on stiff wooden chairs that discourage loitering, Danny seems unhurried—comfortable, even, in spite of the way he dominates the furniture. He talks easily, and his open expression matches the words that tumble out of his mouth. He's telling me about his childhood, how he grew up in a low-income home with three siblings and no father, and the unlikely series of events that landed him, years later, on a Division I college basketball team and then in the NBA. All told, he would end up playing professionally for ten years.

The longer I listen to Danny's story, the more struck I am by the contrast between his accidental path to basketball glory and the very deliberate, highly orchestrated route foisted on young people today who show an affinity for basketball. Or, for that matter, the kids who might demonstrate a talent for baseball, or interest in field hockey, or a knack for soccer. While Danny scrambled his way to the top of his sport with little more than verbal support from his high school coaches, enthusiastic young jocks today (and even some unenthusiastic ones) experience their sport with plenty of adult investment, both personal and financial.

When Danny grew up, adults were in the background. He and his brothers and sister started out in a two-bedroom apartment five stories up on Aqueduct Avenue in the Bronx. His siblings shared one bedroom, and his parents slept in the other—the one with the air conditioner. It was a no-frills place, with beige walls and the odd statue of the Virgin Mary to remind the family of their Catholic faith, as well as a "fancy" room with plastic-covered furniture where children were not welcome. It was of no consequence to Danny; the fun was to be had outside. It was a neighborhood teeming with kids.

He was nine when his father died. "When he was gone, there were certain fears—of being left an orphan," he said. His mother, Mary Murray, started waiting tables at a diner in the Bronx, and two years later the family moved to a three-bedroom house in Bayonne, New Jersey. The place was a wreck, but Mary bought it anyway, for $25,000 cash, and promptly began fixing it up. She found work at Burke's restaurant, where the owners looked out for her and her brood, and after a few years got a job as a custodian at the high school in Bayonne.

In the new neighborhood, Danny and a circle of friends played "unorganized sports" all the time, all day, whatever was in season. The sport that he would go on to compete in professionally didn't come naturally to him as a child or young adult. "My first memory of basketball is failure," he said. He was eight years old and playing at an indoor clinic at the town YMCA. Though taller than anyone else on either team, he couldn't get the ball in the hoop, even when no one was challenging him. "I thought, 'Holy crap, this is hard, and I'm not very good,'" he said. Everyone expected him to be skilled. "But I sucked."

That trend continued in high school. During his entire freshman season Danny sat the bench while his more talented teammates competed. He got "garbage time" only when the team was ahead by miles in the fourth quarter and putting Danny in wouldn't jeopardize the win. As a senior, he finally made the varsity squad, playing about ten minutes a game; more skilled players started before him. But now basketball was fun. He exulted in the camaraderie at practices and fellowship in the locker room, and savored the feeling of striving with teammates to achieve a common goal. "We were never in a race to leave, because it was so much fun," he said.

Danny broke through in the middle of his twelfth-grade season. It was during a huge game, Bayonne against their rivals Marist, at home. Fueled by the stakes, the electricity in the gym, and the intensity of the competition, Danny finally delivered on the potential a handful of coaches had spotted in him. He was on the court for eight minutes, and in that window, his game came alive. He snatched impossible rebounds, made clutch baskets, and covered the court with the kind of speed no one expected from a man of his height.

"It was unconscious, out-of-body," he said about that burst of brilliance. The college coaches who had come to scout Marist's stars suddenly took an interest in Danny. How had they missed this guy? And by the time he left high school, he was offered an athletic scholarship at Fordham University, which, along with a Pell Grant, allowed Danny to attend college for free.

The Cost for Families

Danny's mother reared four children alone on a custodian's salary. Apart from what she paid to get to her son's games at Fordham, she spent next to nothing on his athletic pursuits. Her kids played in cheap town leagues and on school teams, and none used any special gear. Danny wore $15 Chuck Taylors to school and then to practice most days, replacing them when holes opened up on the bottom. Varsity players were rewarded with Nike basketball shoes, which the coaches insisted they put on only during games. Danny earned his pair as a senior and wore them all the time, like everyone else. "It was all most kids had," he said.

How much families spend today is hard to calculate, and estimates vary depending on who conducts the research and which families are included in the survey. One large study conducted by the Aspen

Institute's Project Play—a think tank established in 2013 to address the problems in youth sports—and Utah State University arrived at estimates of family expenses by looking both at families with children who played only in recreation and school leagues, and those with kids who played for private clubs.

The researchers then came up with averages. According to their findings, families today spend an average of $693 a year for every child per sport. The biggest chunk—$196—goes to travel: airfare, car rentals, gas money, hotel costs, food on the road, and every other cost associated with a trip away from home to a tournament or game. Equipment costs were next, at $144 for each child, for every sport. Lessons followed; private coaching, strength and conditioning sessions, and all the other personalized learning opportunities children experience to hone their athletic skills cost $134. After that were registration fees—$125—and finally, camps, which cost families $81 a year, per sport, and per child.

But a study of families with children who play just on private teams reveals a much more substantial parental investment. A 2019 Harris Poll survey of 1,001 select adults—they needed to have at least $25,000 of "investable assets" as well as one or more kids on private sports teams—found that 27 percent paid more than $500 per month on their child's sports. Eight percent spent *at least* $12,000 a year. And though these families weren't destitute, 36 percent reported that they took fewer vacations, and 19 percent added a second job to help cover athletic costs.

Parents are paying up so their children can play. Indeed, so important were their kids' sports that 21 percent of surveyed parents in a TD Ameritrade study were holding off on saving for retirement to keep their children playing. According to these 2019 findings, "Youth sports expenses impact three in four (74%) American parents' ability to save and invest for retirement."

Time outlays also were staggering. Some 19 percent of parents said they devoted twenty hours per week to their kids' sports, which might sound too high to be true, until you consider how much driving and weekend time these activities demand.

How Did We Get Here?

When Danny was playing high school basketball in the 1980s, youth sports were a low-budget affair, and not just for families without wealth. Those kids who played organized sports could choose from town recreation leagues, YMCA teams, Boys & Girls Clubs programs, and for boys, Pop Warner football or Little League Baseball. Team practices and games were carried out close to home, and competitions were held over the weekend. But most of the running around happened outside the team, in parks, streets, and backyards, beyond the reach of parents or officials dictating the rules of engagement.

Many factors turned youth sports into a multibillion-dollar industry, Daniel Gould told me. Gould is the director of the Institute for the Study of Youth Sports at Michigan State University, and he's been examining the changes in kids' athletics for decades. He said the shift began during the 1970s, when raging inflation and a receding American economy brought about cuts in community funding for parks and sports programs. The reductions went deeper after the recession of 2008. "Communities didn't invest as much in parks and sports programs after that," Gould said, and strapped cities and towns generally didn't restore that funding even after the economic crisis waned. That's in part because private clubs and teams had stepped in to fill the gap.

The decline in public spending on community sports coincided with a burgeoning youth sports travel industry. Disney made a big move in 1997 when it built Disney's Wide World of Sports near Orlando, close to Disney World. It was considered one of the country's best multisport complexes. Disney got the idea when it realized that it was missing out on the market among older teenagers, whose interest in the Magic Kingdom had fizzled. At a 2019 conference, Mike Millay, who was present at the creation of the sports complex and worked as an executive at Disney for twenty years, explained how the business began and what prompted Disney to build it.

"Disney created this sports complex to drive people to Walt Disney, to stay in our hotels and go to our theme parks," he said, later adding that "the business of sport in Walt Disney is to drive incremental visitation." Even if the sports complex itself lost money, executives reasoned, Disney would do just fine as long as it drove money "to the mother ship"—the theme parks and thirty thousand hotel rooms that the company owns. It was all about heads in beds.

When I spoke with Millay after the conference, he told me about something unexpected that Disney noticed after the September 11 attacks in 2001. While profits elsewhere on their properties stayed the same or sank, earnings at the Wide World of Sports went up by double digits. It turned out that fear of terrorism wouldn't keep families away from Disney's sports complex. Until then, the company hadn't considered their youth sports business as profitable on its own. Now, Disney altered its strategy. "We could use the expertise of Disney and create metrics and models for youth sports," he said.

The park now comprises 700,000 square feet of usable space for sixty different youth sports, including thirty playing fields for softball, baseball, soccer, field hockey, and lacrosse; a ten-court tennis complex; a champion stadium and fieldhouse; a track-and-field complex; and restaurants and ESPN-sponsored venues where parents can indulge a child's athletic interests—and then, possibly, head over to Epcot or the Animal Kingdom once the game is over.

Disney set a new standard for youth sports travel, and its success didn't go unnoticed. Sports commissions around the country, which for years had focused mainly on bringing prestigious professional games to their cities, saw that youth sports could attract visitors and tax dollars as well.

"What we did, we got municipalities interested in the business of youth sports," Millay said. "Anytown, USA, wasn't trying to build a soccer complex until us. They thought, 'Why can't we do that, too?' We kick-started it and took travel sports to a new level."

Don Schumacher is an authority on sports tourism, helping advise cities on whether to invest in new fields and gyms for their communities; he was a founder of the National Association of Sports Commissions (NASC) in 1992, and led it from 1994 until 2017. When he started working with sports commissions in the late 1980s, Schumacher told me, most of them were privately funded and driven by a sense of civic pride: they sought to host big sporting events to bring exposure to their city. Schumacher's was Cincinnati, and when he headed the sports commission there, he was able to attract the NCAA Women's Final Four, the US Gymnastics Championship, and a number of other major championships. "It was about corporate pride in our community," he told me.

In the late 1980s, commissions and a handful of visitors' bureaus began to compete against one another to nab the most prestigious events. At one gathering of the NASC, Schumacher recalls, someone said, "What about age-group championships?" There were Amateur Athletic Union (AAU) age group championships in about fifteen sports, Little League Baseball tournaments, and lots of other possibilities—why limit themselves to collegiate and professional? "The original cities began to realize that there were different approaches to the sports tourism industry," he told me. The commissions started competing to host youth sports championships as well.

This incidental shift toward kids' sports had cascading effects, starting with the NASC itself. Having begun as a purposeful association of sports commissions that shared information and traded best practices, the NASC morphed into a giant body that included visitors' bureaus, chambers of commerce, parks and recreation departments, and other suppliers like hotel chains, all intent on making money off this newly profitable source of tourism. "The industry seemed to change from specialists in high-profile major events to focusing on room nights, based primarily on youth sports events," Schumacher told me.

The financial crisis in 2008 marked another turning point. Just as September 11 didn't thwart families from making a pilgrimage to the Wide World of Sports, the recession wouldn't stop them from traveling to less-celebrated locations, either, especially those centered around kids. "We found out that though the industry didn't grow, it didn't shrink. And it didn't shrink because parents were not going to deny their kid the opportunity to participate in an event. They were going to do it; they were going to go; they're going to encourage that trip," Schumacher explained. After all, he said, their kid was only twelve once; next year, they wouldn't be eligible for the under-thirteen soccer championship.

Sports tourism wasn't recession-proof. But it was resistant. "That's brought a lot more people into the business. That really encouraged many more destinations, new event owners, and industry suppliers to get into it," Schumacher said.

Since Disney opened its mammoth sports complex, the number of sports facilities in the United States has shot up to thirty thousand, ten times what existed in 1997. Schumacher has called it a "facilities arms race." And what those entities needed to make money were kids—and parents willing to travel and pay the fees. In addition to competing at Disney, kids were invited to play at countless other destinations. Parents embraced the idea that more travel would mean more college coaches laying eyes on their exceptional children.

Some facilities are built in tourist-friendly areas, near fabulous beaches or chic cities that can draw visitors with or without the attraction of a youth amateur athletic contest. But communities without such natural advantages have also invested in sports complexes, betting that snazzy fields and stadiums will attract out-of-town players and their families. When those visitors with wallets don't show up, Millay said, communities welcome for-profit entities to come in and run tournaments.

Perhaps a private club will rent out the place, hire highly skilled coaches, and invite kids to join their elite soccer or lacrosse club. And with that will come the imperative to play a lot.

"If we have more local sports organizations, and more local people offering fitness and services and training, then it's to be expected, in my view, that people who start new businesses are going to tell people that 'your kids have to do this or they'll never get a shot,'" Schumacher explained, "whether that's true or not."

The media, too—and there are many companies—helped expand the youth sports industry. It started with ABC, which provided a template for coverage of kids' sports events when it began televising the Little League World Series, back in 1963. Then, it was a low-key, nostalgic occasion that the network broadcast in part to fill a void; at the time, summer was a desert for major sports. But that changed when ESPN took over televising it. Ratings for the Little League World Series are now greater than those for the NHL playoffs, and the fee to own the rights to cover the series ranges from five to seven million dollars. ESPN turned the humble kids' baseball tournament into an annual television event.

The network didn't start out like this. When ESPN was founded in 1979, it lacked the money and reputation to secure a contract with one of the big professional leagues. In searching for something that had not been televised, the owners noticed that early rounds of the NCAA men's basketball tournament, as well as the NFL draft, were absent from the mainstream networks. They seized the opportunity and bought the rights to televise them, and eventually, having built up a war chest of cash by selling advertising and charging cable operators for offering ESPN packages, gobbled up the rights to broadcast much more: college football, NFL games, and finally the championship rounds of the NCAA tournament. ESPN saw what other media companies had not: the American public had a huge appetite for watching sports at all levels. After Walt Disney World bought ESPN in 1996, and rebranded its sports complex "the ESPN Wide World of Sports Complex" in 2010, the merging of sports and entertainment was complete. ESPN began to televise the High School Basketball All-American Showcase for top basketball teams as well as the Super Bowl equivalent for Pop Warner football players.

Print media also took a greater interest in youth sports, especially *USA Today*. Shortly after the paper was founded in 1982, it began ranking high school teams in select sports from around the country. Some eighty newspapers and twenty TV stations cover the *USA Today* rankings, which expanded to include five sports, Mark Hyman notes in *The Most Expensive Game in Town*. As with the frenzy that ensued after *U.S. News & World Report* started ranking colleges and universities, *USA Today*'s public measuring of teams across the country has affected the way some teams play. And the popularity of this ranking system for youth sports may have inspired others—like GotSoccer, a software company that schedules games and ranks players, and the United States Specialty Sports Association, which rates softball teams—to get in on the business. This fixation on standing or rank makes winning the primary purpose of play.

As Hyman pointed out, "Media is first in line to monetize youth sports."

Who Gets Left Out

Investors who are looking to make a buck probably don't realize it. Parents tootling off to purchase the hottest new Little League bat (the Marucci CAT9 Connect, $299.99 at Dick's Sporting Goods) probably miss it as well. But the downstream effect of the billions now spent on kids' activities are real and corrosive, starting with those who are left out.

"There is a frighteningly strong relationship between social class and every stage of youth sports participation," wrote sociologist Rick Eckstein. The age when kids pick up sports has become linked to family income; the greater the income, the earlier kids start.

Time constraints also push lower-income kids out of sports earlier than high-income children. "This likely speaks to lower-income kids' family responsibilities, such as caring for siblings or earning money from a job, and transportation challenges to attend practices and games," the Aspen Institute reports.

A 2015 study by the Pew Research Center found that 84 percent of kids aged six to seventeen in homes with a family income of at least $75,000 took part in sports, while in families with incomes under $30,000, just 59 percent of kids did. The Aspen Institute's Project Play identified a similar pattern when they widened the income gap and studied physical inactivity: among kids aged six to twelve, 29.9 percent of those with a family income under $25,000 were inactive, compared with 11.5 percent of kids from homes with incomes of $100,000 and above. When the national economy takes a hit, as it did during the recession of 2008, fewer children play organized sports. Participation rates among six- to twelve-year-olds dropped from 45 percent in 2008 to 38 percent ten years later.

The disparity extends to schools. Those with students from low-income homes generally offer fewer sports options than schools with students from higher-income homes. Thirty-three percent of "high-poverty schools"—where 75 to 100 percent of kids are eligible for free lunch—offer no interscholastic sports at all. In schools that do offer sports, funding for those programs has held steady or declined over the years.

Another analysis of youth sports concluded that the varying rates of participation among children from different income brackets "may be linked to barriers that may disproportionately burden low-income families, such as pay-to-play fees, school budgets, family time and commitment required, and potential transportation challenges."

Kids in poor families who can't participate in sports lose more than just opportunities to play and compete, as valuable as those might be. Sports can be a source of hope, a catalyst for change, and one way into an otherwise closed world. Children today who are born into desperate circumstances have trapped talents, too, and when their access to sports is blocked, one road out is shut. All of us bear the consequences of that loss.

How Money Changes the Game

Many parents have asked me over the years if I would "work with" their slow or unmotivated child. "She's a fast runner, but she doesn't like to train and gets nervous before races," one exasperated mother of a ten-year-old told me, looking for advice. I agreed to take the child out for a few "practices," which consisted of brief jogs around the neighborhood. She chatted about elementary school, and I gushed about all the fun we were having. It was dispiriting. She was a perfectly normal little girl who didn't love to run, and spending time with her mother's friend who was a coach wasn't going to change that. On the contrary, my involvement signaled that running was serious business, not a mirthful diversion, and that her disturbing lack of dedication required the attention of grown-ups. Finally, I told the mother that I didn't think my guidance was helping, and we let it go. I haven't agreed to coach a young child since.

I don't doubt that the mother who solicited my help (and for the record, I took no money) wanted her daughter to derive the copious benefits that come from regular running—along with, perhaps, the satisfaction of watching her talented daughter sprint ahead of the herd at the town-wide mile race for kids. I also don't question the motives of the father who asked if I would act as an "outside coach" to his tenth-grade daughter. He'd done the same for his boys when they played baseball, and he wanted his daughter to feel the equivalent degree of parental commitment to her sport. Would I please work with her a bit, try to instill some confidence, and maybe offer some pointers that she'd not heard from her high school coaches? He'd pay me.

I told him no. I've yet to see such transactions work well for anyone involved.

Whether intentionally or not, commercial entities who profit off youth sports are selling the rest of us a story about what kids need—and it's always new, more, better. Children's developmental needs are absent from that narrative. So, too, is the effect of these expenditures on how kids feel about sports and how they play.

Travis Dorsch heads a team at Utah State University that looks at how spending on sports affects families. His research found that the more money parents devote to a child's sport, the less the child enjoys it, and the more pressure he or she feels. At the same time, the more parents pay, the more emotionally invested they become in the outcome of their children's games. "Parents spend money to help their kids flourish, but the effect is just the opposite," he said. Children who understand that their parents might seek a return on the investment they've made lose their athletic verve. The intrinsic delight of playing gets squashed by parental pressures or supplanted by the possibility of a fat extrinsic reward, in the form of a leg up in college admissions.

The pinnacle of athletic achievement used to be the three-sport athlete, that talented kid who could move seamlessly from soccer to basketball to track, and still dominate, her athleticism translating from one sport to another. These kids were the athletic equivalent of the fox in Isaiah Berlin's famous division of people into two types: the fox, who knows a little about a lot, and the hedgehog, who knows a lot about a little. The way youth sports have been monetized has compelled kids to burrow into one sport at an early age, making hedgehogs of them all. Athletic foxes aren't extinct, but they have become gravely endangered.

Jay Coakley explains how this shift happened. The surge in private clubs, travel teams, and expensive sports facilities brought with it adults who depended on these jobs for their livelihood. Though perhaps well intended, Coakley wrote, they "needed youth sports to provide them with year-round income, because they had families to feed, fields to maintain 12 months a year, utility bills to pay, and staff that needed year-round employment." To stay solvent, these businesses needed to persuade parents that year-round devotion to one sport was essential, indeed the only way forward. Coakley calls it "the selling of specialization," an approach to athletics that seemed to yield results in some Eastern Bloc countries years ago. When young Tiger Woods burst onto the scene, his father touting the countless hours they'd spent practicing while Tiger was a toddler, along with the sudden acceptance of the ten-thousand-hour rule made popular in Malcolm Gladwell's book *Outliers*, early specialization grabbed hold.

The cascading effects of this approach have transformed youth sports. Young kids pick one sport and concentrate solely on it. They play to win, practice to sharpen a marketable skill, and work to woo a college coach.

Laura Gump can speak to these changes. A middle school lacrosse coach, former college player, and founder of a camp that is specifically geared to beginners, Gump is fully conscious of the shift in parents' thinking about kids' sports and how youth athletics have changed. Sitting at a sticky wooden table in a local café, she told me about what she sees on her teams and with her camps—the ugly downstream effects of these trends. "The most common question I'm asked in my twelve years of running camps is, 'Is it too late for my son or daughter in kindergarten to try lacrosse?'" These are calls from parents of five-year-olds who worry that they might have screwed up already by not introducing their toddlers to the game. Gump hears the question five to six times before the start of summer camp.

"Sometimes there's self-awareness that it's a ridiculous question," she added, but still she finds it depressing. Gump herself didn't pick up the game until her junior year of high school, and then went on to play in college. More recently, a young woman who coached at Gump's camp was tapped to compete at Stanford University, though she only started playing in ninth grade.

Gump said that there are more tournaments than ever pitching to players and teams. Where there once were fifteen large national tournaments that the most competitive teams would choose from, now, new ones pop up everywhere. "Tournament games are a big business," she said. Private team practices during fall and winter used to be optional, but more clubs are making off-season training mandatory. "Parents and kids are being preyed on like vultures," she said. "They can be sucked in because they don't know any better."

Gump thinks the frenzy started when the most popular lacrosse clubs began offering travel teams to younger and younger kids. Parents flock to these teams because they worry that staying out of it will relegate their offspring to the sidelines; they reason that kids who sign on in second grade will develop relationships with coaches and administrators, guaranteeing them a spot on the third-grade team—and all the teams that follow. "There's a fear of falling behind and getting a late start," she said.

But that pressure doesn't stop once the eight-year-olds make it to an elite club. Then, they need to *preserve* their standing on that team. Gump knows of a sixth-grade girl on a competitive travel team who got hit in the head and badly concussed. Though her parents knew the dangers of allowing their daughter to keep playing, they waffled on how to handle it. If the girl sat on the sidelines for a month, another kid might be moved up to take her place. The girl with the throbbing head would miss out on exposure to high-powered coaches who might come to watch their games. She would fall behind her peers, maybe lose her position permanently, and then what would happen? "The stakes seem super high," Gump said, echoing Coakley's assessment.

Gump's voice rose as she talked, and her cadence picked up. The mother of a few lacrosse players herself, she understands how this environment challenges parents to do right by their kids. She sees the shock on the faces of parents new to the system when they finally realize what's required in time and money, and understands why even balanced parents, some of them former athletes like herself, feel stuck. While they might want to resist the vortex that seizes seven-year-olds and doesn't let up until the end of high school (if then), they wonder if holding back will put their own child at a disadvantage.

"You can stand firm and not put your kid on the travel lacrosse team in second grade, but have you done your child a disservice?" she asked. Maybe that particular group of second graders will gel, become a formidable squad among other seven-year-olds, and stick together for years to come, Gump explained. "But your daughter is left out. She was begging you! She told you!" Fault lies with the levelheaded parent who tried to keep silly external pressures from infecting the family.

Fordham and the NBA

Danny's basketball career at Fordham was a mix of disappointment, hope, and big plays executed at just the right time. The coach who'd recruited him left before Danny arrived, and for the next few years he played inconsistently, in one game impressing NBA scouts by scoring twenty-nine points, and in others stiffening up at crucial moments. He found his groove as a senior and decided to aim for the pros when college was over.

Looking back on his stop-and-start college career, Danny wishes he'd played better for his team and coach. He also laments that mistakes on the court triggered more flubs and further self-loathing, and he wonders how he might have developed if he'd been encouraged through slip-ups rather than beaten down. There were moments of joy during his time at Fordham, but the lower moments crowded them out. When you have tough coaches, Danny told me, they don't let you enjoy the successes for long.

But he wanted to keep going. After graduation, and some false starts with the NBA, Danny played for the Continental Basketball Association, then the minor league of the sport. His play there attracted coaches from the Utah Jazz, who kept him for a year. Danny continued to bounce from team to team, hopscotching from the Detroit Pistons to the Milwaukee Bucks and then the Toronto Raptors, along with a stint in Puerto Rico, a trip back to the minors, and several years with teams in Italy, Greece, and Spain.

Danny found his way to college basketball and the NBA without joining an AAU team—the dominant route today for teenage basketball players to be recruited by college coaches rather than through their high school teams. AAU basketball took off during the 1980s, when executives from Nike and then Adidas made shoe deals with select AAU coaches. These arrangements served both parties well: coaches with sponsorship deals attracted the best basketball talent, and shoe companies got first dibs on upcoming NBA stars. In 2021, virtually every American player in the NBA played for a "grassroots" club like the AAU.

Because Danny had no part in this system, he didn't travel around the country to demonstrate his fledgling skills at showcase events, or hone his jump shot at summer basketball camps, or answer to multiple coaches about how to play. If AAU were the route to college ball when he was growing up, Danny says he wouldn't have ended up on a Division I team, let alone a professional one. His mother wouldn't have been able to afford a private travel team, and he wasn't talented enough as a young player to attract a magnanimous coach. "No one was going to say, 'I need that kid, and I don't care if he can't afford it,'" Danny said. "No one would have given me a chance. No one is waiting anymore."

To make it into the NBA today, poor children need to be blazing enough to get the attention of the right AAU coaches, who will then pay the fees. And contrary to the popular notion that the NBA is populated by Black men who grew up in poverty, the unicorns who make it to the pros are 30 percent less likely to be born to unwed, teenage mothers than the average Black male. An economist writing for *The New York Times* who studied NBA rosters and income levels concluded that "growing up in a wealthier neighborhood is a major, positive predictor of reaching the N.B.A. for both black and white men"—a function of noncognitive skills picked up at home, and the height advantages that often come with better nutrition.

Had he grown up in the youth sports environment he sees today, Danny wonders if he'd even have stuck with basketball through high school. Playing junior varsity shaped him as a player, but many kids don't want to play JV past tenth grade. He says that parents often encourage their kids to find something else to strive for when their varsity prospects dim—something sparkly and original, preferably, to buff up their college applications. Danny was a player who needed patient coaches and time to develop, both conditions that youth sports, especially basketball, now lack.

Danny's mother went to a couple of his basketball games during senior year, after the Bayonne/Marist matchup that changed his life. He smiled broadly and threw his head back when I asked if his mother ever questioned the coaches. "She would never complain about playing time!" he told me, the absurdity of the notion prompting a snort.

She didn't grasp the particulars of the sport and kept quiet on the sidelines. In fact, she didn't much care about the game at all. "I don't ever remember her asking me if we won or lost," he said. "Not that she didn't care, but it wasn't important."

Danny struggles to understand why parents pay so much for their kids' athletics—for private teams, coaches, and clubs. In his experience, there's no magic to what makes a successful young athlete. "It has to come from the kid," he says. "They have to really want it." Parents who believe they can will their child into greatness, or bribe their offspring into trying harder, are fooling themselves. "Parents are definitely flushing money away."

After all these years, Danny still loves the sport he made a career of. He coaches his youngest child in recreational basketball and baseball— the town leagues—and always urges his players to compete and have fun. Go down fighting, he tells the kids, take the shot, strike out swinging. He encourages them to brush off mistakes and play the game, whatever it is, with a whole heart. His eyes brightened when he told me about a kid he coaches in basketball who had never played before, and who now regularly goes for the hoop. The boy is on top of the world; he's making a real contribution, Danny said. "It's a great game," he added, reminding me of how it started for me, for him, and for us all: as just a game.

"What Are We Really Doing Here?"

America gets by on money. There's a perpetual scramble to make it, hold on to it, and find ways to acquire more of it. Parents, it turns out, are an easy mark for profiteers. "For Walt Disney World, the bottom line is profit," Mike Millay reminded me. "We found a way to do it in youth sports."

We parents need to be clear-eyed about what's going on here. The tournament fees and distant games and Rinat Fenix Egotiko Quantum Pro Goalkeeper Gloves with a German latex Omega grip that cost about $80 (and are "very, very popular for kids," a salesman at a local athletic store told me) are being pitched to us parents because companies want our money. And we parents can be suckers for our children, buying crap they really don't need because someone promised it would help, and look, the neighbor kid is going to Virginia for a soccer tournament—should we be doing the same for our daughter?

"The more experience you have with youth sports, the more events you attend, the more things you think about compared to other experiences, the more you think, 'What are we really doing here?'" Millay said to me.

These businesses profit off the boundless bewilderment parents feel when rearing kids, the muddle of doubt, heartache, and confusion that defines being a mother or father. Maybe if we pay up for the extra coaching, and spring for the STX Duel U face-off lacrosse head (unstrung, $89.99), Justin will finally get his act together and start caring about school, or at least stop picking on his brother. Maybe he'll even excel on the field, graduate with distinction, march off to Yale, and lead a life of astonishing achievement.

We parents have always wanted our children to thrive. Getting them to play seemed like a smart way to help them along. The infusion of money into the game has changed that calculus.

CHAPTER 2

The Stakes (and Status)

When my kids were little, I often sparred with family and friends about youth sports and their foothold in the suburbs. I wanted no part of the frantic signing-up and incessant scheduling that these activities required, and poo-pooed it all as a colossal waste of time. Though less barbed, my arguments with friends who had gone in early on kiddie soccer touched on the same themes: organized sports for glorified toddlers were ludicrous, pointless, and so *boring*.

But just a few years later, there I was, shifting my weight from one foot to another on the side of a soggy grass field, cajoling my daughter to "go get it!" For in spite of my vocal opposition to organized sports for preschoolers, my two oldest were now signed up for soccer. I had caved. I'm not proud of that decision, or my reasons for making it.

The truth is that I simply didn't know how to answer the persistent questioning about what sports my kids were playing. "Uh, nothing?"—my go-to response—lost its charm after a while. And it wasn't just submitting to peer pressure; I needed the kids doing *something*. God knows I had enough time alone with them at home, refereeing squabbles over crayons and graham crackers. Organized sports would have to do.

The two older children had their own ideas about participating in the sports that every other kid was playing. Our middle child, Jeff, simply refused to go. He wanted nothing to do with running around a field and kicking a dumb ball, especially with adults watching and clapping and offering unsolicited advice. Our oldest child, Julie, on the other hand, had at least a short go of it. Just five when we wheedled her into playing for a local recreation soccer team, she protested every Saturday morning before practice. When we finally managed to get her dressed and packed into the car, always five minutes later than we should have, her hair would be a tangle of knots, her face blotchy with tears, and her outfit distinctly non-sporty. She retired at the end of the season.

Only our youngest son, Paul, had a genuine appetite for sports, and it revealed itself when he was in diapers. He could swat a Wiffle ball and catch objects with ease. He was eager to play on a soccer and basketball team, and we promptly signed him up when the time came. We'd given up pressing sports on our older children, content to let them decide the terms of their play. Their coolness to athletics made our lives easier, in fact. We took turns going to Paul's games, one of us staying back with the older kids while they hunted for salamanders in our backyard, the other sitting on the sidelines and watching our promising young jock shine.

It wasn't long before I started noticing how athletic ability, even among elementary school kids, conferred prestige. For though it goes unsaid, physically gifted children do indeed gain status, as do the humble parents who brought them into the world. If you spend enough time around a talented young athlete, the fawning by kids and adults is impossible to avoid.

Children make no effort to conceal their awe. After many a basketball or soccer game, someone Paul barely knew would rush up to him and ask for an immediate postgame playdate. Adults are marginally more subtle in their adulation. Many were extravagantly friendly, complimenting Paul on his speed, his steady hands, the way he could vacuum up a ground ball and throw it accurately to first base when he was nine. Some of this, of course, was ordinary politeness, which Bob and I extended widely to other families in turn. What made Paul stand out was how naturally athletic he was, how at home he looked on the court and field. He was just a child, but his athleticism brought him far more attention and acclaim from adults than either of his siblings received for their more private gifts.

This was true for other kids, as well.

It was especially apparent with Tyler, who was a grade ahead of Paul and whose father had played Division I baseball at a powerhouse school. From the time he took up organized sports until the day he left for college twelve years later, Tyler was the darling of other parents. They'd call to him: "Hey, Tyler, how are you doing?" "Nice boxing out, Tyler." "Awesome spiral, Tyler!" Because of his size and athletic pedigree, the kid had a following long before he had the skills.

One year at junior baseball tryouts a group of evaluators (all men, incidentally) came together to divvy up teams. When Tyler and his father showed up, a group of fans clustered around them. Already, the boy had a reputation for strength and speed and towered over his peers. Fathers of punier kids gazed with envy at Tyler's evident physical superiority, while dads who also had played high-level collegiate sports found one another and shared war stories at a high volume. These men all had a similar look: short hair, tidy clothes, fit bodies. They laughed aggressively at each other's quips and took up space wherever they went. When the boys finally made it out to the field, the men examined the action and murmured about the "talent."

Little boys took their turns at the plate and on the field while the evaluators marked up their notebooks. Like many other kids, Paul did what was required: he fielded and caught the ball respectably and trudged quietly off the turf when he was done. When it was Tyler's turn, the energy shifted. Everyone started to watch. "C'mon, Tyler!" a couple of men on the sidelines yelled. At shortstop, Tyler scooped up a ground ball and shot it to first base, sending it over the fielder's head. At bat, he swung furiously and missed, until he connected with one ball and delivered it far out to center field. The league official pitching the ball congratulated Tyler by name. All the judges, in fact, seemed to know him. When Tyler's tryout ended, he endured hearty back slaps from other fathers who congratulated him for his power at the plate.

Paul managed to escape most of the ill effects of excessive attention from the jock sniffers, as we called those adults who genuflected before athletic children. While his ego might have been lifted, temporarily, by the energetic applause he often received, it shrunk back to normal when he returned home to face his older, unimpressed siblings. Their indifference to his play and enthusiasm for the wider world seemed to keep the whole enterprise in perspective. At least for him.

The Larger Landscape of Children, Status, and Sports

It hasn't always been like this. Children have not forever been the wellspring of parental satisfaction—the vehicle through which grown-ups achieve fulfillment. Journalists, historians, and sociologists have been studying this development for years, all of them trying to figure out how and why, during the last few decades, children have assumed center stage in the lives of their parents.

In *Huck's Raft: A History of American Childhood*, the definitive guide to shifting perceptions of children, historian Steven Mintz explores how childhood "is a social and cultural construct that has changed radically over time." From the "premodern" colonial period, when children were considered primitive and deficient; to the "modern" era, when mid-nineteenth-century kids came to be viewed as vulnerable and in need of protection; and until the "postmodern" time, which began in the mid-twentieth century and continues today, when children are thought of as "independent consumers and participants in a separate, semiautonomous youth culture," the very definition of childhood has shifted in keeping with the times.

Mintz identifies three trends that emerged in mid-1970s America that explain how we got to the current postmodern period: a reconfigured family life due to higher divorce rates and more single and working mothers; a shift in parental attitudes toward children as a result of public panics about their safety and well-being; and a drop in economic prospects, which caused many young adults to delay college and marry later. "These trends," Mintz wrote, "combined to produce a mounting concern that young people's well-being was declining and that only drastic measures could help."

In *All Joy and No Fun: The Paradox of Modern Parenthood*, journalist Jennifer Senior expands on Mintz's ideas. She profiles a handful of middle-class families around the country and dives into social history to get at the cause of suffocating parental involvement. She also identifies three reasons for kids' elevated role, which complement Mintz's. Children are scarcer, and thus more precious, making them a source of "existential fulfillment" for Mom and Dad. National sprawl and exaggerated worries about child abduction—the panic Mintz identified—prod parents to turn to organized activities for stimulation. Most important, though, Senior wrote, "hyperparenting reflects a new sense of confusion and anxiety about the future."

There's another culprit here, as well. Former Stanford dean Julie Lythcott-Haims, who was led to write a book on overparenting, credits the baby boomers for triggering the shift in attitudes (and behavior) toward children. They've overreacted to stories about missing kids, fallen for the squishy self-esteem movement, panicked over bleak findings from the infamous 1983 government report on education, *A Nation at Risk*, and bought into "playdates" as the way to encourage child socializing.

"Boomers tried to control and ensure outcomes for their own kids and became their strongest advocates," wrote Lythcott-Haims. By virtue of their massive numbers, the boomers' embrace of these mores has had the effect of changing the way middle-class families reared their children. These norms have become so broadly accepted that few parents would think to challenge them.

And what are those norms? The socially sanctioned way for middle-class families to rear their kids, wrote sociologist Annette Lareau, is through "concerted cultivation," the relentless prodding and sculpting of children by their anxious and weary parents. Lareau arrived at this term after studying the home lives of twelve varied families—white, Black, low-income and middle-income—and finding distinctive commonalities among these varied groups. Working- and lower-class parents allow their kids what Lareau calls "natural growth": a hands-off, strict, and no-nonsense childhood, in which kids are expected to obey authority and fend for themselves with their peers.

But middle-class families, Lareau explains, operate by a different set of norms, namely a dogged focus on organized activities. These activities take precedence over everything, including the adults' leisure pursuits, family time, and gatherings with relatives. For middle-class families like the one she profiles in her book *Unequal Childhoods: Class, Race, and Family Life*, Lareau wrote, "Time spent with the extended family wasn't unimportant. It's just less important than sports."

Unlike the working-class children in her study, who resolve conflicts on their own, middle-class children are accustomed to adults intervening and fixing things, including battles among siblings. Lareau surmises that middle-class siblings fight more often because their full schedules allow for less "face-to-face interaction with members of their own family."

It's not all bad for the cultivated, of course. Lareau observes that middle-class children reared with such intense parental commitment develop a sense of entitlement and a familiarity with how society functions. Brought up in highly verbal homes that foster negotiation and compromise, middle-class kids learn over time how to navigate the systems that resemble white-collar workplaces. Poor and working-class kids with a lot of unstructured time often "hang out" with relatives rather than attend organized sports or other adult-run programs. As a result, they're less acclimated to institutions that operate under different social codes. Some kids will be adept at improvising, but for many it's dropping them in unprepared.

Like Mintz, Lareau believes that economic anxiety is at the root of parents' zeal: "Worried about how their children will get ahead, middle-class parents are increasingly determined to make sure that their children are not excluded from any opportunity that might eventually contribute to their advancement." But it's impossible to read Lareau's assessment of middle-class family life and not be reminded of the mores in my upper-middle-class town. Here in Summit, New Jersey, where 41 percent of households earned $200,000 or more in 2019, wealthy children are cultivated just as vigorously as the middle-class kids Lareau studied; they're watered and pruned, doused in pesticide and stuck in hothouses, all to produce the most eye-popping and flawless flower. While financial insecurity may motivate many, it doesn't explain what propels the very wealthy—those with big jobs and powerful social networks who needn't obsess over their children's future financial security—to cultivate their offspring just as strenuously. There's more than economics at stake.

Jay Coakley offers one persuasive explanation. In his view, the widespread embrace of concerted cultivation is a by-product of Reagan-era policies that emphasized the individual over the group. Having bought into the popular slogan that "government is the problem" and the belief that success can only be attained through private endeavors, wobbly parents came to believe that they alone were responsible for shaping their children's development and character. Columnist David Brooks has written about the same trends. "Society became more individualistic and more self-oriented," he wrote. "People put greater value on privacy and autonomy." Perhaps unconsciously, the masses gradually began to embrace the idea that matters were best resolved individually, or within a family, rather than through mushy community.

Brooks wrote, "A code of self-sufficiency prevails: Mom, and Dad, and the kids are on their own, with a barrier around their island home."

"Due to this cultural shift," Coakley wrote, "the moral worth of parents became directly linked to the actions and achievements of their children." Successful children, especially those who shined publicly in a "culturally valued activity" like sports, were a reflection of good parenting.

"The idea," Coakley wrote, "that the character and actions of children were shaped exclusively by parents led mothers and fathers to dedicate themselves to the success of their children in ways that few parents had ever done before."

It's not just financial worries, then, that drive parents to extremes. It's our very moral worth that's at stake—our station as decent and responsible parents. In this context, it makes some sense that modern parents like me would come to equate children's success with good parenting. And what better way for a child to succeed than through sports?

The Allure of Athleticism

This shift in the perceived value of children—"from our employees to our bosses," as Jennifer Senior puts it—has coincided with the growing prestige of athletes and sports. To state the obvious, top professional athletes are exalted figures, beloved celebrities with rare physical talents that are alien to most of us.

Their cultural dominance is apparent in many ways. The very best are rewarded with riches: In a 2020 *Forbes* study of the one hundred highest paid celebrities, thirty-four were professional athletes—LeBron James, Lionel Messi, and other male sports luminaries, most of them baseball, football, basketball, or soccer players. Pro sports, especially football, capture people's attention and time: Three of the five most-watched TV "series" during the 2018–2019 season were Sunday, Thursday, and Monday Night Football.

And it's not just the professionals. In the 2017–2018 academic year, 494,000 young men and women took part in an NCAA sport, an all-time high for college sports participation—the same year that the NCAA earned more than one billion dollars in revenue, mostly from TV deals. And kids want in on it. A 2017 survey asked one thousand kids under the age of twelve to identify their dream job. "Professional athlete" was the eighth most popular pick for boys—a steep drop from its top position in 2015, but higher than teacher or astronaut.

It follows that when travel teams and private clubs showed up and promised to provide the very best athletic instruction to their children, parents steeped in this environment would lean in and pay up. And that's exactly what they did. Shrunken budgets for public parks, the razzmatazz of new athletic complexes, and the surge in media coverage of sports both reflected and exacerbated the profound change in how parents reared their children.

I spoke to Coakley about the surge in the social value of youth sports. He recalled how his own parents, many years ago, missed nearly all of his games and tournaments, even the biggest ones. They were like Danny O'Sullivan's mother, who busied herself with her own life while her children went about theirs. For a parent to miss his child's championship game today would equate to moral failure, Coakley added.

Parents have come to consider kids' sports participation vital for the development and social status of their children, as well as for the parents themselves. "A good parent is one who invests $10,000 a year on a twelve-year-old soccer player," he said. "Such investments send the message that 'I'm a better parent than you.'" Other ways to communicate that idea include giving up weekends and summer vacations for a child's team duties; paying handsomely for private coaches, gear, and club fees; and acting as coach/administrator/laundress/cook/driver to advance a child's athletic career.

There's a simple reason why youth sports have taken their current form. "The system builds the reputation of coaches and the moral worth of parents," Coakley said.

The Promise of Status

In all my jabbering about kids' sports, not once have I admitted the joy that Paul's athletic success has brought me. How his coordination and speed and smoothness, apparent to all during those frequent games, made me feel rich with satisfaction. How his team's wins, often aided by Paul's electric play, could turn an otherwise humdrum Saturday into a happy weekend. Nor did I admit to how unreasonably bitter and blue I felt when he played flat, or when the coach blocked Paul's path, or when some grossly misguided youth sports body placed him on a third-string team.

Over the years, I've asked many parents why they have done so much to enhance their child's athletic prospects. Not one has shared what their child's athleticism meant to them. "I do it because my kids love it," a mother of two high school athletes told me. Her daughter's three weekly soccer practices; the one-hour extra training session two hours from home; the weekend game in a distant locale; the regular workouts with a strength and conditioning coach—it's exhausting, but Madison loves it, the mother told me with a wan smile. Somewhere lurking behind that smile was private joy over her daughter's evident success.

Status is an awkward and delicate subject. No self-respecting adult wants to be accused of hungering for it, few would admit even to themselves to craving it, and yet the silent yearning for it seems to shape our thoughts and actions. Indeed, the longing for respect is universal. John Adams wrote as much in a series of papers published in the United States in 1805: "A desire to be observed, considered, esteemed, praised, beloved, and admired by his fellows is one of the earliest as well as the keenest dispositions discovered in the heart of man," he wrote in *Discourses on Davila*. "The desire of the esteem of others is as real a want of nature as hunger; and the neglect and contempt of the world as severe a pain as the gout or stone."

This urge is particularly strong in America, which was founded on the principles of democracy and equality. These virtues are all well and good when it comes to the ordering of a just society, but the social consequences could be unsettling. Alexis de Tocqueville spotted the problem when he toured the country in the 1800s, noting in *Democracy in America* that "nowhere do citizens appear so insignificant as in a democratic nation." For if everyone enjoys an equal chance to succeed—a fantasy, but one widely held—then life becomes a scramble to distinguish oneself from the rest. In *Class: A Guide through the American Status System*, the literary critic Paul Fussell puts it more bluntly: "Where everybody is somebody, nobody is anybody." Having separated from Great Britain in part to rebel against the idea of inherited power and position, free Americans had to figure out new ways to set themselves apart. "Nowhere, consequently, is there more strenuous effort to achieve— *earn* would probably be the right word—significance," Fussell wrote.

Having athletic kids is one way to do this. But the role of status-seeking as a driving force behind much of the rotten behavior in youth sports is all but ignored; most Americans, it seems, cling to what Fussell calls our "official myth of classlessness." We prefer less self-recriminatory explanations for these problems: the privatization of sports, the scaling back of public sports programs and spaces, the economic pressures on middle-class families that compel them to pursue athletics as a cheaper route to college. And they're partly right. Parents who upend their own lives to develop their kids' athletic résumés offer alternative rationales for their behavior: they couldn't possibly disappoint their sports-obsessed children, and, anyway, a proper parent must make such sacrifices for their offspring. Giant impersonal socioeconomic forces, combined with exaggerated parental devotion and a sprinkling of confusion, so the thinking goes, explain why youth sports have gotten so twisted.

But the less palatable human longing for status among one's peers also taints youth sports. Take it from someone who strutted with self-satisfaction after her child's rec-league basketball game: We parents latch on to our kids' virtuosity in sports and celebrate it as our own.

The hunger for respect is universal, it would seem—a natural longing that steers our thinking and behavior in ways we don't always realize and rarely discuss. Because we avoid talking about status, especially about how much we parents count on our kids to provide it, we sometimes get off track. Many of us have deluded ourselves about why we're up to what we do—why we go to such lengths to help our children succeed, when what's actually at stake, at least some of the time, is our own pride.

"If others examined themselves attentively, as I do, they would find themselves, as I do, full of inanity and nonsense," wrote Michel de Montaigne, the sixteenth-century essayist whose words remain eerily relevant. "We are all steeped in it, one as much as another; but those who are aware of it are a little bit better off."

Dunder Mifflin Field Trip

"Can we get out of here?" Paul whispered, his eyes gleaming with desperation. He'd just finished the last of several games at a two-day summer basketball camp for aspiring college basketball players held at Brandeis University. I'd come to pick him up and saw the last fifteen minutes of his final game. Ordinarily peppy on the court, that day he trudged around and avoided the action. While other players lunged for loose balls and swaggered up the court, Paul stood around passively and eyeballed the clock. He seemed tiny out there in the giant college gym with a soaring ceiling, and practically Lilliputian next to older and much taller peers. Countless other games were going on at the same time, and the din from parents and coaches braying on the sidelines was deafening.

"I want to go," he told me as soon as the game ended.

"Was it fun?" I asked.

He said nothing and frowned.

The camp wasn't his idea. Someone had mentioned it to me, said that it would be helpful for kids like Paul who were academically minded, a nice opportunity for him to get his name out there. It was the All-Academic Camp put on by Hoop Mountain, a basketball entity—not a club, not a team—that offers coaching and specialized camps around the country. "Last year the All-Academic Camp had over 150 college coaches and scouts in attendance," the camp brochure boasted.

"Can we first get the video of your games?" I asked Paul. Someone had told me that it would be useful for Paul to study his moves at the camp, and that buying the tape would be a smart idea—a way to help him detect and correct his mistakes. The tape was $150, and we'd have to go to the lower level of the gym and order it from the videographer.

"Mom, I just want to go. It's not going to help," he said under his breath. He walked with his head down.

"C'mon, let's just get it," I said.

Throngs of sweaty teenagers clogged the gym and the staircase. When we finally made our way to the lobby, I spotted the booth that had the videos and approached the salesman.

Paul pulled me aside before I got there. "I don't want it," he said. Paul was fifteen, closing in on junior year, and still hovered under six feet tall. Nimble and lean, he resembled a sixteen-hundred-meter runner more than a basketball player, especially among these muscular young men assembled here on the campus. His curly blond hair was too long and sprouted from his head like a wild shrub.

"Let's just order it," I said again.

Paul was embarrassed now, I thought, but later he'd appreciate having it. For the next ten minutes, the jumpy salesman explained how valuable this keepsake would be, how much Paul would benefit from careful review of the tape. When he comes back next year, the guy told me, Paul would be that much more prepared to impress the coaches. I wrote the check, while Paul hung back and away from the transaction.

We walked out of the gym and back to my car. Paul was quiet, while I pattered on senselessly—*What a great opportunity. . . . You never know what might happen. . . . Next year will be that much better.* When we arrived at his dorm, Paul hopped out to collect his few items—a sleeping bag, a stained pillow, and a ratty backpack full of sodden clothes.

"I'm not going back there next year," he said as we headed into Boston. He sat in the passenger seat and stared ahead. "I'm nowhere near as good as those kids, and no one was interested in me."

Here, finally, I shut up and listened. He felt outclassed, physically inferior, and out of his element. Every kid was there to impress. The teams were just thrown-together collections of individuals, all of them eager to amaze a college coach. Kids hung on to the ball and forced their way to the hoop. Because every talented kid on the court would attract the coaches' attention, every other kid was a rival, team or no team. No one passed. It was every teenage boy for himself—*Lord of the Flies* on the court.

"Almost everyone could dunk!" he said. I drove on, receipt of the precious videotape tucked in my wallet and still not registering what was beneath his insistence that he wouldn't go back. I seemed to have lost my mind, deluded by the possibility of sports stardom.

It wasn't until the following year, on a Saturday morning in March, that I abandoned my personal investment in Paul's athletics. The high school basketball season had just ended. By now a junior, Paul had started on the varsity team as a point guard, and the team had had a winning season. They hadn't won a state or county championship, but the team was cohesive and the coach attentive and smart. An assistant coach on the high school team invited Paul to join an AAU team.

This seemed like a vaguely good idea. I faithfully drove Paul back and forth from practices. He knew one other boy on the team, but most of the kids were unfamiliar to him and from other towns. Before long, Paul started to complain after practice, about how the father of another kid showed up and criticized him, how no one seemed connected. I listened and sympathized and began to wonder what we were doing this for.

Then he had his first game. It was on a Saturday in Scranton, Pennsylvania, he told me. And it was early. Other families were driving up Friday night so they would be there fresh at game time.

"We're not doing that," I told Paul. We'd get up early and drive from home.

"Maybe we can stop and see Dunder Mifflin," Paul said about the fictitious paper company made famous on *The Office* and located in Scranton. He found an address online.

That morning, we left our house in the dark and headed west. Scranton was more than one hundred miles away, but the roads were empty and we got there fast. We followed the directions for Dunder Mifflin and ended up at a vacant parking lot.

"I guess they didn't film it here," Paul said.

The game was held in a college gym right off the city's main road.

The wooden bleachers were rickety, and the gym was cool. Hands sunk in my pockets, I hugged my coat around my body and waited. Other parents in the stands were strangers, evenly dispersed among the seats; it was impossible to tell which adults belonged to which team. When the game started, five boys from either side got on the court and started to play. Except for the thump of the basketball hitting the gym floor and frequent screech of the buzzer, the room was mostly quiet. Paul perched on the bench and leaned over, elbows on his knees, chin resting in his hand. I sat across the court, stiff and impatient. Another parent crouching nearby talked about next week's game—a tournament, actually, to be played over two days, in Massachusetts. Before halftime, Paul got out on the court and passed the ball to a teammate who took a shot. In the third quarter, and then the fourth, he played some more. He dribbled around opponents, went for a layup or two, and took a jump shot. Then the game ended. I don't remember who won.

My stomach clenched in anger. What the hell were we doing here? Why was I sitting in a cold gym on a precious weekend morning far from home, watching my bored son play a meaningless game? What a fool I was. When both of us could have been home with the rest of our family, watching *Parks and Recreation*, or playing hearts, or hiking through the reservation nearby, we were sequestered, instead, in Scranton, Pennsylvania, collecting dust in a distant gym for a game that meant nothing to either of us.

Now I had clarity. My son had thrived in a competitive high school sport. He'd developed into a talented basketball player, finally learning how to rebound with gusto and drive in for layups, regardless of the defenders clustered under the net. He'd built close friendships with teenagers he'd otherwise have not known. And he'd grown into a responsible young man, serving as a team captain, assisting the coaches during the summer, and cultivating his already well-developed self-discipline. And it was still *fun*. Wasn't that *precisely* what high school sports, indeed all youth sports, were supposed to be?

Maybe this AAU team would serve other kids' interests. Perhaps it would elevate these boys' play and get them in front of the right college coach, who would recruit them and turn them into champions. But for Paul it was a soulless experience—an assortment of strangers unified only by their desire to impress somebody else, no matter the cost. It took me years to acknowledge how much my son's athletic career mattered to *me*, how much his star performances, when he had them, shored up *my* ego. And while the desire for social standing might be understandable, it's not admirable.

Paul shuffled over to the bleachers. I stood up, buttoned my coat, and felt relief wash over me. We marched out to our cold car parked on one of the hills next to the gym. The sun fought through cotton-ball clouds, hinting at afternoon warmth. Real spring would arrive soon, the hard ground would soften, and tiny yellow and purple flowers would erupt from the earth.

Paul slid into the car. "I hated that," he said.

"We are done with it," I said.

CHAPTER 3

College

A troubling dynamic played out with several talented girls on my running teams. After achieving some success, they began to fantasize about being recruited or sought after by a prestigious college. Parents and other respected adults ginned up the fantasy, and before long the only obstacle to attaining the dream was the unwelcome interference of their lowly high school coach or doddering teammates. The coach was an obstruction, holding the player back for the sake of the team, lacking the expertise of better coaches at other schools, or failing to appreciate the unique drama of the modern college admissions process. Rather than partners in a shared endeavor, teammates were anchors keeping them down or competitors needing to be outplayed.

I got a taste of this during one cross-country season early in my coaching career, after I failed to register our team for a giant race held on the same course as the state meet; the race would have been an ideal trial run for the more important competition later in the season. It was an honest mistake, but I knew I had to accept culpability and try to fix it.

After calling race officials and begging unsuccessfully for leniency, I first went to tell Marie, the one girl on the team who would care the most about my error. I drove up to her house after practice, rang the bell, and told her about my slipup.

"That's OK, Mrs. Flanagan!" she said with genuine warmth, bopping along the cement sidewalk that flanked her street. "It's just a race."

Her forgiveness melted my worries, and I promised that I would find a suitable substitute race.

Having consciously modeled what I thought was the best way to handle an error—first be honest and upfront about the oversight, take full responsibility, apologize sincerely, and then try to repair it—I hoped my approach might teach my runners an effective way to manage their own inevitable screwups. Marie's initial reaction, her sense of perspective about the race itself, gave me hope. And the next day, when I told the team we'd be missing the one race with the impossible hill because of my blunder—I'm so sorry, I'll make it up to you—and they pumped their arms with joy, I thought I'd averted a crisis.

But by then Marie's countenance had changed. That afternoon, she looked away when I sought eye contact. A dark scowl had replaced the easy smile she'd shared so readily the previous evening. While the rest of the team celebrated the change of plans, Marie kept to the side and pinned her arms across her chest. I learned later what had prompted her shift in outlook. After leaving me at my car the night before, she'd gone inside and reported my error to her parents, who promptly expressed their horror. It was Marie's junior year. Though already a top student, they believed she needed that race, the one I'd botched, to impress the college coaches—the very people who could ease her way into an esteemed university. Missing it was nothing short of catastrophic. My bungling and incompetence had threatened their child's future.

While never a stress-free affair, getting into college for this generation has morphed into something loaded and oppressive. It's here where the anxieties about money and status collide, causing even the most levelheaded parents and kids to lose their bearings. And kids' sports have somehow become tied up in the drama.

Why College Is So Loaded

Let's start with the basics: there's a lot of money at stake. The cost of attending a four-year college has shot up to astronomical levels over the last twenty years, way beyond the rate of inflation. To attend a private national university, students pay an average of almost $44,000 per year— a 144 percent increase over 2002 prices. While in-state universities cost close to $12,000 annually, the cost has jumped 211 percent over a twenty-year period. And the "student share" of that cost—what students pay after financial aid—has continued to rise at state colleges. For many families, especially those with multiple kids, what they pay for college will often exceed the cost of their mortgage. "This is the most complex and emotionally fraught financial decision that many families will ever make," wrote business journalist Ron Lieber.

For most households without huge nest eggs to fall back on, figuring out how to fund a child's tuition is a nagging concern. Taking out loans can weigh down a family for decades. It can also damage debtors' mental health, in this case young people at the start of their careers. Without substantial scholarships to lower the price, middle- and lower-income kids going to four-year colleges will likely find themselves in hock at the end of it. In 2019, national student loan debt had climbed to $1.6 trillion, more than car and credit card debt combined. That number is expected to rise to $3 trillion by 2030. Faced with the Hobson's choice of skipping college, with its likely long-term financial penalty, or taking out lifetime loans, with their burden built-in, kids and their parents are bound to feel a bit frantic.

On top of the staggering tuition costs, the stakes surrounding college admissions also feel impossibly high. It's an article of faith where I live that children must go to the most esteemed college they're admitted to, "fit" be damned. It's all to help our children, to set them up for a fuller life, for a future rich with opportunities. "The world, that great doofus," wrote Joseph Epstein in *Snobbery: The American Version*, "respects certain schools." The world is not entirely wrong. Some of the most competitive and remunerative companies won't bother with the dummies at any of the schools rated lower than twentieth in the *U.S. News* rankings. A degree from a top school gives new graduates access to a long list of high-powered alumni who might show preference for jobs and internships from their alma mater, and graduates from Princeton and the like get clucks of admiration from most everyone they meet.

Grown-ups also know that having a child in a top college confers respect to child *and* parents—that the sticker on the back of the car boasting of Williams or Cornell is an imprimatur of a superior upbringing. "So much of this is about parents' emotional needs," said Tim Lear, a longtime college adviser from a private school on the East Coast. "If a top school chases your kid, it's a weird sort of validation that you've done something right." A child's admission to a top college rewards parents with a huge boost in status, something most of us secretly long for.

But there's a big problem. The conventional wisdom among families grappling with the "college process" is that the top schools are next to impossible to get into. A look at admissions data tells the tale. In 1990, 53 percent of students who applied to Johns Hopkins University were accepted. In 2021, it was 11 percent. The University of Pennsylvania admitted 38 percent in 1990; today—9 percent. Jeffrey Selingo, an authority on higher education, shares this and other enervating data about colleges' greater selectivity in his book *Who Gets In and Why: A Year Inside College Admissions*. By all appearances, it's simply tougher for contemporary kids to go to the sort of college their parents went to, assuming those parents attended in the first place.

How Colleges Have Changed

There are many reasons for these shifts in colleges' perceived value and actual cost, most of which work in unison to whip up parental anxiety. Of course, there's the *U.S. News & World Report* rankings, begun in 1983, that grade colleges on various measures—SAT scores of the incoming class, number of applicants and admitted students, percentage of admitted students who enroll (the "yield"), among other metrics— and then order them from best to worst. The usual suspects populate the top of the list, but there's movement from year to year. The rankings became an easily digestible way for families to evaluate colleges, a handy report card to determine which schools were worth applying to. And because of their sway over potential applicants, the rankings compelled colleges to change how they approached admissions. Self-respecting and competitive colleges want to ascend that list, and most figured out that a good way to do that was to attract and reject more applicants. Doing this would bump up their selectivity, a key measure in the rankings.

About a decade after the *U.S. News* lists debuted, colleges also began using direct marketing materials to attract potential applicants. They had help from the College Board, a nonprofit body that owns and oversees the SAT, which began to sell test takers' names and addresses to colleges. Selingo reports that the average student's name is sold about eighteen times over the course of his or her four years of high school, which explains why households with teenagers are deluged with glossy flyers from colleges and universities around the country. The goal of all the marketing is to increase the number of students who apply, to which any observer could only declare: mission accomplished.

To stave off a likely rejection, and to increase their odds of success, kids apply to more and more schools. The emergence of the Common App has made the whole endeavor a lot easier, or at least less painful, for families willing to pay the application fees. The number of colleges and universities students apply to continues to rise. In 2021, after the pandemic disrupted every aspect of collegiate life, the number of Common Apps rose by 11 percent, a new record. And if I sound holier than thou, bear in mind that my then-high-school senior applied to fifteen colleges in 2016.

The college rankings, the marketing, the new tools to apply and assess one's prospects, and of course social media, which thrives on comparison and competition, have altogether turned where a child goes to college into a blunt measure of personal worth. By extension, because a kid's success reflects the parents' work—and *talent*, and *standing*—college admissions seem to say a lot about Mom and Dad, too. In some circles, possibly all of suburbia, this makes a kid's admission to an elite college profoundly, disproportionately, and irrationally weighty.

There's just one problem: for all their telegraphing about their desire to admit the best and brightest teenagers, colleges are opaque about what that actually means. High standardized tests, of course. Top grades, too. But what beyond these no-brainers can students do to distinguish themselves from their equally qualified peers? How to convey how extra special your child is, in just the way the college wants, when admissions offices are swamped with applications and fewer schools even take the time to meet the applicants personally? It had all become maddeningly unpredictable.

But wait. There was one avenue for admission at most colleges that has remained faithful and clear: athletics. As long as universities field varsity teams with coaches who want to win, they'll need new student athletes joining their rosters every year.

Professionalized College Sports

College sports have changed dramatically over the last few decades. Many of these developments have made the prospect of being a recruited athlete more attractive.

One of the most significant was the passage of Title IX, which banned sex-based discrimination in all educational programs receiving federal funds. In sports, this legislation meant colleges would have to expand the number of women's teams and create new slots for them on existing ones to make women's sports commensurate with men's. It took until the 1990s for the full force of the law to take effect, but when it did, the numbers were startling: Just over 800,000 girls played high school sports in 1972–1973; almost 3.5 million did in 2018–2019. In college, about 33,000 women joined varsity teams in 1972–1973; in 2017–2018, there were more than 216,000.

The surge in women's collegiate sports, along with more team options for men, had the effect of doubling the number of students participating in college sports between 1982 and 2020. A few months before the pandemic struck, the NCAA announced that almost half a million college kids played sports—a record high—and that colleges and universities were continuing to expand the number of teams they offered.

College sports also have become vastly more sophisticated and central to schools' identities. Twenty years ago, researchers from the Mellon Foundation concluded that college recruiting had become "more aggressive, professional and intense." These scholars warned that walk-on players were growing rarer and that coaches were taking a larger role in admissions. Even among Division III schools, where any given team's record was an afterthought to most, coaches and colleges had become more intent on winning—a function in part of the ubiquity of *U.S. News* rankings, which amped up the competition among colleges at all levels. Victorious sports teams were seen as a way to build alumni engagement—and a shortcut to more donations. The Mellon researchers warned that professionalized college sports, which celebrated athletes on campus over the rest of the student body, were undermining the educational mission of some universities, and limiting other students' opportunities to compete. To state the obvious, these developments have only accelerated.

This trend toward professionalization in college sports is evident in other ways. A generation ago, coaches at universities were often professors or staff members who stepped up to coach the sport they loved; today, colleges rely on professional coaches with large staffs to manage teams. Likewise, many college coaches used to pick teams the way high schools do, via tryouts. Now, most select their players through an elaborate and expensive recruiting process that can cost even smaller liberal arts schools hundreds of thousands of dollars. In keeping with this professionalization, the rate of disbursements at Division I colleges and universities on athletics often outpaces what they spend on academics.

The question of whether a demanding college career is right for the athlete is almost never under discussion. As we'll explore in a later chapter, in at least one study that compared quality of life between former Division I college athletes and less-active peers, the once-elite players came out a lot worse. But this reality is easily hidden beneath the financial promises and social capital dangled before prospective recruits. As college sports have become more professional, they've also become more attractive to families that are nervous about how their child will ever get into a decent college, let alone afford it.

Advantages for Recruited Athletes

My awareness of this new reality came gradually, when the rumor mill reported on local high school athletes who had been accepted into fancy colleges long before everyone else. Sometimes word got out about soccer and lacrosse players, usually girls, who'd "committed" to Northwestern or Duke in tenth grade. Like most parents with precollegiate kids, I suspect, I was oblivious to the complicated internal machinations going on at colleges surrounding athletes and admissions. What I did realize, what was unmistakable to those even vaguely aware of college happenings, was that celebrated athletes got into top schools earlier and easier than everyone else.

I saw another side of this as a coach. Runners are not typically recruited before junior or even senior year of high school; I've yet to coach a girl who was seriously courted before eleventh grade. But in soccer and lacrosse, there's a mad dash to "secure" the best girls as soon as the NCAA allows, which used to be as early as ninth grade. During their sport's official off-season, many of these girls would float over to winter or spring track to get faster or stronger in their "main" athletic pursuit. If they practiced racing the 100, the thinking went, the girls might get speedier with the soccer ball or lacrosse stick. None of us running coaches objected, as long as the girls' preoccupation with the sport that would get them into college didn't interfere with our work.

But, of course, it often did. Most of these girls went to their club team practices in the cracks of our training and games. Naturally, playing two demanding sports at once, and striving to placate competing coaches and conflicting schedules, couldn't help but affect their running; their quads and calves perpetually ached. This high-stakes juggling also put a strain on them. I recall one girl nonchalantly dashing off from an evening track meet at the Armory in New York City to her travel lacrosse team practice in Randolph, New Jersey. Another girl regularly raced off from cross-country practice at five thirty to get to her ice-hockey team at six. (She also managed five AP classes that fall.) Still another scuttled back and forth between indoor track and club field hockey, always apologizing for having to leave early or for arriving late. These girls were talented athletes and polite humans who were doing what they thought was necessary to get into a superior college. And in return for their relentless exhaustion and chronic stress, all three were recruited for the club sport they played during cross-country or track season.

College admissions in general, and the special carve-outs for athletic recruits, do not lend themselves to simple explanations. Each of the three sports divisions has different rules governing recruitment, including how much (if any), and what type, of scholarship assistance they can provide. There's also great variation among colleges in how they handle athletic recruits, especially at the Division III level. Complicating matters further, colleges generally don't share data on their admitted students, preferring to keep the process shrouded in mystery.

That said, we do know that athletes benefit over other applicants in two critical ways. Most important, recruited athletes are generally not held to the same academic standard as nonathletes: it's easier for athletes to get in. Also compelling, they enjoy a quicker admissions process; while regular seniors are weary and fretful through the spring, most recruited athletes know where they're going before Thanksgiving.

How do academic standards differ for athletes and everybody else?

Scholars at the Mellon Foundation found that athletes at elite schools were admitted at up to four times the rate of even those applying as legacies and from underrepresented groups. They discovered that most male recruited athletes at the Ivies scored much lower on their SATs than the student body at large. In some sports, the deficits were significant: recruited hockey players, for example, scored an average of 177 fewer points than students who weren't recruited, while the gaps in basketball and football were 165 and 144 points, respectively. According to one 2004 study, the academic discrepancy was even greater when GPA and class rank were part of the calculus.

More recent data shows how these trends have continued. A trio of scholars examining information that emerged from a lawsuit against Harvard confirmed that the recruited athletes they admitted were significantly weaker than ordinary applicants. Indeed, these athletes were "14 times as likely to be admitted as those that are not recruited athletes," giving them the highest admissions rate. "Although recruited athletes are less than 1% of the applicant pool, they make up over 10% of the admitted class," the scholars observed.

Sociologist Rick Eckstein, an authority on collegiate sports, summarized how recruited athletes benefit in the admissions scramble: "regardless of sport, gender, or level of play, recruited varsity athletes' aggregate academic credentials (generally measured by standardized test scores) are almost universally lower than those of the entire student body."

Depending on the size of the college and its number of teams, this edge for athletes can have a cascading impact on all applicants. Georgetown, for example, sets aside 158 "slots" for freshman athletes, out of a total class of 1,600; these are essentially reserved spots for the chosen players. The majority of applicants at Georgetown, then—a bit more than 90 percent—are selected without regard for their sportiness. But at Trinity, about half the students admitted early in 2017 were athletes—many, incidentally, for sports that are atypical in low-income areas, like field hockey, crew, and squash. And at Amherst, where almost one-third of each incoming class of 500 is allocated for recruits, competition for the remaining 340 openings is fierce. These set-asides for student athletes reduce the number of available openings for kids who don't play sports, but provide a tantalizing opportunity for those who do.

There's a racial and economic impact of these set-asides, too. When colleges reserve so many slots for recruited athletes, they're expecting to achieve their larger admissions goals—often for greater economic and racial diversity—with the applicants who are *not* athletes. For white, well-off suburban kids, that makes athletics their best hope for admission. Contrary to popular perception, white kids are overrepresented in college sports. Indeed, roughly 61 percent of student athletes on campus are white, higher than their representation in the general student body. In some sports, the percentage of white athletes is especially steep: 85 percent of lacrosse players and 66 percent of soccer players. "When you step back to think about all the teams that most colleges field," Selingo wrote, "the locker rooms are, in fact, dominated by white, wealthier students."

Recruited athletes (and their anxious parents) also profit from an abbreviated admissions process. Nearly all recruited athletes are admitted via early decision, a kind of binding arrangement between the school and the applicant that this is the college they'll attend. Colleges benefit from this arrangement as well, because students admitted early are generally not included in acceptance rate calculations. The more students admitted early, the fewer spots available for regular admission, driving up a college's perceived selectivity.

But many recruits have a good idea about where they're going even sooner. Coaches submit the athletes they've selected for their teams to the admissions offices ahead of the application deadlines. If the flagged candidates satisfy the colleges' internal academic standards for athletes, those athletes will receive "likely letters" from the school, a virtual lock on admission. Even at DIII schools that don't offer athletic scholarships or admissions guarantees, athletes recommended by coaches often are afforded a "pre-read" of their qualifications ahead of time. Melissa Korn and Jennifer Levitz, education reporters for *The Wall Street Journal*, refer to the special handling athletes receive in admissions "as a sort of parallel pathway, separate from the general pool of candidates."

College sports appeal to potential applicants in other ways: there are scholarships to be had. Over the past few decades, the NCAA has multiplied the amount of money it offers athletes, from $250 million in the

1990s to $3.6 billion in 2019—an increase of 1,340 percent. For families who can't easily afford six-figure tuition bills, and who recoil at the thought of forever repaying their student loans, striving for an athletic scholarship might seem like a wise move. And many parents share this dream: a 2019 TD Ameritrade study found that some 50 percent of sports families were investing in their kids' athletics with the expectation that the child would be awarded an athletic scholarship to college.

Never mind that only about 2 percent of high school athletes are awarded some amount of money for a sports scholarship in college, and only at the most competitive Division I and Division II levels. Forget, too, that no more than 15 percent of Division I players receive full scholarships, most often in football and basketball. Disregard the reality that about one-third of all NCAA athletes receive any sports-related financial aid of any kind. Three billion dollars is a lot of money dangled in front of families, and in lower-income homes especially, the prospect of winning an athletic scholarship might seem like the fastest—and cheapest—route to college.

What does all this have to do with youth sports? Families chasing college scholarships need to get their kids in the game. For white middle- and upper-class suburban families who fear that their kids' college options are shrinking, joining the rough-and-tumble world of competitive youth sports seems like the best way to go. "(W)hite upper-class parents, in particular, see athletics as the only viable pathway into elite colleges for their children," Selingo observed.

These motives drive seriousness and excess on the sidelines and playing fields. To be good enough for a college team, kids have to start early and play often. They need the best coaches, and the most competitive leagues, at younger and younger ages. If these kids have any chance of making it to Bowdoin or Brown, or Alabama or Duke, they need to make the third-grade travel team. And down the road, they must show up at the right weekend tournaments and three-day regattas put on by their travel teams, for it's at these showcase events where college coaches scout for future players, where all that sacrifice is expected to pay off.

Varsity Blues

Cultivating an athlete fit for college takes a commitment by parents and players. All those practices, games, and training sessions—someone has to manage logistics for the child. And suppose the kid has no interest or talent in sports. Suppose the *parent* has no enthusiasm for orchestrating the whole endeavor. If only there were a way to seize the admissions advantages recruited athletes receive without enduring the sacrifice and inconvenience of actually being one. . . .

Perhaps the whole scheme was inevitable.

For the uninitiated, Operation Varsity Blues is the name that the FBI gave to its sweeping sting operation against the dozens of people across the country who carried out crimes in exchange for secure spots at elite colleges. The fifty-seven defendants implicated in the scam committed bribery, fraud, and racketeering, among other assorted illegalities, to advance their child's college prospects. In its simplest terms, wealthy parents paid college coaches for spots at prestigious universities.

Rick Singer came up with the plan. Having been a legitimate college counselor for years, and before that a high school and collegiate coach, Singer figured out where the soft spots were in the admissions process. He correctly discerned that college coaches have astonishing muscle in determining which applicants get admitted and understood that coaches have few overseers checking their work. With top colleges drowning in applications, admissions staff had come to rely on the coaches' word about an applicant's athletic credentials. Colleges had also become increasingly fond of early decision applicants, the avenue through which most college recruits apply.

Singer was intimate with the desperation parents felt to get their kids into top schools. When he told some about a "side-door" route he'd identified that would virtually guarantee admission, many parents seized the opportunity. The "side door" was typically a substantial payment to Singer via his bogus foundation, who then turned around and paid coaches and test falsifiers who were in on the scheme. (It differed from the generally accepted but mysterious backdoor route to an admission's offer—a multimillion-dollar gift from the fabulously wealthy to the chosen college—in that it didn't cost as much. Because it involved overt bribes, the ploy also was illegal.)

All coaches needed to do was vouch for the athletic qualifications of these select applicants, some of whom were angling to be recruited for sports they'd never played. Singer altered the kids' applications by inserting made-up athletic credentials. Parents helped by paying the bribe, keeping up the ruse with their children, and supplying action photos as needed. Devin Sloane, to name one father, insisted his son dress up in water polo gear and pose for pictures in the family pool. These shots were photoshopped later to appear more authentic and accompanied the boy's application to USC as a water polo recruit.

When the story broke in March 2019, it was met with fury—and fascination. There were celebrities—like actress Felicity Huffman, who paid $15,000 to shine up her daughter's SAT scores. There were millionaires—like former Pimco chief executive Douglas Hodge, who forked over hundreds of thousands of dollars to doctor four of his kids' applications. There were elite institutions—Georgetown, Stanford, USC, already the object of so much awe, corrupted from within. The judge who presided over Huffman's trial expressed a commonly held view: "The outrage is a system that is already so distorted by money and privilege in the first place."

Because it exposed unsavory actors doing deplorable things, Varsity Blues was an irresistible story; the characters' obvious privilege and shameless criminality made them easy to condemn. But it also revealed one way that these millionaires and other big shots are, awkwardly, just like us: they too are enamored of elite colleges, frantic about admissions, and desperate to find an edge for their children. Rather than invest in their kids' lacrosse or tennis careers and drive them hither and yon to out-of-state tournaments and conditioning clinics, they took shortcuts to make it look like they had.

This massive cheating scheme shined an unforgiving light on the nexus between college sports and admissions. "The recent Operation Varsity Blues scandal is generally laid at the feet of an evil entrepreneur and the entitled parents who hired him," Eckstein told me. "But there would have been no 'scandal' if universities had not already built a very welcoming back entrance only available to recruited athletes."

Playing for a Purpose

In some ways, it all makes sense. The dramatic changes at colleges and universities over the last twenty-five years—from prohibitive prices, to ramped-up sports teams, to preferential admissions for athletes—and, on top of these, the greater prestige associated with the elite schools, have revolutionized what's happening on the playing fields and gyms across the country. Kids aren't running around in their Keds, tossing a Frisbee or shooting baskets at an impromptu game of pick-up basketball. More often, they're marching in uniforms, listening to the coaches with the clipboards, and striving to differentiate themselves from their peers. Their sports have a *purpose*. For many families, that purpose is transactional: kids play to get into college.

By junior year especially (at the latest!) when college coaches are scouring for fresh talent, high school athletes need to demonstrate their ability. This is why Marie's parents erupted when I, a rookie coach fixated on what running can do for your soul, flubbed the race entry. This is also why, if you live in certain neighborhoods, the conversation among friends with young children often drifts to tryouts and tournaments and teams. There's no escaping it.

While we weren't looking, youth sports had become a means to another, much greater end.

PART II

THE SIX PARADOXES OF
YOUTH SPORTS TODAY

Kids who play sports and join teams can derive vital benefits from their athletic endeavors.

Having played multiple sports myself, I appreciate the enduring advantages that athletics have given me. Even now, I lumber out the door most days for a five-mile run or install myself in a gym to be beaten up by a trainer. This is why my husband and I prodded our own three kids off the couch and into the game, with mixed results. Health! Discipline! Friendship! And it was for these salutary purposes that I began coaching cross-country so many years ago. I had hoped to share with a sliver of the next generation the gift of running, a daily practice that has buoyed me for so long.

But the changes that have swept through youth sports threaten that promise. Heather Bergeson, a pediatric physician who works in sports medicine, sees the downstream effect of these hopes and dreams in her waiting room, in the form of a torn ACL. "I think that we're going to lose the benefits of youth sports," she told me. "We just corrupted it."

It's not the sports themselves that are flawed but the way we do or don't deliver them to kids that's so costly. It's the arrangement we've allowed to develop, with perverse incentives that celebrate excess and promote greed. It's a system—ad hoc, decentralized, with no one in charge—that forces parents of aspiring athletes into servitude. And it's too much for a majority of children from low-income families, who have neither the wealth nor the time to devote to this overblown undertaking but who would gain from playing sports the way they were intended: in moderation, and without extreme adult interference. "It's a model that's dysfunctional at best, broken at worst," Tom Farrey, who heads the Sports & Society Program at the Aspen Institute, told me.

Let's take a tour of six of the paradoxes this warped system has spurred.

CHAPTER 4

The Myth of Character Building

One summer, my restless and energetic mother cajoled me and my siblings into joining her at the public tennis courts in our hometown. None of us knew how to play, including her, but she was determined to rouse us into trying. We weren't a summer camp family—too expensive—but the sight of her five children loafing aimlessly around the house, absorbed by *Love, American Style* and whimpering for her to please turn on the air-conditioning drove Mom to act. She launched a campaign to get us to play. For the rest of the summer, some combination of siblings would accompany my mother to the hard green courts next to the high school and try to grasp the basics of the game.

This was in Madison, New Jersey, a largely white middle-class sub-
urb that was just far enough from the action to be spurned by Wall Street
hotshots, but close enough to New York City to attract a healthy blend of
managers, electricians, and teachers. Football ruled, and the high school's
head coach was adored (among some) for his apparent toughness. But
gallant sports like tennis and golf, where the emphasis leaned toward skill
development and sportsmanship, also had a following.

We were four girls and a boy. I was the youngest. The oldest of my
sisters and my brother couldn't hack the game. Tennis was too maddening: balls hit too hard sailed over the fence that circled the courts, requiring search parties in the poison ivy–infested woods; balls hit too
softly gasped to the net or dribbled onto other courts; 95 percent of
"play" time was devoted to retrieving balls, apologizing to other ama-
teurs, or cursing the wretched racquet for another betrayal. But three of
us stuck with it, along with Mom, and over time we got so we could hit
the ball over the net with some regularity. By the end of that first summer, and the summer after that, and with the help of some lessons my
parents had sprung for during the winter, we could play a reasonable,
not thoroughly embarrassing game of tennis. As with softball and running, the other sports I played as a kid, tennis prodded me to grow and
learn in ways my nonathletic endeavors did not.

Like most parents, mine viewed athletics as vehicles for self-knowledge
and character development. While they enjoyed any fleeting success we
had (along with companionship on the tennis court), they nudged us to
play in hopes we'd pick up a little resilience and self-discipline, along
with some useful lessons in how to work with others. Dad also believed
that lounging was a moral lapse, and that teenagers really needed something to do. Though they might not put it this way, the adults I know
today who are enthusiastic about youth sports think much the same. They
encourage their kids to play because they believe, as I do, that athletics
play a vital part in child development.

And coaches think so, too. "If my livelihood is really dependent on getting a kid to throw a ball through another team's goal, I will have a tough time justifying my existence," Jack Bowen, a water polo coach and sports ethicist, told me. All the training, the expenditures in time and effort by kids, parents, and coaches, is intended to be about more than accumulating wins.

There are valid reasons to hold this view. Child psychologists and development experts agree that youth sports are instructive. Philosophers, too, have long considered athletics a vital arena for growth, and some of their modern ilk echo that view. "Sports can be a catalyst for learning the higher virtues," Bowen said. Because most kids choose to join teams, and are highly motivated to improve and learn, "sports are uniquely primed to teach ethics," he added.

I've witnessed that growth among the hundreds of runners I've coached—the natural way they come to inhabit their bodies, the evident pride they glean from training and racing, the glimpses of dawning self-knowledge they sometimes reveal. But that kind of development is not guaranteed. We like to believe that sports are inherently wholesome and valuable, but what kids pick up on the playing field depends entirely on the environment. And that environment is unlike the one most parents grew up with. Saturated with money, amped up by the stakes, and altered by the cost of college and admissions office maneuverings, the youth sports ecosystem—and we're central to that, parents—may not be building character but eroding it.

Myths and Values about Sports

In playing sports, we all subscribe to myths of what they mean and what they can do for us. Jay Coakley and I spoke at length about this in the fall of 2017, shortly after he'd retired from full-time teaching at the University of Colorado. His abiding preoccupation is what he calls the Great

Sports Myth: the popular notion that sports are intrinsically good, that those who play absorb that goodness, and that sports invariably foster personal and community health. It's an unexamined nostrum that few are willing to challenge because the myth reinforces entrenched cultural messages about the value of competition and the belief that success goes to those who deserve it. "We assume sports build character and teamwork, but there's no research," he said.

I also spoke to Richard Weissbourd, a child and family therapist who runs the Making Caring Common project at Harvard, a national initiative that aims to highlight kids' moral and social development at home and in schools. Weissbourd believes that one of the most pernicious myths that adults hold about sports is that they magically reveal a child's true character. According to this narrative, a boy who stares down a tough pitcher at the bottom of the ninth in a championship game shows that he's made of the right stuff—strong, impervious to nerves, good in a foxhole. In fact, he's just demonstrated that he's capable in one particular kind of setting, in one particular *game*, which may or may not be transferrable to the classroom, with family, or among friends. The reverse is also true: the kid who bobbles the ball in a close game or abandons a sport in frustration may be confident and dogged elsewhere. In truth, Weissbourd has said, "sports don't reveal a lot about what kind of person you are, in the most important ways."

What coaches and parents emphasize is apt to align with one of the two distinct sets of American values that sports reflect in the United States. The first set includes toughness, grit, resilience, bravery, and sacrifice—warrior qualities that matter deeply to some communities, especially the working-class and low-income, Weissbourd wrote in *The Parents We Mean to Be*. Sports are thought to reveal these virtues, and kids who show them on the field are glorified for them. Subscribers to this myth believe that the principal goal of youth sports is to expose kids to adversity, so they learn to manage and overcome it.

Wealthier, often suburban, communities, on the other hand, tend to adopt a different myth. They are apt to view youth sports as a way to transmit cooperation, self-esteem, and empathy. Here, sports are cheered for teaching kids how to work together and have fun.

Most communities and teams contain some mix of both value sets, contradictory though they may be. The sports-are-about-toughness mob sometimes condemns the sports-should-be-fun group for awarding participation trophies. (Ninnies!) The sports-should-be-fun crowd quietly lambasts the sports-are-about-toughness team for making too much of athletics, of blowing it all out of proportion. (Knuckle-draggers!) From my vantage point on the sidelines, these purported values tend to be flexible, bandied about by parents depending on how athletically talented their child is and their own investment in her success.

Both environments can help or hurt kids' development, Weissbourd wrote. An exacting coach who rewards effort, expects work, reinforces the message that hardship can be confronted and overcome, and who dials down gratuitous praise can spur moral growth. But a more radical variant of this sort of coach, who writes off a child as weak for failing at a crucial moment in a game, say, can set off a tsunami of debilitating shame. Sports that emphasize teamwork and fun over toughness, on the other side, are less weighted and fraught, allowing all kinds of kids, even the athletically average, to make friends and frolic. But kids in these "fun" environments often receive confusing messages from grown-ups who at home downplay the importance of winning but then shriek at umpires and shout instructions to their child during games. They also miss out on the deep satisfaction and character-building possibilities that can come from truly competitive play.

My own experience taught me that sports can be challenging *and* fun. Indeed, upon discovering running, I learned that the fun—and the growth—sprung from the challenge.

Growing Up through Sports

I started playing softball when I was six, tossing the ball back and forth with my sister Kathy on our slanted front lawn, then catching long, high fly balls my father hit to me out in the street. I joined the town league as soon as I could, which for a girl growing up in the 1970s, right after the passage of Title IX, was sixth grade. My team was named Home Life, after a now-defunct insurance company, and our assortment of middle schoolers practiced twice a week on a lumpy field around the corner from my house. Every Sunday, we put on our lemon-yellow uniforms and played a seven-inning game.

My mother coached us. This was a shocking development, as Mom already was locked into a brutally unrewarding schedule that revolved around feeding five kids, keeping her humble consulting business afloat, and attending desultory evening meetings for all the nonprofits she assisted. But *The Feminine Mystique* had lit her up. She started criticizing Nixon during dinner and asking my father to bring his dishes to the sink. Around the same time, she signed up to coach my softball team. It never occurred to me to ask her why, but I imagine she was desperate to escape the imprisoning kitchen, if only for a while, and to model female leadership for her four daughters. My lone memory of that season was hitting a grand slam, a singular feat I never repeated.

In high school, a tiny Italian woman who played in a women's league coached us. Coach Mara was passionate about the sport and determined that we would be, too. We practiced Monday through Saturday, fielding balls on the hard gym floor when it poured and setting up an infield in the teachers' parking lot when it drizzled. Every day, she drilled us in game situations, strategy, and technique, and lectured us about making softball our top priority. School, family, and friends would have to come after softball if we wanted to be champions, she told us. We would have to sacrifice, commit, and suffer.

Our team was packed with able and experienced players who sparkled during practice but who somehow always crumbled during the big games. After a loss, Coach would call us into the locker room afterward and harangue us about our careless errors. *How many times had we gone over that play?! You* know *you have to back up the throw at first! What were you thinking trying to throw out a steal to second with a runner on third?* She'd fling up her arms as she spoke, calling out some girls by name but more often simply ranting about our haplessness. She was exasperated and befuddled, interpreting our inexplicable midgame wretchedness as a mark of her deficiencies as a coach. Because we all respected her, we never protested these dressing-downs. We were as mystified by our failings as she, and when she quit at the end of our disappointing season, we blamed ourselves.

Next season, new coach. He was young, a former baseball player, with thick honey-colored hair that swept across his forehead and an exaggerated nose that seemed to swallow up his face. He yelled at us, too, but more indiscriminately than our prior coach, without considering the sensibilities of the individual. But some gel that was absent the previous year appeared organically this season to hold us together, and our reflex to panic during close games abated.

The midseason games are lost to memory, overshadowed by tragedy in my own home.

It was a gray afternoon on a Thursday in April. Our team was scattered around the field, waiting for ground balls and flies that our coach was hitting out to us at random. At shortstop, I had a good view of the road adjacent to the field and quickly identified the fat AMC Pacer pulling into a spot next to the first-base line as my father's. Not for one second did I think to myself, *What's Dad doing here on a Thursday afternoon?* I'd been expecting him. That morning, one of my sisters had been rushed to the hospital. Details of her story are not mine to tell. But her persistent fragility became an ongoing feature of our household.

Dad walked up to the chain-link fence around the field and signaled to me. I looked at my coach, pointed at my father, and Coach nodded at me: *Go.* Dad was wearing a suit as if he'd come from his office in New York. He thrust one hand in his pants pocket and gripped the rusty fence with the other. My sister was in the ICU at Morristown Memorial Hospital, he said. Mom is there with her. She should be OK. Don't leave practice early—come afterward. He wasn't one to crumble or cry, but he looked worn-out and off-balance, humbled by this family catastrophe that couldn't be fixed by tinkering with the numbers. His kind brown eyes were extra soft.

I jogged back to the field and resumed my place at shortstop. The team was quieter than usual for the rest of practice, probably out of respect for my situation. I was certain everyone knew, but no one said, "Oh, I'm so sorry," or asked, "What happened?" We just kept on throwing around the bases, scooping up balls in the dirt before they slipped through our legs, and swinging at easy pitches our coach tossed across the plate. The rhythms of play were a comfort. So, too, was the intangible bond that connected all of us to one another. My teammates, my friends—they were there for me without saying a word.

Our season progressed, and we advanced to the final round of the state tournament, winning the game handily; it wasn't even close. After our on-field celebration, we made our way back to the empty school parking lot and bounced home. We're state champions! Never before in school history! Sauntering through the halls on Monday, still buoyed by the win, I glanced around at the cliques gathering at lockers and lunch tables, at bored teachers standing guard at their doors, and waited for them to say something. Friends in the cafeteria who'd heard about the win said, "Hey, congratulations," when they saw me, then turned back to their tuna fish and Jell-O. With my fellow jocks on the softball team, it was different. *Remember when you dove for that line drive and got the double play? Can you believe Deb hit two triples?* For us, the game was still on, our victory still thrumming and alive inside us. Even today, forty-odd years since that win, I recall striding up to the plate and smacking the ball out to center field, rallying our bench.

But the jubilation was hard to hold on to, even for us. Our team captains hosted a barbecue the following weekend to celebrate, and we all gathered at someone's house. Subsets of friends within the team splintered off, some of them piling on top of each other on the family room sofa, like they had at the end of the championship game. When we all sat down together with our burgers and salad, conversation sputtered. It had been a week since our win, and five days without practices, and already the bond that held us together had started to fray. I left the party with an ache in my stomach for the intense camaraderie we'd lost. The dissolution was inevitable, I'd come to learn; that kind of passion can't be sustained on memories alone.

My last season of softball was abysmal. Most of the players from our championship team had graduated, and the girls coming in to replace them were inexperienced and unskilled. On top of it, the school had dumped last year's coach for mysterious indiscretions and replaced him with a happy-go-lucky gym teacher who always smiled and kept things breezy. At practice, he'd hit a dozen balls to the infield, give a few of us a chance to bat, and call it off at four fifteen. He was agnostic about our terribleness, congratulating us for showing up and celebrating our half-assed efforts. He couldn't have been nicer, and he was unbearable. If I remember right, we lost every game.

It's clear to me now that my childhood experiences playing tennis and softball were about as good as they can get in terms of character growth. By throwing me into excruciating but ultimately trivial situations that were absent from the rest of my life—bases loaded, two outs, two strikes—they compelled me to grapple with what felt like intolerable pressure. I learned I would survive. Playing for a rotating cast of coaches and with an ever-changing group of teammates, I learned how to get along, and how to work with others. Most important, engaging in serious play on the tennis court and softball field helped me figure out who I was: self-conscious, trapped in my own head, and inclined to anxiety and self-flagellation. Despite these handicaps, I began to think of myself as an athlete, as someone who could achieve things physically that most others couldn't. These were the early stirrings of confidence, an alien state of mind for me that became more manifest as I grew and moved on to other sports.

Do Sports Build Character?

There's no ironclad proof that sports build character. The results of a meta-analysis on the connection between athletics and character development make that clear: "Forty years of research, conducted by more than 20 researchers studying tens of thousands of athletes and non-athletes from youth, high schools, collegiate and Olympic levels, simply does not support the notion of sport as a character-building activity, particularly as it applies to sportsmanship behaviors and moral reasoning ability."

It's true that coaches can build cooperative team cultures and reinforce useful habits among players. "But that doesn't mean they necessarily creep over to class, school, occupation, or family," Jay Coakley explained.

Furthermore, athletic teams are not the only place for kids to learn how to work together, and it's impossible to determine which particular experience makes a person highly disciplined, say, or genuinely collaborative. "I played sports all the way through college, and beyond," he said, "but I did all kinds of other things, too, that have made me who I am." There's simply insufficient data to tease out the effect of sports on a young person's character vis-à-vis other activities and experiences that also shape development.

But that's not to say that kids don't *learn* from sports, or that coaches have no lasting impact on how children mature. As Weissbourd observes, kids make discoveries through sports, but what they absorb is entirely dependent on the context. If a coach degrades players, makes competition too central to the experience, leaves kids out, tolerates backtalk to the referees, and mismanages parents, then kids will pick up destructive lessons. "Sports can be harmful to kids in these conditions," he said. On the other hand, if the coach is fair and respectful to the team and referees; if she helps kids empathize with players on both teams; if she enables kids to handle loss, and to be grateful, and to respect her opponents, then yes—sports can build character. In short: it all depends.

In the absence of evidence, there are theories and testimonials posited by philosophers, child development experts, and ordinary adults who insist that athletics sculpted their lives.

"My high school sports experiences shaped me into a functioning adult," Maggie Lynch, now twenty-four, explained in an email.

Aidan Connly, a recent college graduate who played high school football and lacrosse, said, "I learned to never quit and to ignore the noise."

Jacqui Young, twenty-seven, said playing volleyball, softball, and basketball as a teenager taught her how to work with others, to appreciate her responsibility to the collective. (Group projects in the classroom resonated in a different way: "They made me feel more put-upon than anything," she said.)

Memories may not be controlled experiments, but the volume and intensity of such reports is striking. Indeed, it seems that every adult who played sports growing up can instantly resurrect a story from the playing field or team bus that had an impact.

Kids can grow from sports in other ways, too. Competitive athletic environments compel them to engage with their own and others' powerful feelings. Before long, they learn to manage the anger, sadness, embarrassment, and joy that playing evokes. If the sports environment is healthy, kids can also learn how to control their aggression. In games, after all, one team or individual is pitted against another, and during that competition the goal is to defeat the other—aggressively, if need be. But once the contest is over, everyone reverts back to human beings again, maybe even friends, and the aggression has to be shut down. "It's hard to imagine a more powerful deterrent to violating another human being," Weissbourd wrote, "than recognizing that our hostile feelings toward another person are a kind of fiction, manufactured by a game, and have nothing to do with him or her at all—that we irrationally invent enemies."

With the right leadership, sports also can invite other moral virtues, including appreciation for an opponent's skill, toleration for a weaker player's mistakes, and respect for an imperfect referee. This kind of "demanding morality," Weissbourd wrote, builds empathy: children learn that their emotions, no matter how passionate, are not paramount—that others' feelings and experiences are equally valid.

Philosophy professor Drew Hyland argues that serious engagement in sports also can trigger two profound interior developments: "the experience of deep, passionate commitment and self-knowledge." Hyland drew on his own time playing basketball to share how deeply it had affected him. "There was no experience in my scholastic or college education that led me to more self-knowledge than my basketball experience, no course or classroom in which I learned more about my capacities, my limitations, where I was willing to compromise, and where I would take my stand."

One of the most lucid illustrations of self-knowledge gleaned through sports comes from Mark Edmundson, an English professor at UVA and former high school football player. In his 2012 essay on sports and character for *The Chronicle of Higher Education*, Edmundson explores how playing football drove the kind of moral growth that warrior communities value.

Physically unimpressive—"I was buttery soft around the waist, nearsighted, not especially fast, and not agile at all"—Edmundson nonetheless had the will to stick with the sport, despite the grueling double practices during summer's dog days and regular beatdowns by the coaches. Flouting the expectations of all, he outlasted more talented athletes and earned a measure of self-respect. "I became a tougher, more daring person," he wrote.

He also vanquished the self-consciousness that had haunted him and learned to evaluate himself by his own interior standards rather than those imposed from others. It was the regular practices, the hard drills day after day after day, that forced this lasting transition, he wrote. And the resilience and persistence he absorbed during football guided him through the long slog of graduate school and the job search that followed.

But there were rotten lessons, too. The daily orchestrated violence made him more brutal. Given the hierarchical nature of sports, he became more interested in power and reigning over others. He realized that he'd grown accustomed to thinking in terms of physical domination and that this mindset would be hard to let go: "Once the punch in the mouth is part of your repertoire—once you've done it a few times as an adult—it never really goes away." And he could see how the culture he inhabited was aggressively homophobic, obsessed with physical supremacy, and consequently hostile to the value of kindness.

A handful of studies corroborate Edmundson's experience. Kids who wrestle and play football are 40 percent more likely to be violent outside of sports than their nonathletic peers. "Players are encouraged to be violent outside the sport because they are rewarded for being violent inside it," said Derek Kreager, who conducted the research. A study involving sixteen hundred male high school athletes found that football and basketball players were two times as likely to abuse their female dating partners as athletes in other sports. Most research on alcohol use among high school athletes shows a positive relationship between the two, though it's not clear that one "causes" the other. The link is especially strong in higher-income areas.

We ferry our kids to the field for the same reason our parents did: because we believe sports build character. But the evidence is lacking, and the milieu in which kids now play is inclined to do the opposite. Coakley believes that the way youth sports have changed over the past twenty years undermines character development. "Sports have gotten more cutthroat and competitive among kids and parents," he said.

"Some kids survive the system because they've joined other activities," he added. "They've made it in *spite* of sports and become a pretty good twenty-three-year-old."

To the extent that there's consensus on sport's contribution to character, then, it appears to be this: what kids glean from athletics depends entirely on a shifting and tangled array of variables. Community values, parental attitudes toward sports, the coaches' manner and methods, the child's own temperament and training, and countless other intangibles determine what kids learn from athletics. Sports themselves are empty vessels, imbued with the meanings we attach to them.

CHAPTER 5

The Parent Trap

Parents' approach to and behavior around their children's sports are central to what kids pick up from them. As with academic achievement, when parents talk about the joy in learning but obsess over grades, in sports we mothers and fathers often deliver contradictory messages. While touting the benefits of teamwork and discipline, we often fixate on the output of the sport, especially the final score. I saw this frequently as a coach, most memorably with one father who promised his fast but indolent daughter an iPod if she finished in the top twenty at a particular race; and more prosaically with a Mrs. Gibley, who immediately asked her daughter after every race, "What was your time?"

To be clear, I was no better. If I missed my son Paul's basketball games, the first two questions I'd ask upon seeing him were the same: "Did you win?" "How many points did you score?" (And then, catching myself, "Was it fun?") Children can see through this hypocrisy, and what they learn from it is that Mom and Dad aren't totally honest, at least with their offspring, and probably with themselves. What Weissbourd wrote about adults' preoccupation with their kids' academic achievement makes sense with sports as well: "It's a kind of contagion, and an escalating contagion—parents keep feeding on each other and ramping each other up."

Here's the paradox: what we're exhibiting as parents isn't a love of the game or a deep appreciation for lifelong fitness. What we're demonstrating, with our desperation for quick wins and visible success, is anxiety about our children and our own status. This is not entirely our fault. As the youth sports industry has expanded, so too have the expectations on us; it takes a mighty backbone to resist these cultural forces. But by obsessing over our children's wins, and prostrating ourselves for their sports, we're presenting adulthood as a dismal destination that's best delayed, or even avoided. When we erupt at coaches and slam their abilities, we're telling our kids that conscientious grown-ups are clowns undeserving of respect. And when our child's athletic development trumps every other responsibility, including to the rest of the siblings or our own spouse, we're insinuating that keeping the family together isn't a priority. Indeed, we're letting kids' games chip away at any family life at all.

What Parents Model for Their Kids

The morning was oppressively hot for mid-June, the kind of sticky day where the combination of sun and humidity make time outside something to dread. The grass seemed to grow thicker before my eyes, and mosquitoes and gnats appeared out of nowhere, like mysterious fruit flies on a rotting banana. The air smelled of grass and mud. Gross conditions, I thought, especially for a weekend lacrosse tournament forty minutes from home.

When I arrived at the playing field—make that fields, scads of them, a vast expanse of grass divided by goals and posts and sprayed-on white lines—I scanned the vista for Paul's team. They were hard to find. Across the horizon, dozens of young men dressed in matching colors took over corners of the turf, while collections of adults watched from the sides. From a distance, they all looked the same, boys on the cusp of maturity, most of them white, and largely indistinguishable in their helmets and pads. I wandered around for a while, peering at different fields and growing increasingly sweaty as I walked. Finally, I found them, and as I got closer, the scene became clearer.

The boys perched comfortably in their chairs, spreading their legs out long and leaning back so far that the nylon backing assumed the shape of their spines. They'd removed their helmets and were cradling bottles of Gatorade and sliced bagels and paper plates loaded with fruit. Shielded from the blazing sun and talking sports with their teammates and friends, they seemed relaxed and happy—in their element.

Some mothers and fathers who'd come to watch stood outside the tent's protective cover, blocking their eyes with their hands and glancing around in pursuit of shade. Other parents gathered behind a long table covered in a checked red tablecloth and acted the role of mess cooks. Men sliced bagels, peeled oranges, and chopped pineapples, and women arranged the deli sandwiches, granola bars, and drinks in a sensible and aesthetically pleasing order. The food and beverages, all bought and delivered by parents, were there to sustain our young warriors, so that these boys could take on the next team of rivals rested and refreshed. As for the grown-ups, it was every woman for herself.

No one had a handle on the schedule, and the boys' coaches, young college men who got the summer gig thanks to the largesse of their high school coach, had disappeared, flinging balls back and forth to each other somewhere out of sight. We all waited. I found a dry section of grass not far from the tent and eased my way to the ground. The sun broiled my scalp, and the humidity settled in. I sweated and stewed. After a while, I got up and stole a chocolate doughnut hole from the box I'd brought for the team. Parents had been advised to bring healthful snacks, but I hadn't found the time to get to ShopRite. The shiny orange doughnut box stationed next to the fresh fruit and bottled water looked wrong—a Styrofoam cup on a tea tray at Harrods.

It was hard to identify what rankled, exactly. The boys were doing what they were told—showing up early for a hot day of play and applying themselves when the ref blew the whistle. We adults (some more than others) were doing our best to help them succeed. The boys needed to hydrate sufficiently, fuel themselves with the right kind of calories, and rest between games away from the sun. And they were too young to drive. Why would anyone want them to be miserable and overheated when we parents had the power to keep them comfortable?

Then and now, it feels boorish to criticize parents for stepping up to help. But much of what we were modeling that day felt wrong. Whether intentional or not, our hovering presence signaled that this tournament, and all others if we're being honest, truly mattered. On the one hand, we were saying: *Sports are fun! Go learn about teamwork and discipline!* While on the other, we were communicating this: *We adults are here to make sure this all goes exactly to plan, because athletic success matters deeply to us.* And if you ask Richard Weissbourd, when parents and other adults lionize the little jocks in their midst, they're contributing to the perception—already widely held by most teenagers—that athletes are at the top of the adolescent pecking order, and by definition superior to the dorks in band or geeks in theater. This can't help but breed arrogance in kids, especially the more talented ones, who surely pick up on our elaborate contributions to their athletic success and understand how important they must be.

Squatting in the brown grass that day, I couldn't shake the feeling that adults doting on teenage boys—or girls, for that matter—signals to kids that grown-ups lead empty and pathetic lives. Thanks to our children, we have something to do this weekend! Don't mind me over here, broiling in this fetid, suffocating, treeless expanse; the wait will be worth it if only I get the chance to watch my son retrieve a ground ball or block a goal or nail a pass. All my other duties—running, visiting my ailing father, catching up with a friend—mean nothing next to this boys' lacrosse game. Watching our offspring play, even observing them cradle their sticks and toss ice cubes at their friends under the tent, eclipses all. To suggest otherwise, to blow off the tournament, to ignore the instruction to provide healthy snacks, even to complain just a little that *maybe parents deserve the shade as much as the boys, and is all this really necessary?* marks you as a heretic. A selfish one, at that.

"I have this image of adults watching passively, waiting, while their kids play," child psychologist and author Madeline Levine told me. "It models a miserable portrait of what it means to be an adult. Then we're appalled when they're eight to ten years behind in entering adulthood."

Overbearing Parents

Ask any coach at any level what makes the work difficult, and everyone will come back with a tale or two of an overzealous, interfering, or obnoxious parent. And it's driving coaches away. Eighty-two percent of high school coaches reported that behavior by parents has worsened over the course of their career. Fifty-eight percent have considered quitting because of the way a parent behaved. And 60 percent of coaches reported having spoken to a parent about her behavior during the last season.

When I first met Mr. Taunus, he came off like a ferret: wiry, energetic, and friendly at the pet store, but sharp-toothed and sneaky when you got him home. He was all smiles and eager to inform me about his latest track workout and road race. Before long, he launched into a mono-logue about proper training, enlightening me about the sport I'd been coaching for years and competing in for decades. It's all about mileage, he told me. The more kids run, the better they will be. Girls can handle as many miles as boys—training is a function of inputs and outputs, you see—and suggesting otherwise is sexist. It's perfectly fine for a pre-pubescent girl to run north of four hundred miles during the summer before ninth grade, including two hard weekly workouts. Why, his own daughter Kate was doing this, and thriving! He knew of young girls in other parts of the state running a lot more.

"That's not going to end well," I blurted out, before telling him what I'd experienced as a coach of teenagers—how too-high mileage with girls can delay menstruation, invite eating disorders, bring on stress fractures, and crush enthusiasm. How many girls who excel before reaching pu-berty will battle the sport and their weight after their bodies have ma-tured. How this mad rush to secure personal records now, before it's too late (for what?), is exactly the wrong way to build a lasting commitment to the sport. But Mr. Taunus knew better. He was in some ways the modern male version of Undine Spragg, Edith Wharton's antiheroine in *The Custom of the Country*, who thought to herself, when facing ob-jection, "If only every one would do as she wished she would never be unreasonable."

Kate looked like a ten-year-old when we met. She weighed less than ninety pounds, her pipe-cleaner profile that of a child rather than a teen-age girl entering high school. Despite her size, she carried herself with a subtle air of superiority, throwing her tiny shoulders back in their sock-ets, tilting her chin up, and racing ahead of her teammates during warm-ups. It was unusual to observe such visible confidence in a girl her age and would have been refreshing if not for her go-suck-it attitude toward me. But her father's disapproval of my conservative approach had not been lost on her. Her contempt occasionally stung, but more often it struck me as sad and absurd—the natural consequence of a parenting style that's comfortable with trashing teachers and coaches in front of kids. It wasn't her fault.

Mr. Taunus could be counted on to show up at every race. He often arrived before our bus, then scampered up to me with a scouting report on the opposing teams, the weather forecast, the conditions of the course ("There's a big root over by mile two"), and anything else he thought I should know, including the proper race pace for our number five girl and the best way to approach that uphill stretch toward the finish. He never arrived empty-handed, always carting a folding chair for Kate so she could get off her feet before a race. He stood nearby, making himself available to her every need. Would she like a ripe banana? An energy bar? A splash of cold water? Kate seemed to relish the attention, even when he got down on bended knee to double knot her racing spikes.

One of the primary developmental tasks for teenagers, psychologists will tell you, is to carve out an identity separate from their parents. But like other hovering parents before him, Mr. Taunus seemed determined to prevent that from happening. He was utterly enmeshed in Kate's athletic career, drinking in her achievements as if they were his own, and moping over her failures with commensurate gloom.

Like other parents before and after him, Mr. Taunus would permit no obstacle to interfere with his child's athletic promise, including a coach he deemed insufficiently talented, ambitious, or attentive. And it seemed that no difference of opinion was too small to dispute, no perceived oversight too tiny to protest. If he had to be overbearing and obstreperous to get his way, so be it. In my experience, parents are most apt to interfere with coaches when they're worried about their child falling behind, in which case they'll happily make a coach's life miserable. But if the team is winning, and the child is playing, parents tend to keep quiet. Even if the coach trains the kids to exhaustion and barks at them like a bond trader, these same parents will look the other way.

Snack Creep

Since I began coaching, and then later when I was on the receiving end of the email chain that included directions on snack content and logistics, a few food-related trends have emerged. The first is the movement toward better nutrition. Fruit, raisins, water, pretzel rods—in. Potato chips, Oreos, cupcakes, doughnut holes—out. Insofar as healthy snacks promote eating habits that lead to clean health and trim bodies, this trend makes sense. Insofar as carrots and rice cakes contribute to an atmosphere of fun, this development stinks—another reminder that youth sports are a serious business, not casual games designed for kids.

The second trend is the organizational expertise that has been brought to bear on parental snack assignments. Thanks to SignUpGenius and regular old email, the scheduling and delivery of appropriate refreshments is now hardened and inescapable. There's no sending along a serving of Chips Ahoy! or stale Wheat Thins for just your child (because *someone* didn't get to the store today) when your duty as snack provider extends to the whole team. In this way, there's symmetry for parents and their children: we're all accountable to the group.

The final development I'll call *snack creep*, an obligation for parents that extends past high school.

On some collegiate teams, parental feeding responsibilities have ballooned to include arranging postgame takeout meals for players at away games and hosting gigantic tailgates for coaches, athletes, parents, and alumni after competitions at home. Here, for example, is an unexpurgated list of "suggested items" the parents of a college rowing team were invited to contribute for a one-day regatta:

- *Whole wheat or Ezekiel bread (4 loaves)*
- *Bagels (2 dozen) and cream cheese (2 containers)*
- *Salads (all types)*

- *Peanut butter and almond butter*
- *Plain Greek yogurt*
- *Granola and berries for topping*
- *Yogurts (individual containers)*
- *Whole fruit—apples, oranges, bananas*
- *Fruit salad*
- *Cheese sticks*
- *Gatorade*
- *Coffee (for coaches and parents)*
- *Water bottles (plastic)*
- *Plates and small bowls, plastic utensils, napkins*
- *Paper towels & plastic tablecloths (3)*
- *Coffee cups, cream, sugar*

Snack creep goes hand-in-hand with the changed expectations surrounding team dinners. At least in some sports, in some communities, it's now customary for teams to gather at a family's home the evening before every game and share a meal, presumably to "get psyched." The parents who host pay for the food. I saw this up close during my son's brief tenure as a lacrosse player in high school. Sometimes mothers (it's always the mothers) took a day off work and put together four trays of lasagna for the ravenous boys, along with salads and rolls and homemade cookies; others ordered a massive takeout dinner that could feed eighteen. Because the team played one or two games a week, these meals seemed to become routine for the boys, and by the end of the season my son would zip in and out of the host's house in twenty minutes—faster than a diner!—so he could get home and tackle his assignments. Team dinners were just one more thing to do, not special gatherings that a kind parent had generously provided.

You might consider these food-related developments trivial, and in the larger scheme of kids' athletics, perhaps they are. But snack creep and excessive team dinners are clear reflections of a warped youth sports environment. They reveal how invested parents are in our children's activities, and how much we've insinuated ourselves into their play. They uncover how vital the sport is, how much this game or that race matters—*to us*. They also tether adults to kids' sports, regardless of the parents' wallet or wishes. Preparing elaborate snacks and meals, and fussing over kids' diets and hydration, are a way for parents to demonstrate their commitment to the sport. As with so much else related to youth sports, the food fixation is more about the grown-ups than it is the kids.

Disrupted Families

A mother of two whose school-aged kids both played on club teams year-round, Kelly was tall and had the carriage of a younger woman but the worn-out, slightly dazed expression of someone who had been through a lot. She told me how she managed the kids' schedules and her other responsibilities, saying, "There are days I can't handle it." Her son played club lacrosse, her daughter club soccer, and both needed to be driven to practices and games regularly. Their home was forty minutes from each. Her daughter played for an elite team that prohibited participation in high school sports, so Kelly had to drive her daughter from school to practice every day—another thirty minutes in the car—while the club team was in season.

"I started full-time work last year, but it was too crazy with the sports and practices," she told me. "Now I work part-time because of sports. It's a full-time job juggling the sports schedule." It's wearying for everyone, with few built-in breaks and relentless travel.

The previous summer she and her husband had spent every weekend apart: he with the son's team; she with the daughter's. "Most people wouldn't know I was married!" she said. There wasn't a single free week all summer when the four of them could escape for a family vacation.

The handful of studies on youth sports and families suggest that Kelly's experience isn't unique. Many parents are put out by the demands their kids' athletics impose on budgets and time. They feel angry and annoyed at their children, guilty about their perceived insufficient commitment to the sport, and resentful of the whole youth sports enterprise. Studies have shown that parents are "mentally and physically exhausted" and "often experienced relief at any break in the sporting season."

There's little research on how competitive kids' sports affect marriages. Given the data vacuum, Travis Dorsch at the Families in Sport Lab at Utah State suggested that what's happened with the US snowboarding team might be true of other sports: "It's very rare to have an intact family with skiers," he said. Snowboarding usually requires parents to split up for months at a time to allow their snowboarder to train, and most couples divorce. It seems inevitable that children's rigorous athletic schedules would affect a marriage. In my experience, parents who are invested in their kids' travel sports speak dispassionately about how rarely they see each other on weekends. They adopt a divide-and-conquer strategy with their children, splitting up in their off time to manage each kid's sports obligations.

Siblings of the child athlete, especially those with varied interests, are also affected by the sacrifices made on behalf of the family jock. Unworldly they may be, but even kids understand that parents spend their money and time on what they care about. And children have a finely tuned radar for identifying imbalances in parental attention and expenditures. The bookworm picks up how readily Dad opens his wallet for her brother's baseball gear, and how eager he is to coach. It can't help but foment resentment among siblings.

Parents' rigorous cultivation of their brood undermines sibling relationships in other ways. Sociologist Annette Lareau found that children who are ferried around from activity to activity have more strained relationships with their brothers and sisters than kids with less structured lives. "The middle-class children we observed," Lareau wrote, "are more competitive with and hostile towards their siblings, and they have much weaker ties with extended family members." In these homes, Lareau often heard blunt expressions of aggression among siblings, including casual references to "hating" a brother or sister. While her findings apply to the multiple activities kids are involved in besides athletics, sports are often the most demanding on families.

And what of the younger child who is dragged along to all the older siblings' games? This leaves its own bitter aftertaste. Ask writer Sarah Miller, who was slung in the family Suburban most weekends for five or so years, all in service of her brother's ice hockey games. "Any unathletic person from an athletic family has spent a lot of time underneath bleachers wondering why they were born," she wrote. Miller told people that the endless excursions and solitude under the bleachers taught her how to write, because the boredom forced her to amuse herself. "My brother played Pee Wee hockey, and my parents treated him like a Fabergé egg and had no idea I existed."

An older sibling's athleticism can also determine how younger ones approach sports. Dorsch found that when parents lavish money and time on an older child's athletics, and the later siblings are close in age and gender, then one of two outcomes will likely follow: brothers and sisters will differentiate—"I'll do something different to get Mom and Dad's attention"—or they'll take after their elder, betting that what worked for the athlete will work for them. Another eventuality might also occur, as it did with my children: the less athletically inclined in the family, indignant over the perceived imbalance in parental resources, will give endless hell to the jock. And when it comes to sports it's hard to argue with them. After all, if the Harris Poll on parental spending for club sports is accurate, 77 percent cut back on family activities to afford them. That can't feel right to a brother or sister who doesn't play.

One of the largest disruptions, though, is immeasurable. "There's a loss of vacation time, and family dinners, and opportunities for connection," Dorsch told me. Heading to Maryland for a weekend lacrosse tournament might mean skipping a cousin's birthday. Devoting a summer to volleyball or basketball might require missing out on a family trip or a summer job. Eating McNuggets in the car three nights a week between extra strength sessions and late-night practice—can this be good for families? When the quest to perfect a child's athletic skill takes top priority, something's going to give, and the family unit is often what gets sacrificed.

CHAPTER 6

Body Slam

If the wealth of research on exercise and sports participation has taught us anything, it's that moderate physical activity at all ages is an unmitigated good. Sprinting,
strolling, pirouetting; hoisting dumbbells, thwacking tennis balls, slapping hockey pucks; splashing and kicking
and stroking the water, dribbling and shooting on a driveway or court, chucking footballs over a field or across
the street—all of these activities and more translate to a
healthier body and sounder mind. And if sports are played
with others, even better—a boon to physical *and* social
health. Hauling the body up and out and around, elevat-
ing the heart rate, forcing the damn thing to move every
now and then, is good for you, full stop. It's a truism I've
experienced myself.

On top of the personal growth and profound connections sports can forge, children who played in middle school and through high school are more likely than their sedentary peers to remain active as adults—a vital component of long-term health. In short, early sports participation is an investment in future vigor and well-being.

And teenagers, especially those involved in varied sports, are better able to handle the turbulence and temptations of adolescence: they feel better about themselves, enjoy richer social lives, and outperform their inactive peers in the classroom. For kids from fractured or dysfunctional families, team sports can do even more. They can provide a refuge from danger, a respite from trouble at home, and a positive experience that sets or resets the path of a life.

Better, better, better—the word is unavoidable when comparing outcomes of teenagers who play sports versus those who don't.

The way we're doing sports now, though, compromises those health benefits. Specializing early in one exercise, playing year-round, adding more games and workouts to an already full athletic schedule—the default mode for middle- and upper-income kids—can damage a young person's body and scar the psyche.

It's not that parents and coaches set out to maim kids. But the intensity and nature of competitive youth sports often have that effect. The rate of stress fractures in kids is "an epidemic," Dr. Heather Bergeson, a pediatrician specializing in sports medicine, told me. Dr. Neha Raukar, a professor at the Mayo Clinic College of Medicine and Science, calls early sports specialization "an American public health disaster."

Our youth sports system, which glorifies winning, tolerates bullying, and normalizes overtraining—much of it done with the complicity and support of parents—also brings lasting emotional harm to some of the young at its mercy. "We all know it's unsafe and unhealthy, but still it persists," Bergeson told me.

It's a paradox: playing sports and exercising are so good for kids, until it all goes too far and teeters over into injury and despair. And just as these kids from higher-income homes are doing too much, children from poorer families are left with little.

Becoming a Runner

Dump coffee into a metal filter and set the pot to brew at seven. Check tomorrow's weather, pick running outfit accordingly. Arrange shorts, bra, T-shirt, Nikes, and socks next to bed, the easier to slip into while groggy, pre-caffeination. Tomorrow's Tuesday, and a gaggle of women will be meeting for our regular speed workout at Tatlock Field, where the track resides, at eight thirty. We're doing nine miles in all, including a two-mile warm-up and cool-down, with sets of 800s and 1000s at 10K-race pace, in preparation for a ten-mile race down the road. This workout comes on the heels of our Sunday long run (thirteen miles, 7:45 pace), an easy six-miler Monday, and a "comfortably hard" seven-mile tempo run Friday (6:30 pace), on the streets of our hilly town. It's all booked, all planned.

When you've been running for as long as I have, it's nearly impossible to recall a period when figuring out the logistics of the daily run weren't foremost on your mind, including when, where, how far, how fast, and with whom. The serious runners I know come up with answers well in advance of the actual run, always striving to adjust for all the variables that might interfere with running—like an early flight on a workout day, or three days of freezing rain during the middle of marathon training. All this plotting about getting our runs in can be tedious, especially for the non-runners in the group, but it's a reflection of how central the sport is to our identity and well-being.

When I started running at fourteen, these OCD-fueled complications were unknown to me. I began at the urging of my oldest sister,

Kathy, who'd taken up the sport with her usual gusto while studying in Ithaca. On summer Sundays, she and I would shilly-shally around the kitchen, search for any alternative to the tedious task ahead, and finally, when we could dither no longer, heave ourselves out the front door. She'd plod ahead of me, and I'd scramble to stay even with her, my thick cotton T-shirt growing heavier with every mile. During the week, I'd scurry along the streets in our shady neighborhood without her, past the water tower, down to the intersection near my old elementary school, and then up and around the road near the back entrance to Drew University. Despite my good intentions, I never got out before 10:00 a.m., and by then any trace of cool air from the night before was undone by suffocating humidity. There was nothing romantic about it.

I don't know when I began identifying myself as a runner—when the sport became a part of who I am rather than an activity I endured. The change occurred incrementally and imperceptibly. But by the time I got to college, with my high school sports behind me, running became a kind of bulwark against the strains of young adulthood. And for a female at a competitive, male-dominated university with a robust Greek system, there were many.

I was no great college runner. It was only then that I even started doing interval workouts, hill repeats, and long runs, which drive improvement; until then, my "workouts" had been six-or-so-mile runs at a comfortable pace. I writhed through my first track intervals—six quarter miles, or 400s, with ample rest between them—at age twenty, convinced that my heart or lungs would burst from the exertion (a workout, incidentally, that the high school freshmen I coach manage with ease). Despite my inexperience, and regardless of the shifting cast of characters who coached us, I remained the fastest runner on our modest team. One tall girl a year younger than I always sprinted out of the gate and got ahead of me, but she couldn't resist turning around mid-race to assess her lead, a provocation that became my accelerant.

After graduating, I went to Oxford for more studies and joined the cross-country team there. No NCAA-like body existed in England at the time to challenge my eligibility, and it never occurred to me to ask. Anyway, the whole athletic system at Oxford bore no resemblance to the American model. In cross-country and track—or "athletics," as they name track-and-field events—no coach organized practices and meets. Captains did the administering and ran the workouts, and runners went along with it. I was the only American woman in the group and couldn't get over the absence of an adult authority telling us what to do. Even more striking was the natural way in which everyone fell in line without being ordered to, like a colony of bats moving by echolocation.

At Oxford, cross-country racing is essentially orienteering mixed with steeplechase: punishing slogs of indeterminate length through ankle-deep mud, without officials or orange cones as guides. We had just a handful of races all fall, each with just one or two other teams, and they were entirely student-run. Afterward, we'd splash the mud off our legs in cold showers near the finish and meet for tea and biscuits with our opponents. Even at the time, I could sense how British it all was: no frills but steeped in good manners and tradition.

I was supposed to be having the time of my life, pickling in big ideas and hobnobbing with fascinating intellectuals, but in fact I was often lonely. At that first practice, I slobbered over the British girls on the team, deploying all the American social tricks I'd picked up over the years, but to no avail. They remained aloof. "In America, you make friends and then you get to know someone; in England, you get to know someone and then you make friends," a British woman who later became a friend explained to me. But little by little, after striving together to get through a bog without losing a shoe, or to cover the distance in a long run around the Port Meadow, a lush pasture close to the city center, the other runners on the cross-country team became my closest allies abroad.

A magnet on my refrigerator shows a 1950s-style woman with a giddy smile and these incongruous words above her head: "Unless you fell off the treadmill and smacked your face, no one wants to hear about your workout." In that spirit, I won't elaborate on the racing milestones that followed. In short, after leaving Oxford I went to Boston and competed for several clubs, where I ran the mile in 4:56, the 5K in 16:44, ten miles in 58:58, and the marathon in two hours and forty-nine minutes, four minutes too many, in 1992, to qualify for the Olympic Trials. I won tickets to Europe and overnight stays at four-star hotels, and saved enough race winnings to help fund my honeymoon.

And there was so much I loved about that. I relished slipping into road races dressed in crappy togs and trouncing the runners wearing shiny new singlets and elaborate watches. (To paraphrase Lance Armstrong: it's not about the gear, runners!) Skipping past winded middle-aged men desperate to prevent a *woman* from getting ahead of them, even during a regular run around town, was disproportionately gratifying. "Don't have a heart attack!" I longed to yell back to them. The elation that came with winning races, and the knowledge that I was better, sometimes, than every other woman there, made training addictive. At the same time, running success was largely invisible to those outside the racing circuit. Puffed with pride about a win or a new PR, I sometimes called home to tell my parents, assuming they'd be equally thrilled. "That's wonderful, dear," my mother would coo, doing her best to show interest in my alien endeavor. Her own mother had said to me once, when I went out for a run around the cornfields in Iowa, "Where do you have to go?"

It was hard to explain why it mattered. But I knew it did. Running fast, then faster still, and winning, was irrationally exhilarating, even when most of the world was indifferent to it. Of course, more than that drove me out the door when I was young and speedy. It was the way running propped me up and kept me sturdy, the way it eased worries and hardened good habits, that kept me at it. Even today, as my mile-pace climbs and my body rebels, these same intangibles compel me forward.

What Exercise Does for the Body and Brain

Exercise: a tonic for what ails us. A tincture for good health. This has been true for me since I was a child and remains so today. Athletics have kept me vigorous and balanced. They protected me when I was a child, gave me an outlet when I was a teenager, and afforded me glimpses of confidence as I grew into adulthood.

Research on the health benefits of exercise confirms my experience. Just learning to kick, jump, and throw improves cardiovascular health during childhood and into adolescence. Playing outdoor sports at a young age slows the growth of the body mass index. Kids who grow up engaging in sports reduce their chances of developing metabolic syndrome, which is linked to heart disease and diabetes in adulthood. Exercise at any age contributes to better sleep, itself a crucial feature of good health. "The single strongest predictor of later-life physical activity," the authors of one study concluded, "was whether he played a varsity sport in high school, and this was also related to fewer self-reported visits to the doctor."

Exercise also improves brain functioning. A 2019 study found that physical activity improved cognitive ability among young adults in three essential ways, "fluid intelligence, cognitive flexibility, and processing speed." It enhances executive function in young children, helping them block distractions and toggle between subjects. Regular exercise also alters how sound is managed in the brain; collegiate athletes were found to be better able to pick up sounds and ignore background noise. Just as critical, exercise enhances the ability to "self-regulate"—to exert control over one's own behavior. Among older adults, exercise also improves word memory. Countless studies involving mice have found that running creates new neurons in parts of the brain related to learning and recall. Weight training has a similar effect: it can improve thinking and offset memory loss (at least with rats). Because varied levels of movement sharpen memory, problem solving, focus, and creativity, writes Annie Murphy Paul in *The Extended Mind: The Power of Thinking Outside the Brain*, school leaders who want their students to excel academically "should be advocating for an increase in physically active recess time."

Along with these advantages, adult women who played sports when they were twelve were more apt to have higher bone density than their compatriots who took to the sidelines as kids, which protects against osteoporosis later in life. Women who exercise regularly also reduce the risk of developing breast cancer by 25 to 30 percent.

A Trinity of Wellness

In *How to Think About Exercise*, Australian philosopher Damon Young explains how physical effort and competition simplify a complex world. Our daily lives are fraught with uncertainty and chaos; we are forever striving to make sense of ourselves. With their strict rules and regulated conduct, sports provide rare clarity: "Exercise can be a reprieve from confusion—from the anxiety that comes with not knowing one's place in the world." Flummoxed in youth by shifting and ambiguous social dynamics, Young found solace in tennis, a sport in which he wasn't particularly talented. No matter: the rules, and the game's clear purpose, provided a respite from angst.

I've stuck with running all these years for related reasons. This sport, more than any others, has rewarded me with the trinity of wellness that all the research on exercise boasts of. The act of stepping outside, pushing the Start button on my stopwatch, and propelling myself from a walk to a gentle jog and then to something quicker flips a mental switch. The old engine has finally gotten going, and with it my brain starts to hum. Thoughts and ideas float up out of the ether and a solution to the paragraph that had given me so much trouble suddenly appears. It's almost impossible to worry while running. Even when times are dark, as they have been so often in recent years, a good run has a way of casting sunlight on the scene.

Feeling sluggish and sore also reminds you of your corporeal presence. If you spend most of your days tucked behind a computer manipulating symbols, it's easy to think of *yourself* as merely your mind—an entity that exists apart from the body. Running obliterates that distinction. A bad run reacquaints the ablest of minds with the stubborn physical laws of the body. *Hey, don't forget about me!* the old carcass signals with its creaks and groans. Like an effortless run, one that's full of strain keeps you connected to the body you inhabit.

Racing inspires an altogether different kind of mental clarity. When the gun sounds, you go as fast as you can, for as long as you can, to beat as many others as you can; it's hard to get bogged down in the existential and inane questions that might ordinarily plague you—*What am I doing with my life? Do I use too much plastic? Am I a good friend?* There's no room for agonizing self-consciousness about whether you're doing it right: on race day, it's a matter of raw will. There's a brutal austerity to it that's absent in other parts of life.

And overcoming these physical challenges, hanging on when you ache to stop, persevering in spite of gravity or the elements or your opponents' greater skill—all of this comes with a hidden reward: self-possession. This unfamiliar sensation started creeping into my consciousness the more I raced and the faster I got. Physical confidence came with it—the sense that my body was capable, especially during a race. When the gun goes off, you have to *move*. You may be slow, you may finish last, but you are igniting some internal motor and compelling it forward.

Logging so many miles over the years has protected my health in countless ways. Most days, I start the morning with a brisk five-miler before work, sometimes with a friend. Afterward, I'll climb over to my desk with a bagel and a jug of coffee and concentrate, absorbing the words on the page and then churning out my own. Peacefulness descends—a feeling of calm open-mindedness. With the clutter cleared, and a social connection restored, all is well with the world. Except for one janky knee, running has brought me nothing but wellness and fulfillment.

Many young people growing up today have had a different experience.

When Katie McCafferty started tearing up the track in high school, running the mile in 4:56 and the two-mile in 10:24, college coaches from competitive Division I schools came after her. She landed a spot at a prestigious northeastern school along with a partial scholarship and threw herself into the work. Though the high mileage and intensity of college training took some getting used to, Katie adored her teammates; they were as passionate about running as she—a welcome change from her indifferent high school teammates—and always supportive and encouraging.

She got a glimpse of the trouble ahead, though, and insight into the gravity of her running commitment, after taking a quick trip home one Friday afternoon in the fall. The coach had called off practice that day, and she wasn't needed back until Sunday for the team's morning run. But when Katie arrived home that night, she got a phone call from her coach. *Where are you?* he asked. *You can't just leave without checking in with me. You need my permission.* She hadn't realized that the coach would be monitoring her movements.

Katie's cross-country season had started well, and she kept getting faster. But during one race, she landed on something sharp and heard a crack in her foot. Katie rested and did the mandatory physical therapy, but when she jumped back into training, she'd lost fitness. Confidence seeped out of her. When she told the coach about the pain in her foot, he called her a "delicate flower." So she pushed harder, and got hurt again, this time in her right hip. For the remainder of her college career, Katie's running followed this pattern: she flogged her body, got hurt, recovered, and resumed training. She also snuck in some stellar performances, earning All-American status as a junior after a blazing mile in the distance medley relay.

Now, years after graduating from college, and having retired from competitive running, she questions her decision to go with an aggressive college program. "It didn't pan out the way I thought," she told me. Though her teammates remain her closest friends, and she treasures the achievements they shared, she thinks the relentless slogging thwarted her potential.

"You're basically a racehorse," she said, there to be deployed by the coach when deemed healthy. "The sport is like a full-time job, it's not a side thing."

She wonders if her college experience as a whole would have been more balanced if she'd not spent so much time on her sport. "I think I'd have been a more well-rounded person if I'd gone to a Division III school," she said. Sometimes she thinks a gentler running program might have given her time to develop, maybe sparing her from the injuries and surgeries that ended her career.

Physical Costs

Competitive youth sports have clouded the link between physical activity and health. For despite the abundant advantages exercise and sports can bestow, the way we provide them now often damages kids' bodies and well-being. This is so in various ways.

In lower-income neighborhoods, the lack of play places and shrinking community offerings, along with the cost of private teams, means that kids from poorer homes don't get to play. Accordingly, they are the least physically active, and suffer the highest obesity rates. Because an overweight child is 70 percent likely to remain overweight or become obese as an adult, they are more apt to experience high blood pressure, diabetes, and high cholesterol. These kids are denied the lifelong benefits that athletics can provide, starting with physical health.

In more stable communities, the intensity of youth sports has driven most kids away. By age thirteen, the majority of kids—70 percent—have given up on sports entirely.

COVID and its cascading disruptions have made things worse. Prior to the pandemic, a little over 18 percent of kids between six and eleven, and 20.6 percent of adolescents between twelve and nineteen, were obese. Another 16.6 percent of adolescents were overweight. Since the start of the pandemic, obesity rates grew to 22 percent for kids between ages two and nineteen, the CDC reported. The upsurge is rightly considered a national health crisis, which Michelle Obama addressed during her stint as First Lady. Today, getting more kids moving will have to be part of the solution.

While inactivity has obvious costs, so too does its opposite. Overuse injuries—the accumulated wear and tear on a young body's muscles, tendons, joints, or bones, the logical result of specializing in one sport too soon—are on the rise. Indeed, "epidemic" is the word that doctors and specialists often use to describe the flood of these injuries they are encountering in their medical practices.

Nearly half the sports injuries middle and high school students seek treatment for are related to overuse. During the past ten years, shoulder and elbow surgeries among youth have increased by five times in baseball and softball alone. Dr. Charles A. Popkin, an orthopedic surgeon who specializes in sports-related injuries among youth, told me that kids as young as twelve come in for surgical repair to their elbows. "There's an epidemic of ulnar collateral ligament tears," he said, referring to the ligament that connects the upper part of the arm to the forearm, securing the elbow.

Up to 20 percent of overuse troubles are stress fractures, most often happening among runners; they're caused by rapid increases in training volume and inadequate rest. Other typical overuse injuries afflict a part of the body that's been subjected to repetitive stress—like baseball players' elbows and swimmers' shoulders.

A variety of acute injuries are also occurring more frequently among young athletes, especially tears to the anterior cruciate ligament (ACL), the flexible connective tissue that connects the thigh to the shin and stabilizes the knee. These occur most often in sports like soccer, lacrosse, and basketball, where sharp twists to the knee are common. Players dread ACL tears, because they usually require surgical repair and months of rehabilitation. Despite athletes' eagerness to avoid them, the number of cases among adolescents continues to grow. Dr. Mininder Kocher at Harvard Medical School found that ACL surgeries among adolescents in the Boston area jumped from about five hundred cases in 2004 to more than twenty-five hundred ten years later—a 400 percent increase. Kocher blames early sports specialization, which puts stress on kids' growing muscles and joints. He also notes that women are more susceptible to ACL injuries, and that their greater participation in sports is adding to the increase in tears.

Endurance athletes, especially runners and swimmers, are disposed to "overtraining syndrome"—a physical and emotional condition defined by exhaustion, sleep troubles, low appetite, and depression. The "female athlete triad" is another risk for adolescent girls who train excessively. The triad refers to three symptoms or conditions that often occur together: low energy levels, sometimes related to inadequate nutrition or an eating disorder; the absence or loss of menstruation; and low bone density. Young women with this condition don't just feel rotten. They're also likely to develop stress fractures and perhaps osteoporosis or osteopenia when they're older.

Head injuries are another danger, especially concussions. Roughly 300,000 high school athletes are diagnosed with concussions every year, most of them occurring in high-impact sports, and the rate of reported concussions among high school athletes has continued to rise. According to the American Academy of Orthopaedic Surgeons, female soccer players are most likely to get concussed, followed by football players, at a rate of 29.8 to 25.2 percent. The sport with the dubious distinction of fastest growth in concussion rates? Girls' volleyball.

Researchers who've focused on head injuries also have called attention to the devastating consequences of frequent blows to the head that fall short of a full concussion. Recurring "sub-concussive" hits to the head can cause chronic traumatic encephalopathy, or CTE, a degenerative brain condition. Those afflicted with CTE often suffer from violent mood swings, depression, and cognitive impairment.

The risks to kids of developing CTE are much harder to quantify, as the effect of multiple hits to the head may not become manifest until many years later. But a first-of-its-kind study of 202 deceased football players conducted at Boston University's CTE Center in 2017 found the disease in 87 percent of the players' brains. Even those who had played just high school football showed mild pathology. According to Dr. Jesse Mez, one of the study's top authors, "The data suggest that there is very likely a relationship between exposure to football and risk of developing the disease." These and other findings on concussions and CTE have prompted a movement to replace tackle football with its gentler cousin, flag football, until kids reach high school.

Of course, injuries are a part of sports. Even the most overprotective parents, it seems, will tolerate their children's athletic injuries provided the damage is short-lived—a few weeks off, maybe a season even, of no play.

But what many parents seem not to realize or acknowledge is that some injuries sustained in adolescence will linger into adulthood. Recurrent ankle sprains, for example, can lead to osteoarthritis. Dislocated shoulders, too—a common-enough injury for competitive swimmers—may develop osteoarthritis within fifteen years. ACL tears also can cause lasting damage. Dr. Kocher found that 50 percent of those who tear a tendon or ligament in their knee will become arthritic within ten years. This finding was corroborated by Britt Elin Oiestad, an Oslo researcher who has studied the short- and long-term effects of ACL tears. "(The) development of knee osteoarthritis (OA) at a relatively young age is unfortunately the reality for about half of the patients with an ACL injury regardless of treatment," she wrote.

When it comes to the wear and tear sports can put on the body, Callie knows all about it. Twenty-eight when we spoke, Callie played intense lacrosse for her high school and club teams before competing for two years in college. "I've had five surgeries," she told me: in 2004 to repair an ACL, two years later to fix it again, as a college freshman to remove hardware and scrape her meniscus, as a junior to "release" the tendon in her kneecap and have another meniscus cleanup, and finally, at twenty-six, to address her persistent knee pain. The last surgery was especially urgent.

"It felt like I was having scalding hot water dripping from my knees to my toes," she said. Doctors shaved under her kneecap and removed scar tissue and told her she had significant osteoarthritis.

Her knees still hurt. "The stairs are always painful. Part of my knee is bone on bone," she said.

Callie's experience may not be unique. In at least one study that compared quality of life measures between former Division I college athletes and their less-active peers, all between forty and sixty-five years old, the once-elite players came out a lot worse. "The former Division I athletes reported significantly more limitations in daily activities and more major and chronic injuries than did the nonathlete controls," the researchers found. Of the seven factors studied—sleep issues, tiredness, worry, depression, pain, physical functioning, and social satisfaction—the nonathletes scored significantly higher in five of them. The findings from this study were replicated later with athletes from Division I, II, and III schools.

Talk about a paradox. Sports are supposed to be good for you. As all the research makes clear, moderate activity does indeed contribute to better health, in all the ways we've come to expect. It's how our system ends up offering them to kids, with either a dearth of opportunities or a relentless emphasis on more, more, more, that's the problem.

CHAPTER 7

Lonely at the Top

Caroline started swimming as a young child and joined a competitive club down the street when she was eight. Swimming was popular among families in her part of Massachusetts, and Caroline's prowess as a free-styler stood out. She was eager to develop and felt it was her duty to achieve her potential. "You're supposed to push yourself and do the hardest thing," she explained to me in a series of interviews.

In eighth grade, she applied to a private school that had an elite swim program. The coach had a reputation for excellence and was known to all in her swimming circles, and Caroline wanted to learn from the best. The school admitted her, and Caroline started training with the team in ninth grade. "There was a time when I loved swimming," she said.

Even with her high hopes, Caroline was astonished by the training load and intensity. During morning practices, which began at six, distance swimmers covered about 5,200 yards. In the afternoon, these same kids often swam another 10,000 yards—or 5.5 miles. On Saturday mornings, everyone swam for five hours. When the coach was disappointed with the team, he'd turn the entire practice into a 10,000-yard race; everyone would have to count the four hundred laps and finish the distance without stopping for a water or bathroom break. If Coach thought the team needed toughening up, he'd assign his infamous run-a-mile/swim-a-mile workout. After swimming a mile, girls and boys would hop out of the pool, put on sneakers, and jog across campus—through woods, over a bridge, and past the football field—to the school's track, where they'd then run a mile in their swimsuits. They would move back and forth, from pool to track, for five hours, always on a weekend.

"Dry-land training" was also a part of everyday practice—work outside the pool to build strength and endurance. Kids would do lunges while carrying a teammate on their back and super-low squats they called "goose walks." They'd lift weights, run on the treadmill, or cycle on the spin bikes. They'd sprint and walk on their hands up and down the slippery pool deck, while one of the assistant coaches chided them to "max out!"

Caroline was a people-pleaser and didn't like to "stir the pot," she told me. But she was disturbed by the team's culture. Slower swimmers were supposed to dive lower into the water if a faster one caught up, or expect to be punched, scratched, or shoved down by the speedier one. Some on the team got a kick out of sexual humor: one girl often yanked her suit down while in the pool "to flash her boobs" at other swimmers, and boys lingering on the pool deck in their tiny Speedos often pulled their testicles out from under their suits so everyone could see. One of the veteran swimmers often left her used tampons in younger teammates' lockers.

Older boys urinated on younger ones in the locker rooms. And the coaches got in on it, too. The respected head coach twice demanded that a shy freshman boy "dance" around a pole in his Speedo.

Caroline avoided confrontations with her teammates. She also strived to meet the coaches' demands, even when they felt impossible or revolting. When Coach held team practice in a pool with excrement on the bottom—the work of a "mystery pooper," Caroline said—she finished the workout despite her disgust. When the team trained in an algae-covered pool during the summer, she kept at it, even though several swimmers developed rashes from the surplus chlorine that some kids on the team dumped in the deep end. And she didn't hesitate to climb the thick rope that dangled from the rafters into the pool, as they were often expected to do, regardless of the way it cut her feet and transmitted staph infections among the swimmers.

Caroline swam through two bouts of bronchitis and a case of mononucleosis because only kids with fevers were allowed to rest. She was tired all the time and sometimes cried in class. Her English teacher noticed and spoke to the coach about it, but Coach just criticized her at practice for being emotional. Being sick was not sufficient cause to miss practice. He scolded Caroline for coughing when she had bronchitis and reminded her that she didn't have cancer.

Though she tried to let her parents know what was happening, and explain how desperate she felt, she couldn't find the right words; mental health had never been a comfortable subject in her family. "I didn't have the vocabulary for it," she said. Caroline's mother knew that practice was demanding but seemed to attribute her daughter's distress to normal teenage angst. Her father was often away during the week, and she rarely spoke to him about her experience. A younger sibling was visibly struggling and devoured her parents' attention, while Caroline appeared to be succeeding in school and in sports.

Caroline considered transferring to another school, but leaving felt impossible. She worried that she'd lose her friends. Her coaches mocked their school's competitors, and she feared being shamed if she went elsewhere. She also was conscious of how much her parents had paid for her swimming over the years. How could she stay at school but quit the team? Perhaps she was the problem. Maybe she found it all unbearable because she was a thin-skinned baby who had to toughen up if she wanted to succeed. She felt so pathetic. So she stayed. "I tried to force myself into that box," Caroline told me. "I believed the adults."

For many kids, especially those who are predisposed to depression or anxiety, the physical and emotional intensity of competitive youth sports has dislodged the nourishing link between exercise and mental health. Instead of easing the mind, sports have hardened it. Comprehensive data is lacking on how widespread mental health problems are among kids who play sports; the absence of any kind of governing body or record-keeper to assess the problem at the youth and high school levels makes it impossible to know for sure. But sports psychologists, mental health experts, and others who are immersed in this environment are sounding the alarm about the emotional consequences of high-stakes sports on kids.

Psychological Costs

"The professional consensus is that the incidence of anxiety and depression among scholastic athletes has increased over the past ten to fifteen years," said Marshall Mintz, a clinical sports psychologist. Mintz has worked with elite high school athletes and their families from New York and New Jersey for more than thirty years. The National Athletic Trainers' Association (NATA) corroborated that view when it issued a sweeping statement in 2015 asserting that many high school athletes admitted to "higher levels of negative emotional states" than their peers. They "have been identified as having higher incidence rates for sleep disturbances, loss of appetite, mood disturbances, short tempers, decreased interest in training and competition, decreased self-confidence, and inability to concentrate." The team of researchers reached this conclusion, said Tim Neal, the lead author, "based on decades of experience dealing with people in high school and with mental health of athletes in general."

Mental health problems are not unique to athletes; rates of anxiety and depression are surging among adolescents in general. Between 2007 and 2017, the percentage of kids between the ages of twelve and seventeen who reported a serious depressive episode jumped from 8 to 13, or from 2 million to 3.2 million kids. The growth in suicide rates is more stark: over that same ten-year period, suicides increased by 56 percent among ten- to twenty-four-year-olds. And it's not just because kids are more open about sharing their worries, Andrew Solomon, author of *The Noonday Demon: An Atlas of Depression*, told me. "There's both an escalation in diagnoses and in the condition itself."

Hypercompetitive youth sports make student athletes uniquely vulnerable to these problems for several reasons. "All these kids are sleep deprived. This becomes a major contributor to anxiety and depression. It has accelerated," Mintz explained. Many are also physically exhausted, denied sufficient recovery time throughout the year and constantly scrambling to keep up with school and sports.

"Overtraining has become a way of life for many of our young athletes," the National Athletic Trainers' Association report asserted. Even some kids who are doing all they're told by their coaches feel compelled to do more. Scott Goldman, a sports psychologist and coauthor on the NATA statement, calls it "ghost peer pressure": the nagging suspicion that others are training more than you, and you'd better work harder still. Inadequate sleep and lingering fatigue invite worry and despair.

The intensity extends to college, where it's especially acute. Every few years, the NCAA conducts what's called the GOALS study (for growth, opportunities, aspirations, and learning of students in college), among a large body of student athletes. It's a gold mine of information. In the 2019 survey, which included data from more than twenty-two thousand men and women, Division I athletes reported that they'd devoted an average of thirty-three hours per week to their sport when in season, versus thirty-five and a half hours per week on academics. On average, the Division I athletes, men and women alike, slept for six hours and fifteen minutes a night while in season. One of the PowerPoint slides shared at the convention said this: "Nearly 30% of female student-athletes compared to one-quarter of male student athletes have felt difficulties piling up so high that they could not overcome them in the month prior to taking the survey." (To be fair, most college kids are struggling, even those who don't compete for their schools.)

The GOALS survey from 2015 included more granular data. In a summary of those findings, the organization discovered that two-thirds of Division I and II athletes spent as much or even more time on their sport during the off-season as they did when they were competing. Almost two-thirds of the men and three-fourths of the women craved more chances to visit home and family. And "high percentages of study participants" sought more time to relax and be with their friends. Kids' athletic performance also seems to matter more to *them*. When I asked Dr. Victor Schwartz, chief medical officer at the Jed Foundation, why more teenagers who play highly competitive sports are troubled, he said, "Kids have come to feel that the stakes are higher and higher, and that there's less room for mistakes."

This view was echoed by nearly every expert I spoke to.

"High-stakes sports take something that's a stress outlet and turn it into something that's a source of stress and anxiety," said clinical and sports psychologist Lonnie Sarnell. "In what way did we mess it up?" Goldman asked. "When we took it too seriously."

The winnowing of interests beyond sports and the narrowing of identity that follows can also unmoor young athletes. Adolescents who throw themselves into one sport think of themselves as "a soccer player," "a swimmer," "a runner." Psychologists call this shrinking of self-concept "athletic identity foreclosure." Even in its most benign form, this withering of experiences beyond athletics can make some kids oddly flat, their personalities stunted by their singular focus on a sport. "They become binary thinkers, good or bad, win or lose. If you took all the structure away and asked them to go play, they'd struggle. They don't know how to be playful or silly," Mintz said.

Athletic identity foreclosure is especially damaging to kids' psyches when it leaves them feeling stuck. How could they possibly abandon a sport when their identity is cleaved to it? This predicament is especially challenging for elite athletes who dream of athletic superstardom. Two-time Olympic swimmer Katherine Starr had this experience when she was unable to abandon her abusive swim coach. "Your personal dream and desire trap you," Starr told me.

And the more closely their identity is linked with their athletic fantasies, the harder it can be for them to recognize what's normal and what's too much. "They're never ones to say 'enough,'" Mintz said.

For adolescents who identify above all else with their sport, the inevitable injuries that go with competitive play can be especially traumatic. A young woman named Isabelle, one of the top lacrosse players in her state at the time, told me how lost and restless she felt after tearing her ACL in high school. "I'd grown up playing lacrosse, and I had no other hobbies," she told me. Unable to play for eight months, relegated to rehab instead of practicing with teammates, she sunk into depression and developed an eating disorder. "Your whole world revolves around it, so when you don't have it, you're like, 'What am I going to do?'"

A study carried out by orthopedic surgeons found that a majority of adolescents who'd torn their ACL showed signs of post-traumatic stress disorder.

Not all physical injuries are as devastating as an ACL tear. Among young runners I coach, for example, the most common physical woes are shin splints and "runner's knee"—painful but usually short-lived injuries that often heal within weeks or months. (After rest, possibly a bout of physical therapy, perhaps orthotics to correct an unhealthy foot strike, and then a gradual return to training, preferably on soft surfaces.) For girls and young women, disordered eating or dieting can leave them more injury-prone and susceptible to bone injuries that may have long-term effects. Even temporary breaks from the sport can be devastating; the more central the sport to the person's burgeoning sense of self, the greater the void when it's wrenched away.

These factors that make young athletes susceptible to mental health troubles—the sleep loss, the physical exhaustion, the perception among kids that their performance *really matters,* and the erosion of identity beyond athletics—are enabled by coaches and parents who either embrace this approach to youth sports or are reluctant to challenge it. Coaches set the tone and establish the training protocols. In most cases, parents actively participate in their children's athletic lives—driving them to and from practice and games, delivering water bottles and orange slices, giving up weekends to advance their child's career. And how these adults behave has a profound effect on kids' well-being.

To be clear, some kids can handle focused, year-round training, Mintz told me. They work hard, love the sport, and are wild about working out, especially if the coaches are positive, and "aren't whipping their asses like rented mules," he said.

But many coaches aren't positive. In fact, many are bullies, whose hostile treatment of young kids generates further psychological harm.

Fixated on results rather than a child's well-being, parents sometimes excuse or ignore what's happening at practice. Like Caroline's parents, some decide that the child must be exaggerating and that some level of grousing is to be expected among teenagers. Others keep quiet because they secretly applaud the coach's get-tough approach, considering it a healthy reality check for their otherwise pampered kids. Many parents also are reluctant to speak up because they fear the coach will retaliate against their child, said lawyer Luanne Peterpaul, who has brought cases against bullying coaches. And some fear ostracism from other parents.

Exercise as Mood Booster

What's so tragic about the flood of unhappy athletes is that moderate exercise is known to lift the spirits. A dizzying number of studies have been carried out that make this clear. Even low levels of exercise—less than 150 minutes a week of walking—have been found to help thwart depression. Just fifteen minutes of daily jogging lifts mood and boosts energy. Most athletes of both genders report higher levels of self-esteem, self-efficacy, and social support than classmates who don't play sports. Inactive students, on the other hand, are more apt to feel lonely, inferior, and fatalistic. And the more sports a student plays, the better the psychological outlook. There's one caveat here, though: athletes in crew, ice hockey, and wrestling show *lower* levels of psychological health than kids who don't play at all.

Girls derive particular emotional and developmental benefits. Those who play sports in high school enjoy higher self- and body image, hold on to their confidence through their teens, and are less apt to get pregnant by accident. "We do know that girls lose their voice in adolescence, and sports provide a buffer for that," said Nicole LaVoi, who heads the Tucker Center for Research on Girls & Women in Sport. And girls who play competitively show a greater inclination to run for political office than their inactive peers. (Boys who play sports also do better in school and have higher educational aspirations than those who don't.) Researchers have pointed out that studies showing these positive links can't prove that playing sports *causes* these outcomes. But the correlations are strong.

The role of sports in women's overall advancement may be even greater than realized. In a landmark analysis that compared life outcomes among women before and after Title IX passed, Wharton professor Betsey Stevenson attributed the rise in female education rates, employment, and pursuit of "male" jobs to the surge in girls' sports opportunities. "It appears as if sports participation induced by Title IX had a large and statistically significant effect on female educational attainment," she wrote. States with more sports options for girls also had a greater concentration of women pursuing jobs in law, accounting, and veterinary medicine.

Finally, sports can be especially powerful for children growing up in chaotic or frightening homes. This has been so for ages. In premodern society, neuroscientist Bruce D. Perry wrote, trauma victims found relief in part by connecting with others and "regulating rhythm through dance, drumming, and song." Structured movements help restore balance to the brain's "overactive and overly reactive core regulatory networks," which are pushed off-kilter by stress. Athletics, dance, and music do much the same in the contemporary world.

A recent study in *JAMA Pediatrics* found that among adults who'd experienced trauma as children, playing team sports in adolescence was linked to better mental health in adulthood. Authors of the study found that the "psycho-social" benefits of team sports were "protective factors" in these children's lives, leading to better mental health into adulthood. Playing team sports afforded this vulnerable population greater self-esteem, more social acceptance, and a closer connection to school. "Team sports participation during adolescence was significantly associated with improved adult mental health, particularly for boys," the authors concluded. The researchers were so struck by their findings that they advised pediatricians to consider recommending team sports to kids experiencing trauma. They also encouraged policymakers to maintain sports options for all. For these kids, sports could alter the course of their lives.

Chaos at Home

It was the year he and his siblings moved into his grandmother's house, after his parents' divorce and his mother's departure, that Jelani Taylor discovered tackle football—or, as he put it, when football "came into my life." He joined the CAW football league, a generally disorganized, low-cost association of young players in Indianapolis from similar backgrounds. "It was for poor people who couldn't pay for Pop Warner," he said, referring to the established youth football program that has a foothold across the country. At eight years old, he played quarterback and immediately fell in love with the game. Other kids on the team depended on him. They became almost like siblings. For the first time in his life, he felt that what he was doing actually mattered.

Jelani played with his older brother. They'd retreat to the backyard and throw passes back and forth, doing their best to avoid the inconvenient hill at the end of the yard. On weekends, when it wasn't football season, he'd play basketball for a team at the local YMCA. Jelani was athletic and enjoyed every sport he played but one: Baseball, which he took up at five. He was exiled to the outfield and couldn't bear all the standing around, all the waiting for action that rarely arrived.

Jelani's life took a turn when his mother came back with her boyfriend. They all moved in together for a time. But it didn't last, and at the start of seventh grade, Jelani and his siblings moved again, this time to their father's house. This home didn't last long, either. One night, their father decided they all needed a fresh start. Along with his siblings, Jelani stuffed his clothes and sports gear into a duffel bag and loaded up their dad's white van. The five of them drove overnight to Flint, Michigan, and moved in with their other grandmother. Within a year, the family picked up and relocated again, to Beecher, necessitating another change of schools. By the end of eighth grade, Jelani had shuffled through five middle schools.

Beecher is an "unincorporated community" of about ten thousand people just north of Flint. Like that larger city, Beecher is poor and floundering. One 2020 review of the fifty worst places to live in the United States put Beecher in fourth, citing its staggering unemployment and poverty rates—23 and 38 percent, respectively. It had no hospitals or stores—no downtown to speak of. What Beecher did have over Flint was its reliance on well water rather than pipes, sparing the smaller community from the lead contamination that affected Flint.

When Jelani went to Beecher High School in ninth grade, he joined a student body of three hundred that was 99 percent African American. The school's academic standing was awful—it always ranked in the bottom five percent in Michigan, Jelani told me, and every year it was threatened with closure. But it had a reputation for athletic excellence. "It was all about sports," Jelani said.

In the fall of his freshman year, Jelani joined the football team. Though he was just shy of five foot seven, he played varsity from the start and eventually played almost every position on the team. When football season ended, Jelani moved over to basketball, and after that, on to track. Jelani's heart was in football, but he never considered giving up the others. "I was raised that you had to play three sports," he said. Anyway, track made him a faster, more explosive runner for football.

Playing sports also kept Jelani out of the house for as long as possible. Home was chaotic. The family would move to one dwelling for a few months but then pick up and leave after the rent caught up with them. Jelani's father struggled to get regular work; a felony from years before made finding a steady job nearly impossible. With money scarce, Jelani and his brother sometimes used their summer earnings to help with the deposit for a rental house. Occasionally, when they couldn't find a home to occupy, the whole family would move in for a short time with one of his father's friends. During part of Jelani's sophomore year, they ran out of options and slept in a family friend's basement. They were homeless like this for about five months.

On weekends, Jelani and his older brother used to finish up their chores right away so they could get to a park to train. They wanted to be gone for as long as possible, and sports were the obvious outlet. Jelani also saw football as the escape route out of Beecher. Though a closer community than Flint, Beecher was plagued with similar troubles. Kids sold drugs to make quick money, a natural temptation for teenagers with immature brains and scant material comforts. Jelani would have none of it. "I channeled everything into sports, so I didn't have time to worry about the other stuff," he explained.

Jelani knew what he wanted—to play football in college, and then in the NFL—and he wouldn't veer from that dream. "I was super disciplined," he told me. He thinks his discipline more than his athleticism is what distinguished him as a player.

He also knew that he would need top grades to make it to the right college, so he didn't let up at school. He had a knack for writing and found that putting words on the page gave him some relief. These two outlets ameliorated some of the uncertainty brought about by all the moves his family had made, and lingering worries about his mom.

Because his family didn't own a computer, Jelani decamped to the library and used the free internet there to contact coaches. He filled out every online questionnaire he could find for Division I and II colleges with football, then called and left messages. Most ignored him. But Cornell's coaches took notice and invited him to football camp that summer. Jelani raised money to pay for the camp and then boarded a plane for the first time to fly east. After Cornell head coach David Archer watched Jelani on the field, the coach knew he wanted this young man to play for him. The following year, Jelani did.

Football shaped Jelani's life, moving him off the harsh streets of Beecher and onto the gentle roads of Ithaca; sports lift some kids. For others, excessive exercise and relentless competition do just the opposite.

Of course, this immersive and intense athletic experience suits some college players. They live for the relentless practices and high-stakes competitions and have the right mindset to juggle sports and school and the social challenges that come with being in college, all on just a little over six hours of sleep. And 90 percent of the athletes surveyed, including those who were anxious, overwhelmed, and homesick, reported that their collegiate athletic experience had sharpened their work ethic, sense of responsibility, and ability to work with others.

Good for them. But not every adolescent can handle a 68.5 hour (athletics plus academics) workweek. Not all will thrive on short sleep. The talented young athlete who's also a homebody might flounder when the college coach lays claim to every weekend and most of summer. A different player might want to explore a semester abroad or pursue the kind of major that's bound to conflict with practice schedules. It's a job, every Division I athlete told me, and not every teenager is suited to full-time, unpaid work.

Moving beyond Suffering

Caroline was recruited to an elite college with a smashing swim team. When she arrived, she was stunned by the relative ease of her college workouts: she swam less than half the distance she'd covered regularly in high school, and spent far less time at practice. Swimmers could sleep in three days a week! They could leave practice if they had a class! NCAA rules limited what college coaches could demand of their swimmers. In high school, no such boundaries applied.

She set national records in high school and won championship races within the Ivy League, but Caroline has never felt satisfied with what she achieved. She was never the *best*. "It's hard for me to think of myself as a good swimmer," she said. What Caroline is proud of is having survived years of torment on the team. "I was terrified on that deck every day, and physically exhausted, and trying not to get screamed at."

More than a decade after finishing high school, Caroline feels sick about the hundreds of adults who knew what was going on but did nothing to stop it. All the coaches from other teams who visited the pool to learn from the renowned coach. Their own head of school who popped in frequently to get a look at the team. Parents who dropped their kids off for five-hour practices and accepted eleven months of specialized training.

"They partook in it," Caroline said. Didn't any teacher spot the teenagers running across campus in their bathing suits and sneakers, and think it . . . off? Were administrators unaware of how many hours these kids were practicing?

Caroline still grapples with the anguish she experienced as a high school swimmer. She is trying to move away from the belief that suffering through pain is the supreme virtue, and that only desperation and misery elicit growth. After enduring so much to please her coach, now she doesn't know what constitutes a normal boundary. Authority figures terrify her. Cold showers and the smell of chlorine send her into a panic. Sports stories, especially those involving abuse, repulse her. Though she's earned multiple advanced degrees, as well as an undergraduate diploma from an Ivy, she hears her coach's critical voice in her head telling her she's feeble, that she's not good enough. "My general sense of self-worth is completely depleted," she said. "I want to die more days than not."

CHAPTER 8

The Trouble with Coaches

One of the greatest paradoxes of youth sports today has to do with the individuals we put in charge of training our children—the coaches. To be blunt, we could be a lot better. Despite the money sluicing through club teams, travel leagues, and school sports, as well as parents' enormous emotional and financial investment in their kids' athletics, the quality of coaching in America is uneven and sometimes awful. Few are trained properly for the work. Many continue to rely on the primal scream, or even outright physical harm, to spur better performance. A smaller number sexually abuse their charges. And as more girls have flocked to sports following Title IX, fewer women now coach them. For something we claim to care so much about, we don't do an especially effective job of putting qualified people in charge.

Everyone who has played sports has a tale or two about an appalling coach, and I am no exception.

None of my countless coaches over the years ever abused me. This is something of a miracle, as plenty of lechers and misanthropes held positions of authority at my high school during the late 1970s. The vice principal, a greasy ghoul who roamed the halls looking for teenagers to persecute, went to prison years later for sexual assault.

Compared to those creeps, my high school coaches were saintly, and any harsh treatment I received was mainly verbal and rather tame. It wasn't until college that I had my first experience with a lewd coach, and by that time, I was prepared. Newly hired by my university after having been fired from a rival school, as rumor had it, for "inappropriate" behavior with girls, Coach Steve had a roving eye and a vexing inclination to comment on the physiques of the young women on the cross-country team. Despite his own sizable paunch, he found us too fat and didn't hesitate to say so. "You're all a bunch of bubble butts!" he grunted at us while we flailed up a steep grassy hill one afternoon on the university's sprawling campus. When it was time to pick out our uniforms, he insisted that we wear bun huggers, the tight, underwear-like "shorts" worn mostly by skeletal elite runners. He announced this to the team after a tirade about our weight, the implication being that he'd embarrass us into losing it.

At the time I was merely a good-enough runner, still unaware of my potential and fully capable of recognizing—and condemning—intolerable behavior by my coaches; ambition hadn't trapped me, nor had my coach's reputation blinded me to endure the unacceptable. My fellow cocaptain and I reached the same conclusion: our team would not be harassed into wearing spandex bikini bottoms for shorts. We told him that if he chose them anyway, we captains—the most experienced runners on the team, and the fastest—would walk away. He had no choice but to acquiesce. We raced in ordinary running shorts that season, ones designed for normal bodies with actual flesh, and Coach Steve left at the end of the year.

This encounter stayed with me, along with vivid memories of other powerful interactions I'd had with coaches. When I got the call years later asking me to take over a high school cross-country team, I drew on these experiences to figure out how to lead.

Becoming a Coach

"Hi, everyone!" I said to the ten teenage girls stretched out on the patch of grass next to the gym. It was my first day coaching, and my inaugural set of runners. I was forty-one, dressed to run, eager to get started, and a little disappointed at the turnout. Cross-country at a small girls' school was apparently a hard sell.

"Hello," a couple of them mumbled.

A tall girl with long dark hair, a hint of scoliosis, and a large mouth beamed at me. Another held her chin in one hand and picked at the grass with her other. One of the older girls grabbed her feet with both hands and pulled herself forward, nearly touching her knees with her nose. She eyed me warily. Still another, this one skinny and a little goofy, with crooked teeth and sculpted runners' legs, flashed a wry smile.

Like most of my teams in the years to come, this first one included young women with a wide range of talent: one aimed to finish the toughest 5K course in the state in under nineteen minutes, another would struggle to cover the same distance in less than thirty, and the remaining girls would fall somewhere in between. It was my job to bring them all together, to find the commonality among them, and to help everyone get faster. Improvement was the easy part; with a little training, kids can't help but bring their times down. The unifying—converting a group of disconnected and awkward teenagers into one cohesive *team*—was something else.

Aiding me that season was a young man named Michael, a tall and rangy white fellow in his late twenties with a David Cassidy haircut and the sideburns of a vampire. When Michael pulled into the school parking lot in his clunker of a car, often just a few minutes late, he'd smile, quickly avert his gaze, and amble on into the gym. Most days he wore jeans, slip-on sandals with socks, and a puka shell necklace, inadvertently defying the school's prim dress code. He was often unlucky. One day he came to practice wearing a bandage around his fingers, the victim of a wobbly computer that had toppled over at work and landed on his hand, breaking several bones. Another time he consumed sushi so foul and far gone that he was hospitalized for a week and lost twenty pounds.

Starting that first day, Michael and I established a regular practice routine: attendance, quick stretching, and group runs that varied in distance and pace, depending on each girl's experience, followed by more stretching. I would set off with the quickest seniors for six miles around the neighborhood, while Michael would supervise the less experienced girls as they worked to build their base mileage. The next day, we'd switch groups, so we'd both work with everyone.

Like most coaches, I'd had no official training for the job. The athletic director had hired me based on little more than a recommendation from the previous coach, who had intuited that I was qualified. And in the most important ways, he was right. Along with my long experience with competitive running, I cared for teenagers, was rearing three kids of my own, and had enough perspective to grasp how playing sports in high school could ripple through a life. I'd taken up sports as a child, and they mattered to me still. I wanted athletics to matter to the girls in front of me, too.

The best way to do this, I thought, was to guide them to their own personal records, to express faith in their ability to run and improve, and to make practice something to look forward to. I'd expect a lot from them, but my commitment would match theirs—I'd not demand punctuality of them and then saunter in late. There'd be no screaming over a bad race, no humiliations, or dressing-downs. Excellence was the goal, winning the hoped-for by-product. And I would take a deliberate interest in every girl. It wasn't that long ago that I'd been an adolescent aching to be seen and understood.

You don't necessarily know, as a coach, what impact you're having— if the teenagers under your care are learning about themselves, developing discipline and drive, and becoming more capable young adults. Even if it's clear they are growing, you never know your own role in their development. But that first year, one of my girls let it slip. It was a Saturday race in October at a distant prep school, and summer had made a brief and unwelcome return. The 3.1-mile race began on a grassy downhill, then turned into a cornfield and a small cluster of trees, before looping back again and finishing in a chute near the start. While waiting for the gun to go off at one o'clock, the girls grimaced and moaned. It was so humid. There was no shade. The other school had huge crowds cheering them on. It was going to be terrible.

"Yes, it's hot, and it's going to hurt, but you can do it," I'd say, matter of fact. I never saw the use of lying about it, and unlike other coaches, wouldn't shush them for complaining. Instead, I'd just smile, remind them of their preparation, and tell them to keep warming up.

Kerry, who was phobic about vomiting, was especially antsy, running off to the bathroom at the last moment and warning me that she wasn't feeling well, don't expect much—typical prerace jitters. "You'll do fine," I told her with a grin.

And despite her worries, Kerry took off at the start, stuck with girls who'd previously whooped her, and sprinted through to the finish in record time. She was leaning over, arms on her hips, breathless and damp, when I found her at the end. Her narrow face gazed up at me, and her blue eyes widened with surprise. "I didn't know I could run that fast!" she said to me, elated. Rather than flashing her usual ironic smile, this time she beamed with genuine delight.

She was more capable than she'd thought, stronger than she'd realized: personal growth, courtesy of cross-country. And I saw this again and again over the years—this sweet dwelling, among the girls, in their own possibilities. They were untested; none knew the limits of their strength. Kathryn, for one, began running as a freshman. When she showed up at cross-country, she didn't say much, except to make fun of her failed audition for the tennis team. She was striking at fourteen, slim and green-eyed with legs up to her neck and feet too big for her body. As gentle as she was—I have a photo of her holding my daughter's gecko and stroking its cold-blooded back—Kathryn trained with a passionate intensity, fighting to get faster and to pass anyone in her way. And she discovered, over the course of her first season, that with preparation and encouragement she was blazingly fast. When she finished high school four years later, having set various records in track and cross-country, she went on to run at a competitive Division I college. She remained luminous and kind but now possessed a visible strength.

Megan's story was more typical. She was young for her grade, chatting incessantly with new friends, whining about every workout, and finishing her first 5K race in close to twenty-eight minutes, an uninspired debut. But something shifted as she began to improve. When the workouts yielded results, she traded out her baggy basketball gear for actual running shorts and arrived at practice early. By twelfth grade, Megan would come to practice armed with everything she needed—a post-run snack, a stretching routine designed to loosen her belligerent shins, water, a GPS watch, sunblock—and talk to me about race performances happening nationally and overseas. By the end of that last cross-country season, she'd dropped almost nine minutes from her logy first race three years before. More important, she seemed to own her body and her running—they belonged to her.

But during that first season, Kathryn and Megan were unknown to me. I was muddling through with my team of ten, figuring out how to coach while the girls were learning how to run, how to race. Still, I relished working with them and savored their improvement as much as they did. I couldn't imagine ever lashing out in anger, let alone in the middle of a race.

Untrained and Bullying Coaches

The guy stood there, clutching the stopwatch in his right hand and snarling under his breath. He was bald, about my height, and, like me, an indoor track coach. We were stranded together with other coaches in a special section near the finish, away from mere spectators, the better to keep an eye on our high school runners and capture their times. It was an 800 race we were watching, four laps around the stifling indoor oval, and the bald guy and I were shoulder to shoulder.

"That's terrible!" he shrieked at the girl from his team as she loped by, on lap two. Little beads of sweat collected beneath his nose, and wet spots broke out on his long-sleeved blue shirt. He shifted from foot to foot and sighed theatrically, a deep frown punctuating his face. The girl came around again, and he glanced at his brown clipboard. "That's terrible!" he bellowed, trying to get her attention, to light a fire under her with shame. She sputtered past us, straining to keep up, glancing over when she heard him howl.

Experiences like these, along with the chilling revelations about Larry Nassar, prompted me to run an experiment. I wondered what would appear in the way of news stories if I set up Google alerts for "coaching abuse" and "coach sex." How widespread was this problem with predatory or belligerent coaching?

I soon learned that there were more horrors than I could have imagined. Since establishing this morbid notification system, at least one ghastly article a day has appeared in my feed involving cases against youth sports coaches from across the fifty states. Most often, the harms have fallen into three camps: physical abuse disguised as training; emotional exploitation masquerading as tough love; and sexual offenses and innuendos cloaked as innocent misunderstandings. And though the rough outlines of these stories were similar, each contained its own squalid details.

To mention a few: In April 2020, two former runners at South Pasadena High School sued track coach Pierre-Jonas Hernandez for sexual abuse, claiming that he touched them lewdly in an empty boys' locker room when they were underage. High school baseball players in Maplewood, New Jersey, told the Board of Education that their coaches had called them "pussies" and losers, berated them for making mistakes, and benched players who objected. Parents of football players in Texas sued coaches at Hamshire-Fannett High School for negligence after the excessive exercises the coaches required put several players in the hospital; the boys were ordered to do hundreds of jump squats over three days as punishment for leaving a locker room dirty. None of these stories rose to national attention.

Sexual abuse is a small piece of the mistreatment young athletes experience and is universally condemned. But more run-of-the-mill harms—roaring at players for fumbling plays and addressing mistakes with physical "corrections"—are considered normal, even admirable, in sports. This is so despite evidence that emotional cruelty is the "gateway" to other kinds of mistreatment, said Celia Brackenridge, the late women's sports scholar who spent decades researching such harms. "To prepare an athlete for abuse, some sort of emotional abuse usually occurs first," she explained when we spoke. Many coaches, especially those who require early specialization in one sport, also impose such excessive training on young players that it verges on physical mistreatment.

Some of these transgressions are a function of the coaches' scant training. Of the roughly 7.5 million who work with children and teenagers, about four million are volunteers; these latter are the ones helping out with Little League, youth soccer, and CYO basketball. But less than 5 percent of these coaches receive "relevant" instruction, according to the National Committee for Accreditation of Coaching Education, a reality I observed when coaching my young son: after signing up to coach, I showed up to practice without having attended a single training session. The interscholastic level isn't much better. Just 25 to 30 percent of coaches in schools get training. Recognizing the deficit in coaching education, the Susan Crown Exchange—a foundation that works to support youth development—pledged to instruct a million coaches in social and emotional learning by 2025. They have a long way to go.

A handful of findings over the years suggest that bullying by coaches is common. In one study, 36 percent of coaches surveyed "angrily yelled at a player for making a mistake." Another 10 percent encouraged an athlete to retaliate against an opponent who plays "dirty." Of the 8 percent of coaches who admitted to making fun of kids on their team, 20 percent did so "often." Thirty-five percent of the surveyed kids said their coaches yelled at them for making mistakes, and 27 percent reported that their coaches promoted retaliation on the other side. Overall, according to investigators, "youth always reported problematic coaching behavior more often than did the coaches themselves." And bullying coaches have a profound effect on team conduct. A study of nearly twenty thousand college athletes that looked at coaching styles and their effects on players found that an abusive approach cultivated an atmosphere that tolerated cheating and was less inclusive overall.

Bullied kids, including those who are targeted outside sports, often suffer psychologically into adulthood. A team of researchers found that anxiety, depression, and suicidal thinking persist for years among kids who were both bullies and victims. As well, both victims of bullies and bullies themselves were more apt to experience bad health, troubled relationships, and economic hardship as adults. "I'm starting to view bullying the same way I do abuse in the home," the head researcher said.

Laurence Steinberg, the Temple psychology professor and authority on adolescence, told me that coaches who yell at kids have merely adopted the misguided American fable about cruel coaches getting results. "It's a cultural meme almost," he said. But this is exactly the wrong way to handle teenagers who already are highly emotional, often anxious, and intensely aware of their peers. "It can't be good for them," Steinberg said. Getting screamed at publicly will likely intensify kids' anxiety and prompt some to withdraw or quit. And verbal mistreatment at a tender age can leave psychic scars. Dr. Kody Moffatt, who specializes in pediatric sports, told me that verbal battering by coaches "can shake kids to the core."

One of the greatest ironies of this coaching style is that it doesn't improve performance. "Yelling doesn't work," clinical sports psychologist John Sullivan explained to me. Getting screamed at will trigger an athlete's fear response, meaning she'll seek to fight, flee, or shut down— not the building blocks of high performance.

Indeed, a coaching regime that relies on punishment as a form of motivation will flounder. "Punishment practices don't achieve goals, don't build team unity, and don't create better players," Moffatt told me. The kids and teams that manage to perform well with a punitive coach do so in spite of those methods. Plato was right: "Nothing taught by force stays in the soul."

I can't say if coaching abuses have gotten radically worse or more common over the years; the lack of oversight of youth sports and hundreds of thousands of coaches who move on and off teams make it impossible to measure. I can say that the emotional cruelty, lack of training, and occasional lapses into physical or sexual abuse among coaches should concern everyone who cares about kids and values sports.

Consider Caroline, from the previous chapter, who swam for an esteemed coach on an elite high school team. Celebrated for producing champions, her coach was erratic and unforgiving. One day, he'd be nice and tell the team he loved them. Another day, he'd rage about how spoiled and anemic they all were, especially if they cried. Even as he used his belt to thrash stragglers into the pool, he'd smile and laugh and make a joke out of needing to hold his pants up. Sometimes he'd give the swimmers special T-shirts as a reward for their performances and make a big show of his support. On other occasions he'd berate them for no apparent reason. He told Caroline and other kids he spoke harshly to that getting the coaches' attention meant they had talent. This applied, apparently, even to the group of girls he labeled the "geek squad" and to a diabetic boy he often picked on for fretting about blood-sugar levels.

And he was preoccupied by the swimmers' weight. "I don't need a satellite to tell that you ate a lot of junk food this weekend," he told Caroline and other girls when he observed them on Monday. To keep tabs on them, he measured everyone's body fat once a month. The girls would retreat to their locker room, peel their suits down to their hips, and throw on a T-shirt, so that the special adult brought in to gauge their fat had easy access to their waistlines. Some girls made themselves vomit before being measured; others avoided food for twenty-four hours in advance. When the caliper testing was over, Coach announced whose was highest. "A minute on the lips, a year on the hips," he'd call out in warning.

Though Caroline's parents didn't amplify the hostile messages she was hearing at practice, they didn't object to the coach's methods or yank her off the team, either. "A lot of parents were also the bad guys here," she said. "They were abusive in their own way." Her mom and dad are sorry they didn't do more to help at the time. They just couldn't *see* it, she said. "It was so easy to manipulate the parents."

Where Are the Women Coaches?

There was little I looked forward to less than the end-of-season meeting of all the track head and assistant coaches in the county. These were mandatory gatherings to talk about scheduling, to identify any problems that needed to be addressed collectively, and to pick the runners who deserved special notice for their performances, among other random, unforeseen subjects. When I finally found the cheerless school cafeteria where the meeting was held, I was confronted with something I'd not noticed before. Of the approximately two dozen coaches, assistant coaches, and administrators gathered in the room, all of them the leaders of the boys' and girls' high school track teams in the county, three of us were women. And I was the only head coach.

Title IX famously launched girls into sports, but it has, less famously, pushed women out of it. Since its passage in 1972, the number of women who coach has continued to fall. In 1972, 90 percent of women's collegiate teams were coached by women. In 2014, the percentage dropped to 43. Data on high school coaches is scant, but what does exist indicates that few women lead teams: a 2014 study in Minnesota found that only 21 percent of head coaches, and 28 percent of assistant coaches, were women. At the youth level, too, women heads are atypical. A 2015 study conducted by the Sports and Fitness Industry Association found that just 27 percent of kids' sports teams up to age fourteen are coached by women.

This is so for a few reasons. One is that Title IX brought money to women's sports, which made coaching them more attractive to men, particularly on college teams; now that there was real money at stake, the men wanted in on it. Another is that some colleges responded to the legislation by combining their men's and women's athletic departments and bringing them both under the orbit of one athletic director, typically a male. These athletic directors, in turn, hired those they knew—male coaches. At younger levels, the dearth of women coaches reflects what sociologists Michael Messner and Suzel Bozada-Deas call "institutional gender regimes." Powerful norms about gender explain why women have opted for "team mom"—organizing rides, snacks, schedules—rather than team coach. Tom Farrey at the Aspen Institute's

Project Play suggested that coaching is often seen as a meaningful way for fathers to get involved in their kids' lives. We mothers, presumably, have already had enough of them.

All of this makes sense. When my son Paul started playing organized baseball, I quickly signed on to coach him. Having played softball growing up, I found guiding kids on the infield far more appealing than managing carpools; we were all volunteers, so why not coach? It felt natural to fling balls around, hit soft grounders to clueless kids learning how to play, and to offer counsel on baserunning. But it didn't take long to figure out that I was the only woman doing any coaching of boys, at least those in his grade.

This is bad for kids. Young women who've been coached only by men lose an everyday model of female leadership, as well as exposure to a coaching style that may differ from the macho approach many men adopt. When girls "only see men in positions of power, they conclude that sports are not for me," said Nicole LaVoi, from the Tucker Center. And girls need sports, especially during adolescence, when they often lose confidence.

Boys, too, if never exposed to female coaches, "don't see women as capable, viable leaders," LaVoi told me. Surely the converse is also true: that boys coached by competent women see female leadership the way they do male—an aspirational quality that's unattached to gender. This was true for Leland Jones, one of New Jersey's top distance runners a few years ago. He was coached by an elite woman who ran with the fast pack and shared her enthusiasm for the sport with everyone. "She was definitely a role model," he told me.

Will Ebben, now twenty-four, was coached by women in soccer and basketball when he was a boy. Their example transformed his view of girls' sports and "definitely played a role in how I view female authorities," he wrote in an email. The decline in women coaches during the past several decades has served neither boys nor girls and has eaten away at the perception that girls can grow up to lead, too.

———

As my first season drew to a close, the days shortened. Light drained out of the sky earlier and earlier, and by five it felt like nighttime. Temperatures dropped, and now girls slipped out for their runs wearing shiny black tights, gloves, and long-sleeved T-shirts. When it rained, slick red and yellow leaves littered the roads; I warned the girls to step carefully when they ran downhill. Cross-country would all be over by mid-November, and winter track would begin soon after. But that wouldn't be my last season. I had begun to realize that, at least among some girls, I had the power to spark an interest that could last a lifetime. That by virtue of being on my team, they might adopt a habit that could help shield them from hardships around the corner. I stayed on as an assistant to the winter track coach. And I would continue this work for another sixteen years, always as the head cross-country coach, and off and on as an assistant track coach, at this school and then another.

CHAPTER 9

The Connection Conundrum

Social connections of all kinds have been on the decline in this country for decades. The political scientist Robert Putnam made that clear twenty years ago in his book *Bowling Alone: The Collapse and Revival of American Community*, which examined the collapse in social trust among the American population during the latter half of the twentieth century. Putnam observed several worrying trends in American communities: membership in churches and unions was dropping; philanthropic donations were down; volunteerism had become passe; and casual social connections—like dinner parties and card games—had waned. Rather than mingle, socialize, or engage in some activity that involved the larger community, more of the American population was retreating inward and staying there. Putnam found multiple culprits for this social deterioration including the widespread embrace of TV, a shift in generations, "busyness," and sprawl, but added that other unknowns were also responsible.

In his 2020 revision of the book, Putnam concludes that these unwelcome developments have only worsened. "America has continued to regress in the intervening twenty years—a downward plunge resulting not merely in fraying community ties but also in worsening economic inequality, greater political polarization, and more cultural individualism." Consider that he wrote these depressing words before the dumpster fire of the contested 2020 presidential election and the start of the pandemic. Since then, we've seen upticks in reckless driving, clashes on airplanes, urban violence, student misconduct, and attacks on health care workers, among other toxic antisocial behavior. Dip into Twitter for even a minute, or dare take a stroll around Facebook, and the vitriol will swallow you up, send you scurrying back to the lonely comforts of your COVID cave. Never, in my lifetime, has the hunger for community felt so desperate while at the same time seemed so out of reach.

Sports have the reputation and potential to bring people together. Indeed, of all the rewards that sports confer, connecting with others may be the most sublime. The bonds built in athletics are hard to measure and don't lend themselves to analysis. But they're nonetheless nourishing and profound. In team sports, you might experience all the human emotions over the course of a single season. I don't mean to suggest that other kinds of relationships, those cultivated over coffee, books, or spreadsheets, are any less tight or lasting. But going through such emotional trials in sports is a fast pass to social connection, and a potent way to transcend divisions.

And we are in dire need of such bonds. Kids and teenagers need connection that much more; their mushy, unformed brains cry out for the stimulation that comes from contact with others, some of it denied from years of COVID lockdowns. For those who play sports, they require the companionship that comes from the shared struggle to compete hard and win. Team sports are especially important now, as they are that rare arena in which hardened boundaries between varied social groups begin to break. The playing fields also offer support, companionship, and healing to kids who are cycling through painful life events outside of sports. Connection and community are what kids need when their family unit isn't enough, and athletics can provide this fellowship in ways that few other activities can.

But youth sports have gotten bogged down by the forces that are tearing us apart in other ways. Indeed, the culture of individualism Putnam bemoans is apparent everywhere in the way we provide athletics to kids. The fixation on winning, pursuit of personal glory, and divisions between the haves and have-nots—the defining features of kids' sports—wring out the greater social benefits that athletics naturally provide. The paradox is that one of the very best antidotes to alienation—playing sports with others from varied backgrounds—has been twisted so far around that now competitive youth sports contribute to the loss of social connection that kids want most.

Connection Is at the Root of Human Thriving

Connection is the antithesis of loneliness, the antidote to alienation. When we join with others and recognize our common humanity, some of life's hard edges soften. Hope appears. Because healthy relationships are so central to a good life, they're especially crucial for kids. Children who grow up with strong bonds to others are more apt to flourish.

We know all this because of an extraordinary longitudinal study of human growth conducted by Harvard University beginning in 1938.

Dubbed the Harvard Study of Adult Development, the project involved regular in-depth interviews with two wildly distinct populations that were singled out for analysis: 268 undergraduate boys at Harvard, and 456 young men of the same age growing up in Boston's poorest neighborhoods. The original research team followed this population of 724 men year after year, interviewing them about their life satisfaction, careers, and families, and conducting medical exams to assess their health. When the first scientists on the team were too old to continue, another generation of researchers stepped in to carry out the interviews and conduct the analysis. This project, which continues today, is widely considered the longest-running study of adult development.

Its most significant finding, said Dr. Robert Waldinger, a psychiatrist at Massachusetts General Hospital who heads the research, is that close relationships are the key to good health and happiness. "Social connections are really good for us, and . . . loneliness kills," Waldinger revealed during a 2015 TED Talk that summarized the findings. More than career success, wealth, fame, education, or background, high-quality personal connections sustained over a lifetime are what delivered physical health and a sense of well-being among the men studied.

When it comes to teenagers, less-celebrated surveys reveal a similar finding. A study published in *Pediatrics* in 2019 found that adult men and women who had reported a high degree of "connectedness" when they were adolescents—defined as "a sense of caring, support, and belonging to family and school"—were in better condition than their peers who'd reported no such connection. "Family and school connectedness," the authors concluded, "may have long-lasting protective effects across multiple health outcomes related to mental health, violence, sexual behavior, and substance use." Earlier, narrower studies have determined much the same. One report found that teenagers who had been attended to by caring adults—not necessarily their parents—did better going forward than those who hadn't. The authors assert that policy makers and program directors who are concerned about how kids develop should find ways to encourage relationships between young people and adults.

Psychotherapist and author Lisa Damour concurred. When I asked her what teenagers need to be mentally sound, she answered, "Loving relationships with adults! Loving relationships with adults! And it doesn't have to be a parent."

As Putnam has observed, social engagements of all kinds are on the decline. Some of this has to do with the widespread use of technology, he noted, though social media affects relationships in complex and varied ways. Among kids who would otherwise be ostracized or alone, online relationships can be a path to connection. Still, he wrote, while "offline friends matter a lot for our happiness . . . online Friends appear to have no such effect."

As a hopeless phone addict and Twitter enthusiast, I hesitate to blame technology for the epidemic of loneliness. But the changes in behavior among the girls I've seen and coached has persuaded me that the ubiquity of phones has altered adolescents' social lives. When I started coaching, before phones and social media took over, the gathering places at school used to be noisy and bustling bazaars, where some kids shouted greetings to one another from across the gym and others collected in circles to share stories with their friends. Shy and self-conscious teenagers retreated to their corners, but without a socially sanctioned electronic pacifier to keep them there, they eventually spoke up; the sheer awkwardness of appearing friendless would compel most to acknowledge another uneasy kid by their side. And little by little, having successfully confronted the social anxiety that kept them quiet, they might make a tangible friend, and begin to ease into conversation and companionship.

More recently, when walking through the narrow hall outside the gym before practice, I was struck by the quiet all around me. The corridor wasn't empty—teenagers were milling about, waiting for their team to gather—but the kids were mostly silent, heads bent over phones and fingers tapping out messages. Withdrawing into online reinforcements is easier than daring to say hello to a real-life acquaintance, especially when you're a wobbly teenager. And one place where phones are neither welcome nor relevant (with few exceptions), and where human interaction cannot be avoided, is on the playing field. This is where social skills are forged and sharpened, and where resilience is practiced and tested.

When the Worst Happens

The day after Aly Carter's brother died, her teammates and high school coach from the indoor-track team drove to Aly's home in Westfield, New Jersey, as a show of support. Cars lined the road outside her house, and inside, friends and relatives huddled together in quiet clusters, comforting Aly's parents and older sister. Aly sat with the team in the kitchen. She'd been crying all night, and her face had gone blotchy and red. Aly told her teammates that her brother had been wearing a seat belt when he died; it had even left lacerations on his body. One of her close friends had come with a basket of knickknacks, and everyone on the team messed around with the toys as if they were back in elementary school. Aly smiled and laughed along with her teammates. For a few moments, she forgot her dreadful new reality.

Aly was a freshman at an all-girls' private school, having moved over from public school that fall. The adjustment had gone well. Since the start of soccer preseason in August, she'd quickly accumulated friends, a function, in part, of her sunny and self-deprecating personality. Aly laughed easily, often placing her own imaginary inadequacies at the center of the joke. Another part of it was her full-throttled approach to soccer. She had been playing for years, and on top of her natural speed, she had hustle—a willingness to practice and play with a relentless energy. Hustle was Aly's edge, she thought, her secret weapon. She brought that same spirit to winter track and lacrosse.

Her brother's death blotted everything out. Aly missed several days of school after the funeral. With her older sister back at college, it was just Aly and her parents at home, the three of them working their way through the rubble. Her parents, Mike and Mary Lou, were flattened, and many nights Aly cried alone in bed. She drew her legs up to her chest, contracted into a tiny ball, and sobbed. In the morning, she went to school and threw herself into sports.

Hurling a lacrosse ball into a goal, sprinting back and forth on the football field in town, catching a ball she'd just thrown against a tall brick wall—practice kept Aly's mind occupied. School was more of a struggle. In the classroom, her mind would drift away from geometry or English and linger on memories of her brother. In lacrosse, she could throw her body into the mix and lose herself in the action. Sometimes her brother's friends from the Penn State golf team would drive up to Summit and cheer for her on the sidelines.

A good part of what kept her going, even allowing for flashes of cheer, were her teammates. Friends from lacrosse and track helped Aly with her homework. The same girls organized a surprise sixteenth birthday party for her. Instead of avoiding discussions about her brother, they brought him up in conversation. Many composed encouraging letters and rousing texts after her brother died. "You are the strongest person I know," one wrote. Others lamented the unfairness of her circumstances, refusing to nullify her heartbreak with hollow platitudes. When Aly looks back on that time today, she remembers her teammates' guileless expressions of love as essential to her survival.

A sense of normal life had begun to edge back. But six months after her brother's death, Aly's father started experiencing random and debilitating headaches. He and Mary Lou first assumed that the stress of their son's abrupt death was the cause. But a series of tests uncovered an aggressive melanoma, which had metastasized to his brain. Aly learned about her father's illness during the indoor-track season. For most of Mike's life, he had been a dedicated runner and repeat marathoner. "I realized how happy all my sports, but especially running, made him," Aly told me. She leaned harder into the sport.

Aly joined the cross-country team as a senior. Charging up the sharp hill on Warwick Road, she would pump her arms mechanically until she got to the steepest part near the top, then drive them faster until she reached the finish at the telephone pole. On the track, she'd jump off the white line with the sprinters and cling to that pace on the inside lane for as long as she could, never waffling or proceeding tentatively just to be safe. And on regular road runs, when most girls would turn right outside the gym's glass doors and immediately lapse into a comfortable jog, she'd surge to the front and go with whoever else could stay with her. When the workouts were over, she reverted to her lighthearted alter ego, mocking her own form and calling out others for their great work.

Aly's resilience was tested that fall on a hot Saturday in the middle of October. Around eleven thirty that morning, our team piled into a stunted yellow school bus and left for southern New Jersey to race against *The* (capital *T*) Lawrenceville School. Set among acres of playing fields, an expansive golf course, and plentiful red brick, the campus had the character of a baby Ivy. Lawrenceville dominated athletically and academically, and its golden student body—fit, clear-skinned, and effortlessly at ease in the world—exuded privilege.

When the gun went off, runners from both teams darted across the grass and down a gradual hill. Lawrenceville's fastest girl quickly tore ahead of everyone, and within minutes separated herself from the pack. Aly attached herself to their second runner, and the rest of the girls followed. As always, I ran from field to field, armed with my stopwatch and notebook, so I could record their mile splits and places, before sprinting to the edge of the soccer field, close to the end.

A girl shot out of the woods, a skinny thoroughbred in a red singlet—Lawrenceville—galloping ahead of everyone, her breathing jagged and strained. Within a minute, the second Lawrenceville girl appeared—and then Aly, heaving in her blue-and-white uniform, her eyes fixed on the girl ahead. As they turned the corner of the soccer field, Aly closed the distance between them, and the two girls rushed forward, side by side, both picking up speed. Lawrenceville parents there for soccer tuned in when they noticed this drama playing out in front of them and let out a sudden chorus of support for their school, and their girl, which echoed across the soccer field.

No matter. Aly's legs quickened, her ponytail jumped, and she began to pull away from the runner beside her. The narrow gap between them grew—two feet, then four, and Aly's rival, unable to hold on any longer, yielded to the inevitable. Aly leaned across the line, and the Lawrenceville girl tottered in behind her. They both collapsed onto the ground next to the finish, sweaty and spent. When Aly finally pulled herself up, tiny blades of grass still stuck to her wet shoulders and wilted top, she opened her mouth into a wide smile.

With her father gravely ill and parents in and out of hospitals, Aly came to rely on her posse of friends from various teams for companionship and support. A lacrosse player from town drove her to and from school every day. Another teammate's huge family welcomed Aly into their home, calling her their eighth child. Before the semiformal dance in December, one of Aly's closest friends and teammates bought satin dresses, pants, and tops for Aly to choose from and delivered them to Aly's home.

In breaks between school and practice, she looked after her father. When he couldn't eat or drink, she clutched a tiny yellow hospital sponge and squeezed drops of water into his mouth. When she got word that he needed emergency brain surgery while she was training in Florida, she flew home that night to be there. All the while, she talked to him in an upbeat patter, asking unanswerable questions and telling him about her day. She took on an air of fearlessness and determination. "She brought this strength to everything," Mary Lou said. And she was always gentle. She was with him when he died.

Lacrosse season started shortly after, and Aly had no intention of missing any of it. The team was packed with her closest friends. It was these girls who had stuck with her during the worst of times—when she was hanging on after her brother's accident, when sudden medical exigencies forced her to leave practice abruptly, when her parents' immersion in hospitals and treatment plans left her alone at home. And after the unthinkable happened, when Aly's father died so shortly after her brother, they flocked to her house with cookies and flowers and offered her the comfort of companionship.

Not long after the funeral, Aly's school hosted its first lacrosse game of the season, and she was starting. Mary Lou stood on the sidelines. Some mothers approached her and gaped. "We can't believe you're here," they told her. Mary Lou said little, but she thought, *Of course I'm here!* If her daughter had the courage to get on the field, she would have the courage to watch.

That season, Aly's lacrosse team rolled over their local rivals. A few games were a battle, especially one in late May against a nearby high school. This was the semifinal game in the state section—one game down the long road of the New Jersey state tournament, culminating in a final championship match. The merciless sun radiated off the spongy grass field and onto the fans who had gathered to watch. Parents, brothers and sisters, classmates, reporters, teachers, and dozens of others spilled over the bleachers, while teenagers clung to a fence at the top of a retaining wall to get a better view.

Aly and her teammates, dressed in blue skirts and white jerseys, each with a big blue number on the back, strutted out to the field. "I was good, and I wanted it, and I had all the confidence in the world," Aly remembered.

Intimate with her teammates, she also knew many of the players on the opposing team, as she'd played with some of them in clubs. "It was an absolute battle," Aly said.

Onlookers clapped and booed, challenged the referee's calls, and paced when the game got too close. As they had so many times before, Aly's team squeezed out a win, beating their rivals 12–10, and earning the State Group title.

The team went on to lose the championship game, but it didn't matter to Aly. They had won so much by then anyway, and everyone was so close, so bound to one another. A photographer captured a picture of her that day jumping into the arms of her friend and fellow captain. Aly's legs are wrapped around her friend's waist, and both sets of arms clasp the other's shoulders, lacrosse sticks in hands. Aly's face is obscured by her teammate's goggles, but the blue ribbon attached to her ponytail sails into the air.

What Makes Sports Such a Powerful Connector?

Along with its other virtues, running for me has served as a social outlet, inviting not only casual but satisfying relationships with a community of runners, but also more profound bonds with a handful of women who've trained together for years. For at least a decade when my children were growing up, Anne and I met on the steps of the YMCA after school drop-off most mornings for our daily run. One of us would bolt indoors to the bathroom, and then after a few moments of commiseration—the snow, our hamstrings, the latest political outrage—we'd settle on a route, click our watches, and lope down the concrete sidewalk outside the Y. Anne is a few years younger than I and a natural extrovert, and within a minute she'd be calling out to half a dozen friends or neighbors while quickening her pace. "Hey, hold up!" I'd have to say to get her to moderate. Before long, we'd be lost in conversation.

What is it about exercising and competing together that creates such durable connections? I wondered.

"It's all about what's shared," said Jim Taylor, an author and clinical sports psychologist who practices in California. "There's shared passion, shared goals, shared effort, and shared outcomes," he added. Especially on true team sports, where the entire group is interdependent, the communal nature of the endeavor is "connective." Kids are more apt to bond with their teammates than their classmates for exactly this reason: the team's goals are collective, while in the class every student strives for herself.

I would add another experience that committed athletes share, which binds them together: suffering. Running may be considered an individual sport, but those who train together, who endure the same punch-to-the-gut workouts, who join a friend for a run long before the sun has edged into the sky, who take on one more staggering hill or repeat mile when their bodies ache for relief—this shared torment builds bonds. It's what made that wet morning with my gang of women runners so magnificent: We had achieved together what psychology professor Paul Bloom calls "the sweet spot," where chosen pain brings meaning to life and connection with others.

Among the girls I coached, nothing brought them closer than intermittent oxygen deprivation or the buildup of lactic acid in their thighs, which they all endured regularly during the season. Perhaps these grueling encounters with their corporal limits constituted the common enemy that united them. Or perhaps, as Damon Young wrote, the misery marked a contrast to the "muggy, monolithic comfort" of everyday life. Whatever the cause, they were always most relaxed and chummy after arduous workouts.

Sports also connect kids (and adults) because they tap into a human desire to belong. "We are tribal beings; we want to belong to something larger than ourselves," Taylor said. The longing for group identity is a function of evolution: humans gathered to protect themselves against predators and to work together to secure food, sometimes against other tribes also on the hunt. That reflex remains, even if our objective circumstances have changed. Belonging to, or just following, a sports team provides a natural outlet for our tribal instincts, an automatic identity that transcends the self.

That feeling of connection is also tied to emotion. "Emotions are what attract us to sports," Shane Murphy told me. Murphy is a psychology professor at Western Connecticut State University who specializes in sports; years ago, he was the head psychologist for the US Olympic Committee. The triumphant fist in the air, the smack of the racket hitting the court, the drooping heads on the losing bench, the pileup of players on the pitcher's mound—these extravagant expressions of feeling are common in sports, no matter the level. And shared emotional experiences connect us to one another in ways that bland, bloodless experiences don't. If you play sports for any length of time, there's no escaping the range of emotions they evoke: shame, fury, delight, joy, embarrassment, pride, despair, envy. And I'm surely missing a few.

Recent research on the brain reveals that emotional experiences and social relationships are especially resonant for teenagers. The adolescent brain is more sensitive than previously thought. In *Age of Opportunity: Lessons from the New Science of Adolescence*, psychology professor Laurence Steinberg explains the dramatic changes that occur to the brain during adolescence. The limbic system, which is linked to emotions, impulse control, and sensation seeking, is "turned on" once puberty occurs, usually in early adolescence. It "starts the engines," in Steinberg's parlance, making teenagers particularly hungry for pleasure. The emotions teenagers feel thanks to their hormonally infused limbic systems are especially intense. "We know that during adolescence the brain is particularly sensitive to emotional arousal," Steinberg told me.

Puberty also activates the parts of the brain associated with socializing, which explains why teenagers are often self-conscious and fixated on their peers. Later in adolescence, the prefrontal cortex begins to develop. It's the seat of rational thought and planning and acts as a brake on the irrational urgings of the limbic system. Teenagers are most apt to get in trouble—to experiment with drugs, drive too fast, and take dumb risks—when the limbic system is clicking along at full speed but the prefrontal cortex, from which self-control emerges, is just getting going.

Team sports, then, with their social dimension and high emotional index, are especially powerful for adolescents whose brains are attuned to their own feelings and receptive to the reactions of their peers. And because the teenage brain is malleable during this period, emotions and experiences that occur in adolescence get embedded, building new neural pathways and locking in memories. This is why coming-of-age stories are evergreen, and why high school memories remain vivid: the brain is wired to capture them. Those of us who had rich athletic lives growing up are more apt to remember team wins, losses, and embarrassments than we are the routine happenings in chemistry class because sports' emotional impact carved a groove in our brains. What teenagers and young adults experience during this lengthy period, then, can have a lasting effect on how that grown-up person interprets the world.

Sports may also provide one answer to the stark social divisions that persist in this country, whether grounded in class, religion, political leanings—or, especially, race. Educating or exhorting others to be better, to listen, and then to change the way they think and behave doesn't work, wrote *New York Times* columnist David Brooks on the last day of 2020. What does, he theorized, drawing on research from the late social psychologist Gordon Allport, is being thrust into new environments with varied types of people over an extended period. "Doing life together with people of other groups can reduce prejudice and change minds," he wrote. "It's how new emotional bonds are formed, how new conceptions of who is 'us' and who is 'them' come into being."

My son's high school basketball team consisted of mostly white, middle- and upper-middle-class kids from our town, along with a handful of Black kids and some boys from economically marginalized families. Even from the stands, it was easy to see that their shared love of basketball and hunger to win overpowered lunch-table affiliations. Race, class, age, religion—all of these entrenched divisions were eroded over time by the boys "doing life together" on the basketball court after school. They became friends, as teammates usually do, without scolding or prodding from adults.

Under the right circumstances, sports are uniquely suited to bring diverse groups together; I have observed that breakdown in social categories among the girls I've coached and felt it with my fellow runners. The gang of eight women who climbed the steep hill on Woodland Avenue during a downpour many years ago included some with multiple graduate degrees, one whose education ended with high school, a few of us knowledge workers, one who cleaned apartments, and another who was a nurse. We weren't a model of diversity, but nor were we identical in our view of the world. On that morning run, and on many others before and after, our common purpose overwhelmed the superficial differences that can interfere with genuine attachment.

I spoke to Richard Lapchick, author, activist, and founder of the Institute for Diversity and Ethics in Sport, who has spent the better part of his life working to erode racial injustice through sports. He told me, "I don't know of any place in our culture where if you get in a huddle, it doesn't matter if you're white, Black, Latino, rich, poor, young or old, gay or straight: you're going to lose if you don't pull together." This is the "miracle of sports," as he put it in a video address to a women's leadership group, the way the pursuit of a common goal—to win—dissolves trivial differences and invites cooperation.

Of course, it's naive to believe that sports are *inherently* hostile to bigotry and exclusion. Research suggests that hazing and other forms of intra-team ritualized nastiness, ostensibly intended to build team bonds, are common in collegiate and high school sports. One study found that

47 percent of high school student athletes reported being hazed in their sport. Indeed, with half a second of reflection, you can probably recall tales of sports' hazing in your own community—or remember experiencing it yourself. A few years ago, the girls' high school soccer team in a neighboring town made the news when some freshman players revealed that seniors routinely bullied them, including circulating what they called a "slut list" of attractive incoming players. This was small potatoes compared to the football team in Wall Township, New Jersey, who in 2021 apparently abused younger players with a broomstick and sexually assaulted girls off-campus. Or, for that matter, the basketball players in San Diego who threw tortillas at their opponents after narrowly beating the mostly Hispanic team. Such violations of teammates' and rivals' basic humanity would seem to dispel any faith in the "miracle" of sports.

Brandon Whiting is a former NFL defensive lineman who now educates coaches and parents on sports and racism through Positive Coaching Alliance (PCA), a national nonprofit (of which I am a part) that promotes a constructive approach to youth sports. Like Lapchick, Whiting believes that sports are uniquely suited to combat intolerance: they compel teammates to recognize one another as individuals, rather than as representatives of a group. But Whiting cautions against thinking of sports as some utopia that's free of prejudice. He is mixed race, and when he was growing up, he sensed that even his Little League teammates— friends on the field, all clad in the same uniform—kept their distance when the game was over. He's also conscious of racial stereotyping that lumps Black men and boys with athletics. Today, when Whiting walks into stores, perfect strangers will ask him what sports he plays. "I'm a whole human being—I like reading, and science, and astronomy," Whiting said. "But what they see is 'you must be good at sports.'" It's a particular burden for Black kids with no interest in athletics.

After George Floyd's murder, PCA refreshed its commitment to grappling with racism in athletics. Like US Youth Soccer, USA Volleyball, US Sailing, and other sports governing bodies, leaders at PCA, including Whiting, recognized that the organization had a duty to act. Because athletics are so central to building community among different types of people, large youth sports organizations embraced the need to counter racism within their leagues. But racism in sports is complex, Whiting noted, requiring a "purposeful" approach that goes beyond verbal commitments. For its part, when PCA took a closer look at the five hundred Little League kids it served in one area, the organization discovered that only nineteen came from low-income schools. "Something is going on there," Whiting said—structural impediments to participation, in other words, that would take more than enlightened coaching, or commitments to inclusion, to repair. How can sports build bonds among diverse groups of kids when some of those groups never make it on the roster?

Whiting is inspired by the sociologist and civil rights activist Harry Edwards, who has argued that sports are the right arena in which to agitate for human rights. There's a long history of professional Black athletes using their platforms to press for change. Edwards's research helped PCA create its curriculum on combatting racism, which emphasizes the need for difficult conversations among coaches and players. The course doesn't offer up particular solutions to racial problems on teams. Instead, it encourages coaches to be open and honest, to be mindful of how they talk to their players, and to embrace inclusion above all. "It's 'calling in' versus 'calling out,'" Whiting explained. "If I can't do it here, I can't do it anywhere."

From Safe Place to Community

Jelani Taylor, whom we met in chapter 7, was told that moving from a bottom-tier high school in Beecher, Michigan, to the tippy top of the education hierarchy in Ithaca, New York, would be an adjustment. Teachers and advisers at home had warned him that he shouldn't expect to get A's at such a college. But Jelani wasn't worried. Because he had no prior exposure to Cornell—"we never talked about Ivy League schools growing up," he said—he wasn't intimidated by its exalted reputation.

"I knew I could do the work, even without the experience," he told me. He had a work ethic, honed through sports, that he would carry over to his studies. He'd done the same in high school.

Though Jelani was often the only African American man in his classes at Cornell's hotel school, he experienced his classmates as friendly and welcoming. The bigger shock was the financial chasm that separated him from his peers. An assumption of wealth permeated the campus, with professors and students alike speaking casually about luxury hotels, expensive cars, and international travel. It made sense given the nature of their studies, but for Jelani it felt alienating and unimaginable. "If you're not outside of it, you don't see it," he said.

It helped that Jelani had two roommates, also on the football team, who came from similar backgrounds. The three of them lived in a "forced triple"—a room meant for two that was overstuffed to sleep three—in Jameson Hall, a high-rise dormitory on Cornell's north campus. The space was jammed with beds, dressers, and desks, but it was conducive to bonding, and the three of them became close friends. He also remembered what his parents had told him over and over again while he was growing up: no one knows your story, so don't blame them for not understanding you. Even more central to his adjustment was the football team. As he had in high school, Jelani poured himself into the squad. He dreamed of playing for the NFL, and strived to get faster, stronger, and more capable. "The team was my home base," Jelani said. "I didn't feel too uncomfortable because of football—I wasn't completely alone."

And a big part of that was Coach Archer. After a disappointing season his junior year, Jelani began meeting regularly with his coach to discuss ideas large and small: practice schedules. Styles of play. How do we organize the buses? Sweatpants or warm-ups? They got into deeper matters—personnel, even how the defensive coaches yelled and screamed on the Fridays before games. Could that be addressed? Jelani wondered. Sometimes they talked about family, about life. "Jelani always had his shit together," Archer said.

The start of Jelani's senior season was rough. Having beaten Marist in the first game, Cornell lost the following four, the result of careless mistakes, too many turnovers, and general inconsistency. They squeaked out a win against Brown, then lost again to Princeton and Penn. But during the last two games of the season, something clicked among the players. First, they defied the long odds against Dartmouth, beating the heavy favorite by two. Then a week later, they routed Columbia, 35–9, in what Jelani considered a flawless game. "The team came together at the end, and we left it better than we found it," he said. That had been his goal all along.

Jelani's leadership during his last year at Cornell amounted to much more than a handful of wins on the field. Not only was Jelani "the most complete player" Archer had worked with over his fifteen years of coaching; the young man was also the most effective captain. How Jelani communicated up and down the chain, the way he carried himself on and off the field, his consistently constructive approach to problems. Jelani changed the way Archer viewed the players. During that last season, the coach established a "players' cabinet" so he could hear what the team was thinking. Citing Jelani as a model, Archer began to encourage players to follow their own hearts, and to be themselves. "He transformed how I look at the program," Archer told me. He realized that football didn't belong to *him*; it was the players' team.

Jelani acted as a kind of translator for the coaches' wishes—converting Archer's words into action on the field. He could communicate, execute what the coach wanted, and motivate the rest of the team to get it right. Whenever Jelani spoke to the coach, he brought up other players' concerns. He never fixated on his own performance—it was always about the team. Archer remembers that Jelani presented his thoughts in just the right tone—serious and respectful, but assertive. What Jelani did for Archer is just what he'd done for his family growing up: he'd translated his younger siblings' inchoate demands into communication his parents would understand. He was gifted that way with languages. He could move between different worlds, make sense of their distinctive expressions and perspectives, and find a home for himself in both. "I speak Ivy League, and I speak Beecher," he said. "That's my role in life."

It was football that gave Jelani Taylor community. All the players on his Cornell team had been through so much together; they'd survived hundreds of punishing workouts and shared aching disappointments along with exhilarating wins. If he had to rank his most important relationships, he'd put his girlfriend on top, followed by his siblings, and then all the people he's played football with. He and his teammates were so united, so interdependent, that he was able to look beyond himself and discover a sublime beauty in the collective. "That type of bonding, you couldn't get from anything else," he said. And of course, Coach Archer, with whom Jelani still communicates.

"We were so close," Jelani said. "That's my guy."

The pandemic put an end to his dream of playing for the NFL. He still loves football, of course, but he's done pining over it. "I knew there would be life after football," he said.

"I'm fine with it now." Anyway, he'd already gotten more from the sport than he could have possibly imagined. "I feel like football was the single most important thing in my life in terms of influence," he said. It was like another parent, he added, guiding and molding him into the person he is today.

He thinks of the sport as his first love, and is stunned by what the game did for him. "It helped me to be the well-rounded person I am today," he said.

He can't believe he grew up in Beecher, went to college at Cornell, and from there discovered new opportunities and internships that bettered him that much more, even helping him come to terms with his itinerant childhood. When he was growing up, he said, football was "a safe place—a place to run to." Now, he's well past that, living the good life in an airy two-story loft in Seattle. "If you do it the right way," Jelani said, "sports can be terrific and life changing."

"They Carried Me"

The connection that comes with being a part of a team is one of the most compelling reasons why kids should play sports. Jostling in the locker room, trading secrets between sets of push-ups, striving as one to make it through a final sprint: all of these experiences, accruing over the course of a season, generate attachments among teammates. Doing this hard thing together cements the bond. *Together, collective, connection—* the very words sing to me. If enduring eighteen months of a quasi-lockdown has taught us anything, it's that being with others is essential to a fulfilling life.

Joining a team is at least one remedy to the crisis of alienation so many of us are living through. It's also a strike against the profound social divisions that plague us. Closer to home, young people who play sports get an introduction to the kinds of deep connections that stay with you, and that might even change your life. It's one of the most compelling reasons for kids to play sports, join teams, and stay active.

And this is why the corruption of youth sports matters. The defining features of kids' athletics today—the money, the intensity, the specter of college—have disrupted the natural bonds that grow when children and teenagers strive and compete together. For when the stakes seem so high, as they do to many families now, the pretense about self-sacrifice and teamwork evaporates, and it's an ugly race to the winner's circle. The lesser team gets dumped. The community league is abandoned, replaced by a glossy travel team. Teammates or coaches who threaten their path to greatness are dismissed. Poor children are left with no team at all. Of all the ill-effects our youth sports ecosystem has introduced, this loss of connection and community among teammates may be the saddest.

Aly is thirty-five now, but she looks and acts much as she did in high school, often mocking herself and finding the fun in living through a pandemic with toddlers. A wistfulness is there now, too, along with a few tiny creases around her bright eyes. When reflecting on the tragedies she endured as an adolescent, Aly credits her teammates and coaches for getting her through. "Even though there were so many holes in my own family, I never felt that way," she wrote. "They carried me (and still do)." She can't quite get her mind around all that happened when she was growing up and how she survived. When I showed her a draft of this chapter, she wrote, "I look up to the girl in this story!"

How is she doing now, sixteen years after her world fell apart? "I have hard and anxious moments and days, of course," she said. "But so many more moments of happiness and gratitude."

PART III

TAKING BACK THE GAME

CHAPTER 10

What Parents Can Do

Any of us elders offering advice to younger parents about how to manage their kids' athletic lives are, as Oscar Wilde said about second marriages, placing the triumph of hope over experience. Because more often than not, the very people coming forward as I am here— the pundits, the former coaches, the remorseful authors— are the same ones who fell prey to the excesses with their own children. Do as I say, not as I once did. Perhaps we're stricken with guilt over our foolishness, or mystified about how we too, sensible people who fancy ourselves as knowing better, got swept up in the fever.

"In retrospect, it was a mania," David Brooks said at a symposium on youth sports about his own oversize investment in his son's baseball career.

In his book on the commercialization of kids' sports, journalist Mark Hyman admits that he'd "frittered away frightening sums of money on the baseball education of my sons."

And in a talk on his daughter's adventure in competitive youth softball, author Michael Lewis said he devoted as much time to her sports as he did his own literary career—about thirty hours a week. "It didn't occur to me that it was weird," he said, shaking his head in disbelief.

But here we are.

Let me be clear: there's much we parents can do to make our kids' sports experiences, and our own family lives, better. Even if we can't shake up the NCAA from our kitchen tables, we can adjust how we approach T-ball and soccer tryouts, including when to dive in and when to depart. We can rethink our own roles in this drama, look again at what we really want for our families and how we're going about it. For despite the chorus of protests from many a bedraggled parent who feels trapped by her kids' frenetic sports schedule—"It felt like you didn't have a choice," one mother of a star high school lacrosse player told me—there's nothing inexorable about it. We do have agency. Those of us occupying the middle class and above, at least, possess the capacity to deploy it.

I offer here a framework for evaluating your child's sports options that puts what matters at the center. Consider it a reminder of what most of us view as important, and a fresh way to look at the dilemmas we often face when our kids play sports. The framework consists of four main pillars to keep you grounded in reality: look at your child; keep your family whole; strive to keep perspective; and model the behavior you want them to learn.

Look at Your Child

This father I know takes pride in his appearance: dark hair, cut and sculpted just so; freshly shined shoes, even on Saturdays; slippery button-down shirts tucked into slim, pressed pants. He carries himself like the Wall Street guy he is, a man who traffics in contracts, abstractions, and loose talk of million-dollar deals. His son seemed cut from a different cloth: meek, uncoordinated, and what we used to call "husky"—the antithesis of slick. The father believed that sports could build a man and so decided to turn his Tootsie Roll of a son into a jock. The two of them could be spotted on weekends in the weight room at the Y, the boy huffing under a forty-pound barbell while his father egged him to *push, push.*

I wonder if that dad ever looked at his son, if he really understood what the boy cared about and gravitated toward. Could he see the glint of desperation in the boy's eyes as he heaved the bar over his head? And where was I looking, for that matter, when my son shriveled in the passenger seat beside me after a lugubrious two-day summer basketball camp? "You did fine, you did fine!" I told him, undaunted by my ignorance, trying to rouse him to good cheer. Had I looked, and actually listened, perhaps I would have understood that these were my dreams, not his. That he'd rather have gone to the pool with friends, or poked around the food stalls at Faneuil Hall, than attend a soulless sports camp at the start of summer.

Parents who are deeply invested in their kids' athletic achievements can lose sight of the child wearing the running shoes or dribbling the ball. Marshall Mintz, the sports psychologist, often sees this in his practice. "They don't know who the kid is or what he's about," he explained. Parents hire Mintz to toughen their kids up, to impart some psychological tricks that will grant their kids confidence and poise. "I tell them, 'It's not about tightening tiny screws and gritting their teeth better. Not every kid can go there,'" he said. Some parents stop asking if the child enjoys the sport or even wants to continue playing. "There's an emphasis on achievement at any cost, even if the cost is the physical and emotional health of the student athlete," Mintz said. The competitive frenzy of youth sports can warp a person's judgment, can move a parent away from the child's best interest.

I spoke to a renowned psychiatrist years ago about all the parenting conundrums he'd encountered in his practice. He told me that most parents' problems with their kids would be solved if they got to know them a little better. Go out for a meal once a week, one-on-one, with your child, he advised. If you *look* at the strange little human sitting across from you and listen as they talk about what animates (and deflates) them, you might be better prepared to guide them to their natural interests.

FOLLOW THEIR LEAD.

Is there a way to say this politely? Many of us parents suffer some confusion about our role here, when it comes to our kids' athletic lives. We seem to believe, somehow, that our children's physical abilities reflect *our* skill, drive, genetic code, and willingness to sacrifice—that *we're* the shadow heroes who made it all possible, not the scrappy wee child out there on the field. Yes, yes, we drive them, feed them, coax, encourage, and puff them up when the situation requires, give up our weekends sometimes and put them first. But are we responsible for their success or failure, their enthusiasm or apathy? Allow the words of this mother of three grown daughters, herself a collegiate athlete in her time, to answer it. "If my parents looked at my lacrosse playing as a reflection on them, I'd have thought, 'Are you crazy?'" She shook her head. "You're just not that important to the situation."

Another way to say this: it's not about you. Though we like to cast ourselves in the lead role, we parents are supporting players in our kids' lives. Step back. Let them take the lead. This advice is a cousin to the Aspen Institute's Project Play principle, "Ask Kids What They Want."

And every sports psychologist I spoke to uttered a version of it themselves. "Let the kids direct the action," sports psychologist Ross Flowers advised. "Follow the child's lead." It may seem self-evident, but in my experience it's the sort of lesson we as parents need to keep reinforcing to ourselves. We had our time. It's their turn to decide what sports they want to pursue—if any at all.

JUST LET THEM PLAY.

Organized sports are not the only, or even the best, way to encourage physical activity and promote healthy development. Why not just let them play? Peter Gray, a research professor in the psychology department at Boston College and author of *Free to Learn*, is an authority on the value of free play and its decline. He bemoans the "careerist approach to childhood," wherein performance and achievement are the primary goals. In Gray's view, kids are well equipped to manage their own entertainment, without the supervision of adults.

Gray argues that kids who play informal sports amongst themselves learn more when adults aren't standing around enforcing rules and keeping score. Child-directed play teaches kids vital lessons that are absent in T-ball, kiddie soccer, and other organized sports for young children. For one, when kids choose their own teams, and the team roster varies day-to-day based on who is available and how many kids show up, the whole notion of team identity withers. Play is in pursuit of a good game, not a win for the arbitrary assortment of players on one or the other side. Likewise, in kid-run games where everyone is free to quit, the children have more incentive to keep it fun for all, lest the game collapse; along the way, kids learn how to compromise and negotiate. The goal of kid-directed games is fun. "Real life is an informal sport," Gray wrote. The soft skills children pick up while playing games of their own making better prepare them for life.

But it's not safe! you might protest. *How could I leave my nine-*

year-old at the park with a group of kids, where predators and child abduc-
tors lie in wait? The facts about child endangerment, when you look at
the data, suggest otherwise. Indeed, years ago Lenore Skenazy launched
the Free-Range Kids movement to help parents think more realistically
about risk, and to consider what children lose when they're shielded from
every possible danger, no matter how remote.

Despite the horrifying number of school shootings in schools across
the country, the research on child safety is largely reassuring. Roughly
twenty thousand children and adolescents between the ages of one and
nineteen died in the United States in 2016. In 2020, the leading cause
of death for kids was guns—29.5 percent—followed by car crashes.
Drug overdoses and poisoning were next, then cancer, suffocation,
drowning, congenital anomalies, heart disease, fires, and chronic respi-
ratory disease.

Between 1990 and 2016 the rates of assault, murder, and robbery at
the national level dropped almost by half. Researchers at the Brennan
Center for Justice concluded that "Americans today are safer than they
have been at almost any time in the past 25 years." Let me underscore
here that our greater safety applies to all kids, not just the children
who've been bubble-wrapped and kept out of harm's way.

What about stranger danger? The real peril of child abduction may
have been exaggerated to begin with. Reports of missing children
dropped 40 percent between 1997 and 2014, and most of those were
runaways—tragic, to be sure, but not random kids plucked from the
playground. Of the hundreds of thousands of kids reported missing
each year, just 0.1 percent are found to have been abducted by a stranger;
most abducted kids are grabbed by the "non-custodial parent." Again,
that's a *terrible* thing. But it's not the ubiquitous hazard it can feel like
for fearful parents desperate to protect their children.

"If it was safe enough for you to play unsupervised outside when you
were a kid," a reporter who analyzed the crime data concluded, "it's even
safer for your own children to do so today."

ENCOURAGE A VARIETY OF SPORTS.

If your child expresses a sincere interest in playing organized sports, and your own schedule and budget allow, promote a diversity of athletic activities: mix soccer with running and dance, basketball with tennis and tae kwon do. Sports draw on different skills and temperaments; if your child resists sports with balls, she might find her place in exercise that relies solely on the body, like running. And remember that the sport doesn't have to be organized and managed by adults to be valuable.

It's not about helping your child identify the one sport she can play—and play, and play, and play—because with this, at least, she can shine. If you've not gotten the message yet, let me repeat it here: until at least puberty, children should not specialize in one sport. What your neighbors' children are doing is beside the point.

Don't take my word for it. College coaches, orthopedic surgeons, sports psychologists, athletic trainers, and academic authorities like the Aspen Institute's Project Play implore you to give your kids' bodies and minds a break. Invite them to play different sports, and hold off on specializing.

In *Range: Why Generalists Triumph in a Specialized World*, David Epstein explains why it's wise to pursue a broad array of skills. To specialize is to narrow and perfect one's abilities in a single domain to the exclusion of others. Specializing like this works in "kind" domains that have clear rules and discernable patterns, and feedback is prompt—think chess and golf. But in "wicked" environments, where rules are scattershot or unknown, the setting unpredictable, and feedback opaque—think emergency rooms and psychiatrists' offices—success comes to those with an array of experiences. It's the individuals with range, who have different skills on which to draw to discover solutions, who tend to thrive in a complex world. Epstein laments the way American culture fosters early and intense specialization, how it "would have you decide what you should be before first figuring out who you are." Parents' determination to "choose early, focus narrowly, never waver" when it comes to childrearing is misguided and unhelpful, and that extends beyond the world of sports.

Or heed this warning from Jay Coakley: "Parents who allow their children to engage in early specialization in sports are no different than a parent who would let a child eat only apples until their health suffered."

Even a thirteen-year-old, he added, should not be allowed to make long-term decisions that involve sports. "Constricting a child's experiences, relationships, and identities is never good for development," he concluded. Follow their lead, in other words, but not when there's a cliff up ahead that's out of their view.

BUT IF THEY DO SPECIALIZE EARLY, PROVIDE OFF-RAMPS.

You might protest that some sports require early specialization for high-level success. The best gymnasts and figure skaters often start devoting themselves as preschoolers! The fear of missing out lurks: *If I wait until she's capable of making the decision herself, she'll be too old to compete.*

Dr. Jim Taylor, a former competitive ski racer and sports psychologist who has worked with professional and Olympic athletes in a dozen or so sports, is keenly interested in parenting and youth development—and is the father of two teenage girls who ski as well. I asked how he advised his clients. How do conscientious parents introduce a sport that requires such early specialization? Is there a way to do this without shutting down the child's ability to have a say?

"Very difficult question," he wrote back. As a general principle, kids should drive these decisions, not parents, he told me. And in sports that demand early and narrow focus, children should be introduced in stages, allowing them "to experience what it feels like to have progressively greater involvement in terms of time, energy, and opportunity costs for other activities," he wrote. If their enthusiasm wanes, kids also should be allowed to give up the sport without regret about wasted time or stymied personal development. And before parents make decisions involving intense sports specialization for a child, they need to take stock of their values and be honest about the costs and benefits that go with that decision—for the child, the family as a whole, the marriage, and the siblings. In short, invite them to try many sports, even those requiring intense early commitment, but do so with open eyes and ample opportunities for the child to change course.

LET THEM QUIT.

Sarah loathed cross-country, and because she often found ways out of practice, the training rarely got easier. When her teammates improved and she stagnated, she only grew more desperate and upset. I encouraged Sarah to draw on her frustration as a source of motivation—keep trying, you will get faster, it will get better—but my counsel never penetrated. The entire season unfolded like that. And despite her cheerless first year, she returned as a sophomore—her morose attitude and aversion to training still intact.

After one especially unpleasant race deep into the season, I pulled her aside to talk. "Running is hard, but it shouldn't be pure misery," I said. "Cross-country is not for everybody, and there's nothing wrong with that." She looked up at me. "Why not try something else?" Sarah said nothing, and then shoved her hands in her pockets and looked puzzled. Weren't perseverance and grit the most valuable, sought-after attributes? Wasn't quitting the mark of a loser?

We coaches want our players to love the sport—or at least learn to love it—and you'll hear few of us touting the virtues of giving up. But changing course isn't failure. Humans resist the idea of renouncing something they've already devoted time and money to: it's the sunk-cost fallacy. Kids have also been fed the idea that wretchedness makes one tougher and stronger and more equipped to face the real world. But as David Epstein asserts in *Range*, knowing when to opt out of some activity or work can take more courage than staying put. "In the wider world of work," he wrote, "finding a goal with high match quality in the first place is the greater challenge, and persistence for the sake of persistence can get in the way."

TOLERATE NO ACTUAL ABUSE.

Open your eyes. *Watch your children. Listen to them.* If they're often crying before or after practice, or dragging at all hours, or oddly quiet about what goes on behind locker-room doors, reevaluate the coach and the team. Don't throw accusations around, but look again. It might be a bad fit with your child and the coach or the team. Or it could be worse.

I need to add that the word "abuse," like "bullying," has suffered from what psychologist Nick Haslam has labeled "concept creep": when an idea is applied more frequently "downward" to include a broader range of subjects, and "outward" to embrace similar concepts. Thus, a word like "trauma," which once had a quasi-objective and narrow definition, has ballooned into an all-purpose term to describe an everyday bad experience. "I'm traumatized by that phone call with Comcast," you might overhear if you live in my house. What's traumatic, in other words, is subjective, a feeling defined by the person on the receiving end of another's action. Comcast's merciless help line, which bumped me from one representative to another for a full forty-five minutes, was abusive! Greg Lukianoff and Jonathan Haidt illuminate this cultural trend in their blockbuster book *The Coddling of the American Mind: How Good Intentions and Bad Ideas Are Setting Up a Generation for Failure.*

What do you consider abusive? Is it OK for the coach to make indentured servants of your children, by requiring them to attend five-hour practices for eleven months of the year, say, as Caroline's swim coach once did? Is it fine by you if the coach belittles and swears at children when they double dribble, or miss the bus, or forget their uniform? What if the coach enjoys a subtler form of mistreatment, like pulling out the scale and making a show of who on the team is fattest? As a parent, I'm comfortable calling this bullying and abuse, even if it falls short of knocking kids' heads around. Don't tolerate it, no matter the coach's reputation.

But let's be careful, parents, not to get cavalier with the term. The coach with a zero-tolerance policy for punctuality or missed practices; the coach who loses her temper occasionally after a languid performance by the team; the coach who bumps your kid to junior varsity without warning: they're not abusers. You might not agree with them. They might be sloppy, or a little rough around the edges, or terrible communicators. But they're not child abusers. And unless you suggest she should be, your child won't be traumatized, or suffer PTSD, by being benched unexpectedly for half a game.

Keep Your Family Whole

Michaeleen Doucleff is a science reporter for NPR who studied how Maya, Inuit, and Hadzabe (a tribe in Tanzania) communities approach childrearing; she wrote about these populations in her book, *Hunt, Gather, Parent: What Ancient Cultures Can Teach Us About the Lost Art of Raising Happy, Helpful Little Humans.* Doucleff found that these children tend to be more content and self-sufficient than their American counterparts. They are not provided an endless stream of special toys and games, nor presented with boundless activities devised to keep them entertained. Instead of being diverted off into a (hyperstimulating, Technicolor) kid realm, children are welcomed into the adult world. They learn by watching the grown-ups around them perform real tasks, and help the family by performing a modified version of that task.

Childhood is treated as a kind of slow apprenticeship for adulthood, not a separate universe designed to cultivate children's delight.

What to make of the American way, I asked Doucleff, with its early enrichment classes and manufactured fun? Not only do children not need them, she said; these diversions are "a huge disservice." The "magical kiddie worlds" adults provide to their offspring—"Mommy and Me" classes, travel baseball, playdates organized around a child's friendships—"erode children's membership in the family and ultimately their motivation to help their parents." These diversions exempt them from duties at home, encourage the notion that the child's "fun" is more important than contributing to the family, and discourage them from figuring out how to entertain themselves alone. As Doucleff observes, is it any wonder that a child who's been immersed in experiences meant to titillate their senses balks when asked to fold the laundry?

If your goal is to cultivate a well-adjusted, responsible child who contributes to the family, then limiting T-ball, youth soccer, and its ilk may be wisest. Western parenting customs that put the child at the center— usually with the goal of engendering happiness among the young—also fragment families and erode self-sufficiency. Short of boycotting organized sports activities, there are ways to minimize their impact on the family.

START LATER.

To keep your family whole, delay organized youth sports for as long as you can. Wait at least until the child begs to do them. Or even hold off until the child can largely take responsibility for the activity herself—sign-ups and transportation included, she advised. And when that time comes, if it ever does, think about your whole family, including the siblings who will get left behind or drug along, as well as you, the parents—and not just the jock with the demanding schedule.

STAY LOCAL FOR AS LONG AS POSSIBLE.

Kids don't need to travel across state lines to have a worthwhile sports experience. Town recreation and Y leagues, if you're lucky enough to have them, provide everything young kids and their parents need. They allow children to play with friends and neighbors at civilized hours, and usually don't impose burdensome travel requirements on parents. Without having to traipse to Albany or Long Island for an all-day soccer tournament, parents might actually have a minute to empty the dishwasher, pay the bills, or even share a meal with the whole family. By staying local, you'll also be doing your part to keep youth sports cheap and accessible to all. Town teams shrink when families who can afford more opt out for the "elite" teams. And the longer you cling to the local options, the more attractive they become to others: parents flock to what's popular.

Here's a reminder, fellow parents: to be a loving mother or father, you needn't supplicate yourself to the customs and bylaws of random travel leagues. You have your own life, too, which might involve more than road trips to muddy fields in desolate parks away from the rest of your family. And like the person who skipped *Lost* and never cared particularly about the show's debacle of a finale, if you avoid the travel leagues entirely, you'll never know what you're missing.

OBJECT EVERY NOW AND THEN.

"Fuck," the mom—I'll call her Jane—said when she opened the email from her daughter's travel soccer coach. It arrived the day before a one-day tournament in Lake Placid, about ninety minutes from Jane's home in Middlebury, Vermont. One of the teams her daughter's squad was scheduled to play had forfeited. Now, Jane's daughter's team of fifteen-year-olds had just one game on the docket, at 4:00 p.m. But the forfeit wasn't the issue. Hoping to offset the girls' presumed disappointment over the lost game, the coach had scheduled an exhibition match for the team at 9:00 a.m. In his email, the coach asked Jane and the other parents if they were interested.

To arrive in time for the exhibition, Jane and her daughter would have to pull out of their driveway before 6:30 a.m.—even that would be pushing it—and then, after the exhibition, wait until 4:00 p.m. for the final game. *OK, sure*, some parents wrote back. *We'll be there*, said others. Jane was reluctant to object, because what kind of mother wouldn't relish spending her Saturday encamped on the cold bleachers in upstate New York, or even traipsing through the local outlet mall for six hours, if it supported her daughter? But Jane balked, and after tossing out some grace notes about the effortless win, she spoke up. *Maybe we don't need the exhibition*, Jane wrote back to the coach. *It's fine with me and my daughter to play the one 4:00 game.* Before long, other parents followed her lead, and the coach canceled the exhibition. "Everyone was just afraid to be the first to say it," Jane told me.

If you raise your voice against some of the excesses—be they sunrise games in distant states, or catered team dinners once a week, or a suggestion that every kid buy the new warm-up shirt (the possibilities here are endless)—you might find that other parents, and even coaches, will happily get behind you. They were just waiting for someone to go first.

JUST SAY NO.

I'm afraid our son won't be able to play two seasons of club soccer this year; one will do.

Sorry, but no, our daughter won't be attending summer sessions this time.

Thanks for offering, but our family will be away for the holiday this year, and our child won't be able to make practice on Christmas Eve or Yom Kippur.

That strength-training camp looks amazing, but it's not for us.

No, thank you: we have other things going on.

It's not that hard. All the sports extras dangled before parents and kids as if they're absolutely essential, even critical, are not. Unless it's an in-season varsity sport, where kids' commitments to their teammates and coaches should take precedence over most other activities, opting out of extraneous, ridiculous, and highly inconvenient endeavors attached to youth sports should be an option. It's *your* family, not the team's or the league's. And if your child is benched for a game or even expelled from a team for missing a fifth-grade lacrosse tournament—oh well. The world will continue to turn. These are children's sports, not the Olympic Trials.

KNOW THE COACH.

Of all the girls I've coached, Erica stood out in one way: She seemed to have been sprung from the head of Zeus, fully formed and wholly independent. That is, except for a brief encounter with her mother during Erica's senior year, I never saw, spoke to, or communicated with her mother or father during her entire high school career. Neither attended a single race, and there were probably forty-five in cross-country alone over the four years that Erica ran, to say nothing of track. Neither showed up for my preseason meetings with the parents, or the final hurrah when cross-country ended. Had I not known otherwise, I would have assumed that Erica was an orphan.

Coaches understand that working parents cannot attend every, or in some cases any, competitions. What felt off about this—and why parents should get to know the coach, even just through an occasional email or phone call—is that they trusted me without having a clue about who I was. The opportunities for abuse between coaches and athletes are many, and they're more apt to happen if the parents are utterly absent.

It's easy for parents to forget how much time coaches often spend with the kids on their teams, and the accidental influence we wield. Erica and I weren't joined at the hip, but she spent hundreds of hours in my company, listening to my pep talks and race analyses, watching me engage with her friends, manage unforeseen problems, and lead the team. And more than any teacher, I suspect, I saw Erica at her most vulnerable, sobbing after a painful race, and beaming when she ran the 800 faster than she thought possible. Though she seemed unfazed by her absentee parents, Erica's inscrutability made it impossible to know.

Coaches wield enormous psychic power over their charges, and parents would be wise to check in with those coaches from time to time—to send a friendly email, go to a game or two if possible, and attend one of the many parent/coach meetings. Not to offer up suggestions on how to run a better practice, or to request special dispensation for your child, of course, nor to suck up, flatter, or curry favor on their child's behalf. (We can see right through that—you're not as subtle as you think.) Lay eyes on your child's coach to make sure she is a sound individual who warrants your faith. Along the way, you might find she's human, too, and undeserving of reflexive hostility.

One key thing to keep in mind: as you get to know the coach, and begin to evaluate his quality, look beyond the win/loss record. Hendrie Weisinger, a longtime sports psychologist, told me that he advises parents to "look for coaches who are not into sports but are into parenting, because they have more experience." In this case, he means experience with real kids, who may or may not have the "mental toughness" or "grit" that's so vaunted by many coaches, at every practice or game. You want a human being running the show who understands that kids' sports are about a lot more than trophies.

Strive to Keep Perspective

When asked how they handled their children's sports, nearly every older parent I interviewed wished they knew then what they know now: that sports really don't matter. The way your kids play when they're young, whether they score or foul out or get named captain or awarded MVP. Their performance doesn't make any real difference. Their athletic success is unimportant. "My regret now," one mother of two said, "is that we didn't just do shit together like go hiking, camping, wading in a river, and other stuff as a family instead of all piling into a car on Saturday to go to some idiotic soccer match."

Psychologist Madeline Levine put it like this: "We lose our own compass because we let this get so important. All the things that seem so life-altering when they're younger, when they get older, you think, 'That didn't make much difference.'"

But keeping perspective can be hard to come by, especially in kids' sports. Look at that ten-year-old who can dribble with his left hand, eyes closed, while your giraffe-like child trips over his shoelaces and scores for the wrong team. How do you keep perspective when he looks so inept next to the boy who dashes off to AAU practice after recreation-league games? How do you take the long view when doing so seems to handicap him now?

It might help to consider how this fascination with youthful achievement, a distinctly American obsession, harms nearly everyone. According to Rich Karlgaard, author of *Late Bloomers: The Power of Patience in a World Obsessed with Early Achievement*, the fixation on early, visible excellence—academic, athletic, and otherwise—blunts kids' different strengths. Young achievers who've felt the pressure to excel right from the womb often feel brittle and exhausted from their relentless striving. Parents become easy prey for "the child-enhancement industry"—tutoring services, specialized coaching, "educational" games for infants—that erode the family unit.

And among the multitudes of kids who haven't acquired flawless credentials in their teens, the failure to shine early can have more lasting consequences: feelings of inferiority, recurring self-doubt, and the suspicion that their inability to stand out at a young age puts them at a permanent disadvantage. "We're stunting their development, closing their pathways to discovery, and making them more fragile," Karlgaard wrote. "Just when we should be encouraging kids to dream big, take risks, and learn from life's inevitable failures, we're teaching them to live in terror of making the slightest mistake."

It's possible to slow the clock, Karlgaard said. "Parents lack confidence, and think they have to go along with it," he told me. He encourages them to quit "outsourcing" their children's development to tutors, coaches, counselors, and camps as the way to get ahead.

"Listen to them and be actively interested," he said, and recognize that kids develop at different rates and have varied abilities. He compared the emphasis on standardized testing as the sole model for success with the folly of evaluating a talented distance runner on how far she can throw the shot put.

"We have to get to know our kids," he added.

While reflecting on these ills, it might be a good time to talk to your child about maturation rates and how they vary. Tell him that it can take time to grow into your body, and that the smooth operator at ten might peter out at twelve. Remind him of the uneven trajectories of some of sports' biggest stars: Michael Jordan, relegated to JV basketball until his junior year of high school; Lionel Messi, cut at 11 from his youth soccer team; pitcher Mark Buehrle, rejected twice from his high school baseball team. And listen. If your child consistently mopes and moans before games, make a change. Suggest they try another sport, consider switching teams, or take a break from that activity. Fresh opportunities will appear, and their bodies will continue to grow stronger.

And look inward. Does another child's physical superiority, as temporary and elusive as it may be, inspire you to question your "parenting" and to reconsider your earlier decision to keep sports in moderation? Catch yourself. Step away from the crowd on the bleachers, change the subject when youth basketball comes up, and remind yourself what's important. Hint: it's not how well your fifth grader can rebound, no matter how often the mob seems to think it is. Youth sports through high school are meant to build character, connection, and health, all of which are more likely to be achieved when parents' keep these activities in perspective.

WHY YOU SHOULDN'T FRET ABOUT SPECIALIZATION.

Some of the most prominent athletes in the world played multiple sports growing up. Roger Federer, tennis legend from Switzerland, played soccer, squash, basketball, and handball; he leaned into tennis during adolescence. Tom Brady, who needs no introduction, enjoyed basketball and baseball in high school on top of football. When not perfecting her corner kick, soccer icon Megan Rapinoe competed in track and basketball during high school. A study comparing international Olympic *medalists* with Olympic *participants* found much the same: the medalists started training later in life, devoted less time in childhood and adolescence to one sport, and played multiple sports before and after their Olympic careers ended. If the tippy top of the sports world consists of athletic impresarios who played a variety of sports growing up, why should your mere mortal of a child follow a different route?

Because my son's not Patrick Mahomes or Steffi Graf, you say, and needs every advantage available! And forget the pros, what if she wants to play in college? A study of Division I athletes carried out in 2016 found that most of these highly competitive athletes didn't narrow their athletic pursuits until high school. Even then, of the 343 men and women the authors examined, only 16 percent had specialized as freshmen. "The majority of Division I athletes were not classified as highly specialized through high school," the authors observed, concluding that "it does not appear that early specialization is necessary to become a Division I athlete."

College coaches, too, want players with a range of sports skills and experiences. They look for healthy kids whose bones and ligaments won't crumble after a few tumbles or missteps—a reality that's more common among kids who specialize early. They seek out kids who crave competition, as David Archer, Cornell's head football coach, told me. A multisport athlete is involved in physical contests across the year, not just in one intense season. They also value kids with varied athletic experience because that equates with exposure to different kinds of teams and coaching styles, giving kids broader perspective and, with any luck, making them more receptive to feedback. As well, a young person who hasn't invested ten thousand or more hours in one sport alone before college will probably show more upside. About those who specialize young, Clemson football coach Dabo Swinney said, "There's just not that much room for them to get better." He pursues the multisport athletes.

OK, you might say, forget about college. What if I want my child to have the opportunity to play sports in high school? If she doesn't focus early like everyone else, she'll fall hopelessly behind and never have a chance. Not so, says Garland Allen, a longtime athletic director and coach who founded inCourage, an organization aimed at improving youth sports. Children do not need specialized skill training when they're young. Parents would help their younger kids most by offering them a variety of sport and play options. It need not be organized. It need not be in one sport alone. And it need not require a commitment to travel. Indeed, sometimes the kids who focus early and play year-round burn out by high school and find that their technical skills exceed their physical development, he told me. The children who haven't made an early career of one sport, on the other hand, are fresh. "It's beneficial to start later—there's greater room for growth," Allen said.

M ore tips on how to keep perspective:

- *Ask yourself some questions. One mother of two now-adult children put it this way: "How devastated would you be if your child said, 'I want to quit'?" If the mere thought is inconceivable, you've probably lost perspective. Here's another: How quickly would a stranger find out at a cocktail party that your child runs/plays basketball/does karate? If it's less than five minutes, she said, you're probably too obsessed.*

- *Listen to your elders. And for our purposes here, that would be parents like me who've been through this, come out the other side, and possess the perspective we once lacked. "I'm not anti-sport," a mother of three who was once deeply invested in her kids' athletics told me. "It's just not that important. It's what your values are, and what you do, and what kind of person you are, and what you think about." A father of three, reflecting on his families' adventures in the travel team circuit, said this: "Making the A team means nothing relative to future opportunities." A mother of four, who recalled mourning her son's decision to quit high school basketball, said, "He quit. We lived on. Now I can hardly remember it."*

- *Practice "distancing." In his book* Chatter: The Voice in Our Heads, Why It Matters, and How to Harness It, *Ethan Kross, a psychology professor at the University of Michigan, offers tips on how to develop perspective during high-stress moments. He advocates adopting the view of a fly on the wall, or looking at yourself and your behavior from an outsider's vantage point. Rather than ruminating about a problem from the first-person perspective, which sometimes amplifies the misery and fury, step back mentally and examine it as if you were a third party, like the proverbial fly. This mental exercise can help restore perspective.*

- *Picture yourself advising a friend with the identical problem. It's easier to be detached and rational when counseling others.*

- *Travel forward in time and look back from there. Kross advises challenging yourself to think about how this incident will strike you in a few months, years, or even decades. What will sixty-year-old you have to say about thirty-five-year-old you abandoning an old friend over a soccer slight to your child? Here's what I'd tell myself:* Get a grip, woman.

Model the Behavior You Want Them to Learn

Let's go back to first principles for a minute. When you reflect on how you want your children to "turn out," think of the traits that matter to you. Many hopeful adjectives come to my mind: resilient, self-sufficient, industrious, kind. *Responsible* is the attribute that a majority of parents across the political and socioeconomic spectrum want their children to be. If you share that view, you might consider that a preoccupation with youth sports, with all the excesses and distortions they evoke, can undermine those developments. Acting insane on the sidelines, berating the coach in public and private, and scrapping any semblance of a life outside our kids' sports are not apt to inspire good citizenship among the young.

RESPECT THE COACHES AND REFEREES.

I don't imagine that this plea will slay the demon ego when the coach has perpetrated some profound and public injustice upon your child. If you consider yourself capable of reason, and recognize that children look to their parents as models for how to behave, you might realize that butchering the coach or referee in front of your kids sends a clear and ugly message: This so-called coach, this adult person who was tasked with managing a kid's team, deserves no respect. It's perfectly acceptable to rage when somebody like that screws up or disregards your wishes. But if you think your child isn't paying attention when you criticize, mock, or sabotage the coach, you'd be wrong.

For the love of God, just treat coaches like human beings. Offer to help, say thank you often, and keep your criticisms private, even from your child. Assuming the coach isn't a bully or a predator and is well intended toward the team, treat them with dignity. There are at least two good reasons for this: you're modeling decency to your children. They'll learn from you that even the lowly eighth-grade swimming coach who can't seem to get out of his own way deserves respect, even kindness. If you can't bring yourself to be civil for this reason, consider the guidance of psychologist and author Lisa Damour, who told me that friction among the grown-ups provokes anxiety in children. Your kids will be more settled with their sport if you make peace with the coach.

MISS SOME GAMES.

The father showed up at every race. Had school rules not forbidden it, he'd have stood by, hands in the pockets of his low-slung jeans, and offered his counsel at every practice, too. Of his two children, one was a fast and determined runner, and he seemed transported by her success. Inconsequential dual meet on a Tuesday at four? He'd be there, armed with watches and water bottles. Championship race on a Wednesday at one thirty? He'd be there, too, way ahead of the bus. No race was too insignificant or inconvenient to skip. Eventually, his obsessive behavior got the best of him. Caring as much as he did about his daughter's success, he gradually came to worry as much about her teammates', scolding them, behind the coaches' backs, about their lousy diets, half-baked race strategies, and middling effort. Some girls blew the whistle on him, and school leaders barred him from future races. This was terrible. "She won't be able to race if I'm not there!" he said of his fifteen-year-old. His years of hand-holding had made her so dependent that she'd be paralyzed by his absence.

Mom's or Dad's presence in the bleachers should not determine how well a high school kid plays. Attending every one of your child's competitions, if you have the luxury of doing so, is not in their interest. Be engaged enough to know the coach, but do yourself and your child a favor: Miss the occasional meet. Skip the odd game. Model a happy adulthood and cultivate your own interests rather than feed off theirs.

GET A LIFE.

Madeline Levine is a psychologist with nearly forty years of experience who has also written influential books about the woes of modern children and their parents. When we talked in 2018 about what's happening in competitive youth sports and how they've disrupted families, she lamented how parents' excessive involvement suggests that grown-ups lead dull lives. All that sitting in the stands, clapping and cheering, carving out space from our own lives to celebrate our child's—it's a mistake. She regrets throwing herself full throttle into her kids' games when they were young. "I should have been with my girlfriends having lunch, or with my husband, or reading, doing things that nurture me," she told me. Cultivating her own interests would have signaled to her children that growing up isn't so bad. It also would have made her own already full life that much richer.

No parents I'm acquainted with long for their grown sons and daughters to take up long-term residence in the family basement. One powerful way to deter that is to make adult life more appealing. Flee the bleachers at the middle school gym, skip the tournament at the school across town. Resuscitate your own interests and relationships instead.

Limping Along

"Mine are all maladjusted in some ways," Jennifer said, a force-of-nature kind of woman, and a mother of four, about her now-grown children.

Let me tell you about Jennifer. Close to six feet tall, possessing a baritone voice with an oddly youthful twang, Jennifer is hard to miss. When out walking with her posse of friends, all of them wrestling with dog leashes and poop bags, she's the one flashing a giant smile or tilting her head back in laughter. The most authentically outgoing person I've ever known, she also upends the stereotype of extroverts as shallow. She's an enthusiastic and engaging talker but also listens like a trained therapist—leaning in, nodding at the right time, fixing her intelligent brown eyes on yours. And she's not one to gloss over the prickly parts of motherhood, like confronting her sons about pornography, drinking, and sex. She's sensible to an extreme, particularly with her now-grown kids: she set boundaries, insisted on decency, and loved but didn't indulge, among other virtues. All along, she has seemed to take motherhood in stride, embracing her kids' triumphs and defeats with grace while marching forward with her own pursuits. She put it like this: "I limped along like the rest of us."

And now, the kids grown, this verdict: all maladjusted in some ways. Leave it to Jennifer to arrive at the pithiest, most honest assessment of her kids—of all kids, I should say, including yours and mine. Try as we might to be superb mothers and fathers, and I believe all of us *are* trying, we're going to get stuff wrong with our children. We'll let our own fragile egos cloud our judgment. We'll emphasize hard work when what they really needed was comfort; we'll relax the boundaries at the very moment that guardrails were most urgent; we'll preach about grit and determination, or empathy and kindness, or the need to cooperate, compete, score, get going, get to it, buckle down, lean in, focus, *try*, for God's sake—when they just wanted us to *listen*. We'll prattle on—maybe not you, but I—without considering, or considering enough, the little individual in front of us. And how can we? We're all exhausted and distracted and doing the best we can, which isn't always so terrific.

And because, in my experience, kids' stubborn little natures and personalities remain constant, and we grown-ups sometimes muddle things, they will all have their own "issues." Or, to use Jennifer's phrase, they're maladjusted in some ways. Even the blessed children I spotted in a black Range Rover yesterday, who couldn't see out the back windshield for the Yale, Stanford, and Harvard decals covering the glass, will stumble. A superior education guarantees nothing.

What am I trying to say here? That once you accept the inevitability of imperfection with your kids—and your own fallibility as a parent— it gets easier to see what matters. And what *doesn't* matter is Charlotte being demoted to the B team, or Sean getting bumped to JV. Congratulations, Lily, for being named captain, and kudos, Jake, for your winning goal! But the heady joy of these achievements, and others like them, will wither soon enough, and their accumulation is no defense against misfortune.

In short, try this: encourage your kids to play and be active, of course. Help them find what they love, whether it's athletic or not. Then get out of their way and find your thing. Despite the messaging you'll hear everywhere, you and your family won't suffer from avoiding the elite youth sports orbit. Rather, you'll save money, preserve your sanity, and hold on to your whole family.

CHAPTER 11

How Coaches Can Help

The mother of a runner I coached called me one afternoon while I toiled in my airless office. We'd not spoken often, but she'd always been generous and supportive, and her voice wavered when she began. "Denise thinks you're disappointed in her," she said quietly, before telling me about her daughter's emotional struggles. Life was bearing down on the girl, all the pressure she felt to outshine and outperform her classmates. Something I'd said or not said or insinuated or suggested or ignored was adding to the girl's despair.

"I just thought you should know," the mom whispered.

I thanked her for the insight and promised I would be clearer with her daughter about my pleasure with her progress.

Mary Helen Immordino-Yang is a neuroscientist at UCLA and an expert on learning, psychology, and the brain. "You have a very powerful role in a young person's life," she said in our discussion about coaches and their impact on teenagers. You're educators, she said, in her multisyllabic, neuroscientific argot. Coaches have an important, structured role in how kids think, learn, and behave, she went on. During adolescence, teenagers' pliable brains are especially receptive to emotions and peer influences, two characteristics of team sports. The physicality of athletics, as well—the moving through space, banging into barriers, colliding and swiveling and leaping—lends itself to clear and simple learning. And because coaches spend so much time with kids in these charged settings, they get a fuller look at the young people in their care.

"Coaches have a privileged view of kids," she said. And so, we have a duty to be concerned not just with winning but with "helping them grow into happy, motivated, ethical citizens."

But how do we do that? Whether you're working with children, tweens, or adolescents, your mindset should be clear: "Every coach should want the person looking back at him in the mirror to be the one he would want for his own child," said veteran swim and diving coach Suzie Hoyt. This is the north star of humane and effective coaching. Treat every child on the team the way you'd want your own child handled. A variation of this maxim applies to working with parents, too: engage with mothers and fathers the way you'd want your child's coach to behave with you.

With Kids, Show Strength and Warmth

Years ago, an older man who has served as my unofficial mentor gave me some advice. We were talking about teachers and learning—what gets kids to listen to the person at the head of the classroom. I was discussing strategies, approaches, theories on education. He interrupted me finally and said this: when the kid thinks I want to be that person—that's the teacher who inspires. Then we talked about memorable teachers in our own lives, the ones who lit something in our hearts, and the truth of his insight hit home. Kids listen and learn when they observe the teacher and think, *I want to be like that*. It's a variant of the adage about sales, that the customer buys *you*.

The same is true for coaches. High school kids look at what you're wearing, assess how you talk, observe the way you handle snafus, wonder about your personal life, all in service of the question, "Is she my kind of person?"

Bobbi Moran, now a high school athletic director, found that person in her seventh-grade gymnastics coach, who also trained her in field hockey. "She embodied all that I wanted to be: strong, confident, honest, fair, competitive, and inspirational," Moran told me. A master of the push-up and enemy of gum, the coach exemplified physical strength and personal guts; if you were caught with Wrigley's at practice, you ran until it was time to go home. She also possessed a gentleness and authenticity that Moran, especially, responded to.

"She was genuine," Moran added. "I think that is what mattered most to me as a teenager." Later, when the coach encouraged her to try field hockey, Moran took the leap, quitting soccer as a high school senior and throwing herself into the stick sport. "That one decision changed the trajectory of who I am now," Moran told me. Thirty years later, the two women remain in touch.

Research suggests that two qualities in combination are universally admired, for men and women both: strength and warmth. "Strength is a person's capacity to make things happen with abilities and force of will," wrote John Neffinger and Matthew Kohut in *Compelling People: The Hidden Qualities That Make Us Influential*. "Warmth is the sense that a person shares our feelings, interests, and view of the world," they added. We admire strength and appreciate warmth, and those who convey both draw us in. The two qualities together signal competence and trustworthiness, and this blend makes them persuasive.

How to convey strength and warmth? There are many ways:

CONNECT.

You couldn't miss her. If you had your eye on the track, you'd see right away what distinguished the one high school girl from all the others: her sweatpants. It was a brisk, early-spring afternoon in suburban New Jersey, and about half a dozen girls—including the one in sweats—were racing the 800 at a trivial local track meet. The girls scuttled around the windy oval, all but one wearing small shorts and tiny singlets, their schools' names stamped across their chests. I shivered in my black peacoat and yelled encouragement to the runners, especially to the lone girl in the sweatpants and long-sleeved shirt. When they crossed the finish line—2:50, 3:01, 3:06—a coach or two was there to record their times, and a couple of teammates clapped. Then most of them dissolved into the crowd and returned to the bleachers.

"I cannot believe you were wearing sweatpants in the eight hundred," I told the one girl as she rounded the corner by me.

"My coaches didn't say anything," she grumbled back. She was cold. She hadn't run the 800 before. It didn't seem to matter to anyone that she was out there doing a long-distance sprint in thick, billowy pants with the aerodynamic properties of a parachute.

"I cannot believe you were wearing sweatpants in the eight hundred," I said to her again, shaking my head in dismay. Then the girl— my daughter—shrugged and popped into my car.

That my daughter's track coaches were indifferent to her performance should not have come as a surprise. (Note to non-track runners: NO ONE RACES IN SWEATPANTS.) She didn't sizzle in workouts, or show up to practice with an ingratiating smile, or stand out for her leadership potential. She was a normal teenage girl who had a talent for reading the room, and what she read was this: none of the coaches cared about her.

"Mom, the head coach doesn't know my name," she'd told me earlier that season. My daughter's invisibility to the track coaches spurred a predictable reaction in her: she didn't care about her performance.

During my research for this book, I surveyed a handful of coaches around the nation who had been singled out for excellence by Positive Coaching Alliance. I asked these celebrated leaders what's most important for their coaching colleagues to know.

"Connecting. Connecting. Connecting," wrote Meredith Prior, a women's lacrosse coach in Massachusetts.

"Know your athlete beyond the x's and o's of your sport," wrote Patty Waldron, a swim instructor in North Carolina.

"We must see our athletes as human beings and get to know them," wrote Savannah Linhares, a girls' basketball coach in California.

"Know your athletes!!! Know their circumstances and what's going on with their families, help where needed, and build trust," wrote Charlene Crowell, who runs a boys' youth basketball team in Alabama. I could go on, but you get the point. Connection is the first principle of effective coaching.

If you must, start small. Know everyone's name.

BE POSITIVE.

Suzie Hoyt is committed to building a nourishing team culture. Her positive style starts with the conviction that she must be the coach she'd want for her own children. Hoyt came by this style organically, a function of intuition, years on the pool deck, and her own experiences as a swimmer with assorted coaches. She adored her summer swim coaches, who were attentive and enthusiastic, but recoiled from their AAU counterparts, who never uttered a kind word. Hoyt has a mantra she shares with her swimming and diving teams: *I will find a way or make one.* Every season, she writes the Latin version of this saying on top of the whiteboard where she posts the team workouts.

"The most important thing a coach can do to make sports more fun and sustainable is to remember the definition of the word 'PLAY,'" she wrote. Kids should be enjoying themselves with their friends, and coaches can encourage that in countless ways.

- *Celebrate accomplishments of all sizes, including those of beginners.*
- *Invite teammates to call out their peers for doing well; it's on everyone to be positive.*
- *Be scrupulously fair in following team rules, as there's nothing more demoralizing for a squad than when the coach exempts the best players from discipline.*
- *Insert games into the routines. Her team practices "swimming golf" during the winter and plays water polo on Saturdays. "Allowing kids to feel happy and comfortable being themselves in a safe space helps promote longevity in a sport," she offered.*
- *So much comes down to the coach's attitude. Don't take yourself so seriously: We're teaching them sports and games, not the nuclear codes.*
- *Remind yourself that high school kids have duties outside the team, and respect those other pursuits. Get to know the whole person. "I have learned that taking the time to listen was one of the most important things I could offer my athletes," she added.*
- *Never forget that they're kids.*

FOSTER AN INCLUSIVE CULTURE.

It's not so easy, as a coach, to evaluate honestly the team culture you've created. Despite our best efforts to be welcoming, bad stuff can slip in.

One year at the start of my career, when girls had just returned from summer break, I made the mistake of asking them collectively, "So, what did you do over the summer?"

The school where I worked was populated by many affluent families, some of whom enjoyed lengthy trips abroad in July and August.

"We just got back from Paris," one girl announced breezily.

"I spent two weeks in London," said another, offhandedly.

A third girl piped up: "We went to London, too! Did you ride that Ferris wheel thing?"

As they stretched, some of them began chatting about European cuisine—and I belatedly realized how this may have affected others on the team whose families lacked the resources to visit Hershey Park, let alone Heidelberg.

I didn't make that mistake again. But I undoubtedly made other, subtler errors, that had the same alienating effect. Not all kids who play come from comfortable homes with two engaged parents and a secure social safety net. Indeed, in 2020, 16.1 percent of Americans under age eighteen were living in poverty, according to the U.S. Census Bureau. Most youth sports coaches, though, have yearly family incomes of $75,000 or more, while less than 10 percent of coaches have family incomes under $25,000. If we're to understand and cultivate a sound athletic culture, we coaches need to take steps to understand the varied kids under our care. You can't be a warm, strong coach if you're unaware of kids' unique circumstances and varied backgrounds.

The same can be said for trans kids. All young children, no matter their gender identity, should be welcome to play on same-sex teams, even if it diverges from their biological sex. Sports among pre-adolescents are about having fun, connecting with others, and developing an interest in athletics. Before the hormones that shape adolescent bodies kick in, trans girls and boys should be included without reservation.

Making room for trans kids in high school sports that are organized around sex differences is a murkier matter, at least for trans girls. If you've been coaching awhile, you probably have strong ideas about how to strike the right balance between fairness and inclusion. (I know I do.) But here's the thing: we high school coaches don't get to decide. Our state houses or state athletic associations are the arbiters of these matters. Whether you believe trans women and men should be allowed to compete without restriction in high school, or are convinced that such unfettered competition would wrongly penalize biological females, my guidance here is the same: be compassionate. Whoever is on your team, set a standard for kindness.

As previously noted, many sports governing bodies are offering instruction to coaches on how to build inclusive teams. The National Federation of State High School Associations offers a course on understanding implicit bias. Positive Coaching Alliance helps coaches talk about race. There are courses and workshops available for those who look. And now, past my coaching years, I wish I'd taken them.

FOCUS ON PROCESS, NOT OUTCOMES.

You might have seen this illustration of an iceberg. The one I'm imagining looks like a bulbous white mountain that's submerged in a blue ocean. Above the water line, which in the drawing is literally a black line, the top tenth of the iceberg is visible. What's beneath the waterline is the bulky rest, a giant blob of ice that would be imperceptible to anyone paddling by in a little canoe.

In my mind, the top of the iceberg, the part you can see, is labeled "visible success." Beneath the waterline, the majority of the iceberg, keeps the top portion afloat: work, perseverance, dedication, consistency, resilience. These qualities are the foundation of success; without them, the iceberg you see is just a "bergy bit," as the oceanic experts call them—relatively small, rather insignificant, soon to melt into the sea.

Kids, fans, the media, and parents tend to fixate on the top tenth of the iceberg. It's what they see. But as coaches, we need to concentrate on what's beneath the surface. Another way of saying this: worry about process rather than outcome. If you're like me, you'll get questioned every now and then about your goals for the team. It's hard not to jump back with "We want to win States!" But a healthier outlook, for both you and your team, is to focus on methods. *Are we doing the right work? Are we doing the work right? What are we missing?* It's better for athletes, too; sports psychologists will tell you that athletes who fixate on outcomes undermine their performance. For sanity's sake, focusing on your process rather than your record will keep you anchored in what you can control. Demonstrating a healthy confidence in your methods also conveys strength to the kids in your care.

RELINQUISH SOME CONTROL.

Whether out of insecurity or indoctrination, I used to coach my girls with the intentional swagger of the authority. *This* is how you do it, girls—shoulders loose, knees bent, no no no, this way, I told them. You have a question? Bring it to me. Twenty-five years their senior, with as many years of running experience, I assumed my main job was to fill their receptive brains with all my accumulated wisdom.

Over time, I learned that strutting around like a little generalissimo, and making unilateral decisions about our practice and game schedule, was foolish and contrary to my purpose as a high school coach. To encourage their leadership, I had to stop hogging the floor and giving them answers. To spur intrinsic motivation, I needed to invite their input on our training methods and race schedule. To tap into their own knowledge of the sport—whether picked up at running camp or through their own reading—I had to welcome their suggestions for workouts, running routes, and everything else.

Giving kids more control doesn't mean renouncing critical thought, or abandoning preparation, or going along with their every adolescent whim. If they asked, "Coach, can we go to Starbucks today instead of the track?" I'd have laughed—and they would have laughed with me. They wanted to get faster as much as I wanted them to and were well aware that skipping a workout would only suspend their progress.

A subtle shift occurred when I adopted this approach. We became less a monarchy, with I the lone powerful authority, and more of a democracy, where their opinions and insights shaped the team. This was *our* team, not mine, I often told them. Having absorbed that message, they seemed to feel more responsible for their training. They also appreciated my respect for their judgment and feelings and continued working to earn it. With this, the weight of the team's success migrated off just me and onto all of us.

There's liberation that comes with not having to know all the answers—or rather, with acknowledging the reality that we don't. Showing humility this way frees you from the burden of having to prove yourself every day. It has the added benefit of making you more appealing to the kids you coach. No one likes a phony or a know-it-all.

MEET THEM WHERE THEY ARE.

A coach I'll call Louisa sighed when she glanced out at the field where her squad of high school lacrosse girls were practicing. This was a new school for Louisa, and a fresh team of players, and by the look of them—their relaxed jogging, tepid throwing, and general aversion to the ball—Louisa knew she'd be focusing on first principles.

"I'm not going to coach them like Division I players," she told me. Having coached lacrosse for ten years, and brought home a handful of state sectional championships, Louisa said she'd work to get the most out of the athletes in front of her. You have to adapt, she said; the goal is growth. She will meet the girls where they are and strive to mold them into legitimate lacrosse players. Working with raw and inexperienced athletes can be exciting, she added, because the space for improvement is so vast.

"It's a challenge, and a different set of goals," she added. "It's cool for me as a coach."

Rather than reproach them when they lose or underperform, as all teams are bound to do, consider our own role in the outcome. If they're sluggish and distracted, perhaps we've failed to inspire. If they're cliquey and disjointed, maybe we've overlooked team-building exercises, or have doted on favorites, or modeled dysfunction with our assistant coaches. We're the leaders: better to interrogate our own role in the result than blame our players. And if they perform worse than their peers on other teams, consider again where they began.

In *The Price of Privilege: How Parental Pressure and Material Advantage Are Creating a Generation of Disconnected and Unhappy Kids*, psychologist Madeline Levine offered a variant of this counsel to parents. She cautions mothers and fathers against fixating on what their children lack, especially in terms of visible achievements, and implores them to "truly love the child who stands in front of us." Coaches need to do the same. Pining for some other, better group of kids to coach rather than the ones assembled before you helps no one. Meet them where they are and make them better.

DON'T GIVE UP ON THEM.

Once again, she came flying across the soccer field, clutching a drawstring bag and preparing her excuses. Depending on the time of year and day of the week, the rationales for her constant tardiness to practice varied: *My mom was late; there was traffic on Morris Ave; a teacher needed me; I had to make up a quiz; someone took my shoes; lab went over.* Meanwhile, every other girl on the team was already immersed in the stretching routine, pulling her foot behind her back to loosen up the quads or leaning against a fence to stretch her calves. "I'm sorry, I'm really sorry," Helen blurted.

We coaches had pulled her aside and spoken to her privately, sensitively. *What's going on? How can we help?* And she always responded just the right way: with contrition over the problem and conviction to have learned from it. For a few days, she'd be on time. Then the old habit would return.

"That girl's a lost cause," I murmured to one of my assistant coaches on the ninth or tenth day of this. A "lost cause": not worthy of much attention, unlikely ever to shine.

I'm not clear when, exactly, I realized how appalling that sentiment was. Most likely, it happened when I sat on the bleachers at one of my son's early lacrosse games, waiting for him to go in. In some of those games, he played just a little—a few minutes at the end of a quarter, or as a short-term sub, to give the better player a rest. He was new to the sport and less trained than his peers, and the coaches lacked patience with his inexperience. Other kids were more skilled, had more hustle, they possessed an instinct for the game that my son seemed to lack. *How can they just give up on him like that?* I thought to myself.

In fact, the coaches weren't giving up on him. They were simply executing their strategy to win the game, which meant my son wouldn't play; too bad for him, but hardly a sign of the coach's moral failing. It occurred to me then that what I had done, casually dismissing a girl for her chronic lateness, was far worse. Helen was a teenager—a glorified child, really—grappling with something invisible to me. As her coach, it was my duty to help her grow. I'd fancied myself a kind of educator, but there I was, tossing a kid aside because she couldn't fix her mistake fast enough for me.

If you work with teenagers for any length of time, you find that some of them, usually just a handful, will touch a nerve. Maybe it's the drama queen who fusses over a scratch, or the mousy recluse who never speaks up; perhaps it's the kid who always forgets his spikes, or the one who smirks or frowns whenever you talk. Yes, they can be maddening.

But they're teenagers, not fully formed beings made of cement. They're evolving little humans who are floundering, some of them, right in front of us. Accordingly, they need to see that we believe in their ability to flourish, even after they've messed up for the third or tenth time. They need authority figures with significant influence over their lives to show faith in them, for as long as it takes.

All of us who work with young people to help them develop athletically need this reminder: we're not coaching grown-ups. They're kids. Children, tweens, teenagers, preadults. Suzie Hoyt, the very positive swim coach, put it best: "All coaches . . . should remember that the athletes are children, even if they are six foot two and have a size 15 shoe."

TEACH THEM LARGER LESSONS.

Bruce Girdler is a coach and elementary school teacher who lives outside Toronto. A junior giant at six foot seven, he played competitive basketball in college and remains an enthusiastic advocate for athletics. Some twenty years ago, he shook up the grade-based model for youth sports in his community and started inviting younger kids to join the middle school teams. It was not uncommon for him to have grades three through eight all playing together. His goal was to train them in the fundamentals of the game, and to teach them a kind of etiquette that they could call on later in life, including how to win and lose with grace. He likes to share "life lessons," he told me, such as: when they're uncertain about a course of action, whether on or off the court, the harder option is usually the right one. He also insists on more prosaic matters: show up on time; say please and thank you; be positive.

During one game, Girdler had the unwelcome opportunity to reinforce the propriety he'd emphasized at practice. His team of mixed-aged kids was up against a squad of talented but disruptive eighth graders who personified everything about youth sports that Girdler loathed: the kids were "rude, argumentative, arrogant, and sucky," he wrote in an email, celebrating gratuitously over minor triumphs, fussing like infants when the calls went against them, and openly mocking other players. Even worse, the opposing team's coaches seemed to encourage it.

The two teams came head-to-head at the finals of a qualifying tournament; the winner would go on to a regional championship. The game was acrimonious and tight from the start, extending past regulation play and into two testy overtimes. Near the end of the second round, when Girdler's team fell behind, he pulled the boys in close to talk.

"This is an important moment," he told them. "Now is the time to show grace and dignity. Show them what sportsmanship looks like. Congratulate them, shake their hands, and wish them good luck in the next round," he advised. The boys reluctantly complied. And while their opponents "celebrated for like forty-five minutes" after the buzzer sounded, Girdler's team cleaned up the plastic bottles, empty chip bags, and candy wrappers left in the gym.

A few years ago, a young man who had grown up on Girdler's team came back to visit his former coach. The boy had not been a star player in his youth: he was neither tall nor fast nor acrobatic. But he rallied his teammates and worked at improving, and eventually played on some of Girdler's winning teams. When the young man, now grown up—losing his hair, a little soft around the middle—approached Girdler, the two reminisced about the old team and talked about the future. Just as he was about to leave, the man finally sputtered out the message it was clear he'd come to deliver. "I need you to know something," he said. "You taught me how to be a man."

Practices and games overflow with opportunities for us to teach good citizenship, sound sportsmanship, and basic decency. We have to seize those moments. One day, the boys and girls in our care will grow up to be adults like us. Consider all that they can learn.

GUIDE THEM THROUGH DISAPPOINTMENT.

When I agreed to coach high school cross-country and track, I didn't realize how much I'd come to care about the girls I'd be working with. My own young brood at home already absorbed so much of my available affection. I had friends, too, many of them fellow runners, who I relied on to preserve my sanity and intellect, and my husband, of course, who went out of his way to make my life easier, despite his own thankless schedule. I didn't expect, at this stage of my life, to discover another genre of humanity to suddenly care about. But these teenage girls softened something in me. It's what Catholics call "an abundance of love": the belief that there's no limit to the amount of deep affection we can feel, that our love just expands to envelop those in our orbit.

As with so many of the girls I coached, Sophie and I connected. A part of that was a function of the time we spent together—hours every day after school, and on weekends, sometimes for two or even three seasons, for up to four years. Most parents don't appreciate the sheer volume of time coaches spend with their kids or recognize how these hundreds of hours of intermittent togetherness generate bonds. It's a variation of the propinquity theory on relationships, which posits that we become friends with those we are physically nearest to—it's location, not a common background or set of values, in other words, that determines whom we befriend. Though I'd never call the girls I coached "friends," I had a kind of link with each of them that was forged, at least in part, through the time and space we shared. And for the girls like Sophie, who experienced joy and suffering and heartbreak under my care, and who, as a senior, was the swiftest on the squad, our connection was stronger still.

Sophie and I both knew that the team's performance was a responsibility we shared. By her senior year, this collection of runners was my fastest team yet, and we were optimistic about winning the major races that had so far eluded us. The first of these championship meets was the most casual, a "conference" meet against other small schools in our county. I climbed onto the stubby bus the afternoon of the race, both nervous and hopeful about our prospects, and told the team that this was our meet to lose. If we do what we're capable of, I told them, we should win it.

Along with the top runners from five other schools, my girls charged off the starting line at Warinanco Park, an oasis of green tucked between urban centers in mid–New Jersey and the site of most of our races. Running from point to point along the course, breathless and nervous about the outcome, I watched the pattern hold: Sophie comfortably ahead of two rivals, and the rest of my girls in position to secure our win. My thumping heart slowed a little, and I dared to believe that we might actually claim this so far unobtainable prize.

With just a few minutes to go, I dashed to the closing stretch, about four hundred meters from the end, to cheer Sophie on to her triumphant finish. And there she was! But the two runners behind her— long-legged, moving in tandem—were closer now, and Sophie looked tense: she had a tight, mechanical move to her shoulders, and a fearful look in her eye. I was too far away to observe the sprint to the finish, and hung back to rally the rest of my team as they came through. When they'd all passed by, I edged my way to the end, desperate for news, and looked to my timekeeper who'd been planted there to record the girls' times and places.

"Did she make it?" I asked, without mentioning Sophie by name.

My timekeeper looked at me and frowned, then shook her head. The two runners had charged past her a hair before the finish line, bouncing Sophie to third place.

That was it. Race over. We were second.

My mouth dropped open while my eyes closed. I said nothing. I walked around the trees near the finish, envisioning the ugly end. It made no sense. Somehow, we'd seized defeat from the jaws of victory, managing to lose what should have been a comfortable win. *What a shitty coach.* I couldn't force a smile, or even approach my team yet about the loss. When I spotted girls from the winning side bounce into ecstatic group hugs, I had to turn away to gather myself. *What a shitty coach.* Then—breathe in one, two, three, four, five, hold it—I went looking for Sophie.

It didn't take long. There she was, mourning with the rest of the team on the cold metal bleachers we always claimed for our races at this park. By now the sun had withdrawn beneath the clouds and the temperature had dropped. Everyone huddled together, their gray hoodie sweatshirts covering half their faces, completely quiet. When I got close, all but Sophie glanced up at me to gauge my reaction. My hard-ass, never-quit, infallible leader remained hunched over with her head in her hands next to her equally stricken mother.

"Sophie?" I said.

She looked up. Her face was mottled and wet, and the ponytail that collected her thicket of hair had gone slack.

"I'm so sorry," she said in a whisper. Water welled in her eyes, then tumbled down her cheeks.

I pulled her up off the bleachers, and we walked away from the team and the crowds. I put my arm around her trembly body.

"I don't know what happened!" she said.

"I know you were trying, Sophie," I told her.

"I'm so sorry," she said again, as we continued to walk. She'd taken a wrong turn somehow and lost her lead. She was still recovering from bronchitis and didn't feel right. Those two girls got her in a split second, right at the finish.

"We'll be OK," I said. Sophie's body shook under my arm.

"These things happen," I said. She stayed quiet, facing away.

"Every race can't be your best," I said, drawing on my list of comforting bromides.

We were both crushed, and we both knew it, and there was nothing we could do. We continued to walk together, my arm around her waist, away from the small gatherings of kids and parents who'd come to run or watch. The race that followed ours suddenly began, and a stampede of boys rumbled past. We barely noticed. I struggled to find the right words.

We finally stopped, and I put my hands on her shoulders and faced her. "Sophie, you've been the leader of this team," I said. "You've worked so hard and given so much. You are always out front, always the one to win. You were trying. That's all you can do," I said.

She shrugged, still devastated. We began to walk again, now back toward the bleachers.

"We'll both learn from it," I said.

"It's not the end of the world."

"There will be other races."

"Onward," I said finally, a command I often gave the girls after they'd braved something difficult. *Look forward.*

Sophie lifted her head. We lumbered arm in arm back to the rest of the team. I still felt awful, and so did she. But we felt this way together.

In time, my sadness fell away, replaced by the routine aggravations and delights of normal life. Joy returned to Sophie a few weeks later, when she led the team to a win at the much more competitive state championship, where she exacted her revenge and trounced the same two girls who'd swept past her on that awful afternoon. Our equilibrium was restored. But I remember that gray day when Sophie and I marinated in the same sorrow as vividly as any of our later triumphs. The connection she and I shared over that loss was invisible and intangible, but as real and powerful as the wind.

With Parents, Empathize and Communicate

With few exceptions, all the coaches I know love their sport and delight in helping young people develop. It's the friction we encounter outside the team, for the most part, that's the trouble: a chronically displeased parent; obtuse or unhelpful school administrators; kids' widening range of hard commitments—chess club, SAT prep, debate team—that get in the way of practice; our ever-multiplying list of duties. All of these sentiments are expressed in the journal I've kept for at least a decade. Intermingled with the moments of joy are bursts of fury and vows to stop coaching at the end of the season. "I feel so sad, so wiped out," I wrote years ago about the job. "It's not the girls, either," I added. "They lift me up."

In the end, I stayed on for several more years. Once the season finished, and I reclaimed my normal life, the pull of the work yanked me back. The tug of the teenagers, actually; it was their promise, vulnerability, and humor that swayed me.

I've learned a few things over the years to keep me focused on what matters rather than ruminating about the obstacles. There's no single solution to our coaching conundrums, but there are ways to minimize how they affect us. And one natural place to start is how we interact with parents.

The best way to get in the right headspace, as they say, when handling parents, is to put yourself in their position. How would you want your child's coach to treat you? What's vital here are empathy and communication.

START WITH EMPATHY.

Goal! Rosemary sat up tall in the chilled bleachers, cupped her hands on either side of her mouth and let out a shriek—"All right!"—before stomping her feet and then clapping violently. There was a furious quality to her enthusiasm, a flush-faced, white-eyed intensity that suggested outrage rather than delight animated her reaction. She was sitting with parents of other kids on her daughter's high school lacrosse team, but Rosemary's raucous glee stood out because she alone was celebrating. Except for parents on the opposing side, that is. Rosemary was rooting against her daughter's team, making a spectacle of her fury, to send a signal to the coach. That bridge troll had refused to play Rosemary's senior daughter for more than a few minutes. In close games, the girl suited up in her clean blue uniform and sat. If the team led by a dozen goals, she'd go in for the last ninety seconds, after half the fans had packed up and gone home. *The girl was a senior! She'd devoted years of her life to this sport, this team, this coach!* When the referee called a foul on the home team, Rosemary jammed both index fingers into her mouth and let out a piercing whistle.

Parents' bellyaching makes some sense when it's put in context. For one, competitive youth sports demand more of parents than their kids' academics. Teachers don't ask Mom and Dad to bring in Powerade for Honors English, or have the biology class over for dinner, or cart a calculus club to a neighboring state every Sunday morning "just to stay sharp." It's coaches who require parents to make inordinate sacrifices. We expect them to plan their summers around sports practices and training programs. We insist that they postpone family vacations indefinitely. We require their kids to devote themselves to *our* sport, to be all in. And we want parents to comply, to deposit their fit and enthusiastic children at our feet, and then kindly stay out of the way.

This is why parents rage when their kids don't play: because coaches' asks are infinite; because teams are more and more restrictive; because the outcome of the season—the wins, the losses, the championships, and awards—has swollen in apparent significance. Parents want their kids in the game. Coaches want to field a winning team. Sometimes that means Caitlin and Noah won't get to compete very much, and we coaches expect their parents to be OK with that. We're all about the team here, right?

It's no wonder Rosemary lost her shit. All parents, in fact, who have invested so much in their kids' sports careers, and who did everything they were supposed to do, are understandably "disappointed" when the whole enterprise comes to nothing—no scholarship, no glory, not even much time on the field. Put yourself in their shoes. After all this, their kids are miserable, and they feel cheated.

It might not be possible to fix the problem, but a coach can strive to understand. And listen.

Sometimes, their concern isn't truly for their daughter's standing on the team but about something deeper and more elemental. Is she going down the wrong path? Should we be concerned about an eating disorder? If you listen and echo back to them the concerns they're sharing with you, what presented itself as anger might turn out to be parental confusion, even sorrow. Coaches aren't clinical psychologists, most of us, but shutting our traps and listening to parents' worries goes a long way to soothing tensions.

COMMUNICATE, COMMUNICATE, COMMUNICATE.

On the first morning of practice on my first day of coaching, when I assumed my good intentions and devotion to running were all a coach needed, I sat down with the team armed with a small notebook and a dull pencil. On it, I'd jotted some thoughts to share with the girls—my expectations, my hopes, a little about my background—and then moved right into the meat of the practice. As best I recall, I didn't meet any parents until the first race, if they decided to come, and after that the end-of-season awards ceremony.

On the first day of practice during my last season of coaching seventeen years later, I arrived at school armed with nineteen copies of our cross-country team handbook. Here, in writing, for every runner and her parents, were pages on my coaching philosophy; our team values; the qualifications for earning a varsity letter; policies on phone use, uniforms, attendance, and equipment. I wrote a section on the daily time commitment, a skeleton of the season's races, a blurb on captains' duties, more on transportation and permission slips, some on what we expect from our athletes and what they can expect from coaches, along with an entire letter to the parents laying out our expectations of *them*. A one-page missive appeared at the end of the handbook, a homemade contract for parents and runners to sign, which indicated that they understood and agreed to our terms. I went over the handbook at the regular preseason meeting for parents that our school put on—another opportunity for coaches to preempt conflict with open communication.

It's a little nauseating, all the lawyerly documentation we deliver to high school kids so they can play sports after school. At the same time, I understand well enough why coaches and athletic departments rely on them. We're trying, however clumsily or bureaucratically, to head off the conflicts that we know will come. Telling parents and kids as much as possible about what to expect before the season even begins is the multivitamin of effective coaching: the goal here is prevention.

Honesty and clarity upfront are necessary but not sufficient; multivitamins aren't antibiotics. What's required is regular, even excessive, communication, beginning with the kids on our teams. Teenagers want to know if they'll be playing varsity or JV, if they'll be starting or sitting out, if they're expected to run the last leg in the relay or not at all. In my experience, telling them sooner is better than later. And to be clear, communicating does not mean merely delivering blustery public announcements. Nor does effective messaging require eloquence and inspiration before the big game; we all loved Coach Taylor in *Friday Night Lights*, but it's not the pregame speech that sparks the win. It's preparation.

Connecting regularly with parents is also essential. As with the kids, it should be done with an ear toward their sensitivities. Protect their time: make sure the directions to the game are clear, get the word out fast if a meet is canceled, give them early warnings about possible delays. Respect their kids: not every child plays varsity, so every message from the coach shouldn't be a tribute to the top players.

Transparency with kids and parents won't avert all clashes. No matter our intentions, we're going to flub a few times, maybe step on a child's toe, make the wrong call. Own up to it: apologies work. Open communication won't neutralize a parent's fury when the coach blocks their child's golden path. Those parents are out there, and words won't mollify them. But talking honestly and frequently to our little constituents and their parents is the best way I know of to minimize conflict and build trust.

They Who Feel the Respect

A man I know sprinkles into conversation quotations he had to memorize from his years at the United States Military Academy—West Point. Though he graduated decades ago, Thomas still can rattle off those strings of words without stumbling. He returns to one quotation frequently, as it captured so well what he and his fellow cadets were taught from the very beginning of their tenure at the military academy. It was the meaning of discipline as defined by Major General John M. Schofield, who shared his thinking during an address to West Point cadets in 1879:

> *The discipline which makes the soldiers of a free country reliable in battle is not to be gained by harsh or tyrannical treatment. On the contrary, such treatment is far more likely to destroy than to make an army. He who feels the respect which is due to others cannot fail to inspire in them regard for himself, while he who feels, and hence manifests, disrespect toward others, especially his inferiors, cannot fail to inspire hatred against himself.*

Thomas was ordered to memorize these words during the early, grueling days at the academy, when he and his peers were sweaty and exhausted from their immersion into military culture. "Even then, it resonated," he told me about Schofield's insight. It was so different from what he'd been taught to believe about leadership from his high school coaches. "'He who feels the respect'—that doesn't sound like the drill sergeant I had as a coach," he remembers thinking. Thomas reflects on Schofield's words whenever he spots an apoplectic coach going nuts at players on the field. It pains him to observe whip-ass coaches modeling a harsh and tyrannical view of authority.

It should pain us all. The best coaches, those with a humane spirit in their breast, intuitively adopt a considerate manner and tone. They're strong and warm, fully-fledged human beings who recognize that their young charges deserve respect as much as they do. Coaches, we're modeling for kids what adulthood means, what leadership looks like. To paraphrase Miss Manners, the guru on etiquette and getting along, let's not add to the rudeness in the world.

CHAPTER 12

Reform Opportunities Post-Pandemic:

Bold Models and Ideas that Work

What's exciting about addressing reform *now* is that suddenly the timing for an overhaul feels right, and essential. For while the coronavirus has done incalculable damage to so much and so many around the globe, it also has shaken up habits and ways of living that once seemed hopelessly entrenched. "We could hold on to the sense of strangeness and make new choices about how we used the hours of our lives," Oliver Burkeman wrote in *4,000 Weeks: Time Management for Mortals* about this pandemic-induced restart. One natural place to begin is with youth sports in America.

The forced stop of athletics at all levels in March 2020—and their very gradual, chaotic, and uneven return—has rattled the youth sports ecosystem. Suddenly it's not clear that all those kids who stopped playing will ever come back to them: among parents with sporty children, 28 percent reported that their kids were no longer interested. This trend was most pronounced among the very young, children aged six to ten. The seemingly inexorable growth of the youth sports industry—it'll get to $67 billion by 2025, one analyst predicted—also has stalled or reversed, forcing some private clubs, coaches, and gyms to fold: 46 percent of parents with kids on travel teams said their programs had shut down, merged, or scaled back during the pandemic. And it looks like that shift might suit some families. A majority of mothers and fathers said they had a "'better' or 'much better' relationship with their children during pandemic-related restrictions." For these parents and kids, returning to the youth sports rat race may have lost some appeal.

Meanwhile, communities already struggling to offer low-cost sports options for kids will have even less revenue, after COVID, to pay for them. Some have already closed their doors: 44 percent of parents reported that their local sports facilities have shrunk or gone away. Colleges and universities as well are eliminating varsity teams, which is sure to have a downstream effect on kids hoping to leverage their athleticism in admissions.

The pandemic's evisceration of youth sports as we've known them has forced a return to first principles. What are sports even for? Is there a better way—one that's fairer, more balanced, maybe even sane—to go about providing them? There are no quick fixes. The youth sports universe contains a vast cast of characters, many with competing motives and conflicting values: parents, kids, coaches, clubs, leagues, public parks, public schools, private schools, the business of sports and fitness, the tourism industry, pediatrics and sports medicine, to name the obvious players.

"It's an oil tanker, no doubt," said Tom Farrey, who runs the Aspen Institute's Sports & Society program. Turning it around will be laborious and slow.

Let's begin with top-down, in-a-perfect-world ideas that shake up our everyday assumptions about sports for kids. They're a reminder that the American approach is not the only or even the best way of keeping kids active and building strong sports teams. After exploring these, we'll examine some grassroots initiatives that have begun to shake up this ecosystem.

Bold Ideas

TRANSFORM INTERCOLLEGIATE SPORTS.

Imagine what would happen if the greatest honor of all—recruitment to an elite college, an athletic scholarship, or preferential admissions at a select school—were suddenly gone? Sociologist Rick Eckstein has thought a lot about such scenarios. In his view, youth sports won't be healthy again until colleges and universities address the incentives that drive the excesses. He wrote, "Any attempts to make youth sports an intrinsically rewarding part of childhood rather than a commodified means to an end must ultimately focus on changing higher education."

Eckstein and I have talked many times about youth sports and their distortions. Learned and expressive, Eckstein has the slightly disheveled look of the intellectual. He also possesses a dark wit, fueled, it would seem, by a weary disillusionment with higher education. He is genuinely appalled by the damage that competitive youth sports have inflicted on kids, many of whom wind up in his sociology classes, and much of his work is centered on shedding the puffery that surrounds sports at all levels. When we met in person, he was wearing khaki shorts and a blue Macalester College t-shirt. He looked as if he'd just left the soccer pitch, which he might well have. While teaching full-time, Eckstein also coached his daughters' soccer teams.

A surefire way to alter the youth sports landscape would be to adopt what he calls "the nuclear option": a purge of intercollegiate sports. If college heads had the gumption to take such a radical step, they could redirect the ample funding now spent on sports to those endeavors attached to their primary mission—education. They could spruce up libraries and classrooms, bump up the salaries of underpaid staff, and increase financial aid for students in need "without the quid pro quo of playing a sport for thirty hours a week." Spending on collegiate athletics has jumped far ahead of what universities pay for teaching and education, often for goods that are unrelated to scholarships, like sports facilities, coaches' salaries, and special services for athletes, such as tutoring and nutritional counseling. Eckstein noted that college costs have gone up three times faster than the cost of living since the late 1970s. Because "the largest increases have been in noninstructional administration and intercollegiate athletics," he wrote, eliminating one big chunk—intercollegiate athletics—would liberate budgets for other purposes.

Adopting the nuclear option wouldn't require excluding sports from campus. Colleges could encourage and fund club and intramural teams instead. Without varsity teams monopolizing athletic space the way they do now, these student-run athletic endeavors would be accessible to more kids. They would promote greater participation and fun and fellow students would run them—much like my cross-country and athletics teams at Oxford. Replacing varsity sports with club or intramural programs would also be more equitable, as high-cost, high-stakes collegiate sports serve a slim percentage of the entire student body: the athletes, their scant fans, and parents drawn in to watch.

Blowing up intercollegiate sports also would obliterate the warped incentives that compel many adults to organize their lives around kids' athletics. Without a potential reward on the other end of it, parents' willingness to hand over fortunes and weekends for their children's sports would surely diminish, if not disappear. Absent the potential for a leg up in college admissions that clubs dangle before young players, the pay-to-play private sports world would serve little purpose. The same would be true for pricey tournaments that entice players with the promise of college coaches watching from the stands. As the money saturating the youth sports industry dried up, kids who still wanted to play could return to more casual, low-cost options, on town leagues and local teams. Cost barriers that block lower-income families would fall, and more kids could play.

A likelier, if still remote, solution would be to preserve varsity sports but eliminate the athletic scholarships and admissions advantages that go with them. The Division I and Division II schools that award financial aid based on athleticism could dole out funds to students according to need. For their part, Division III and Ivy League colleges that purportedly offer no athletic scholarships could dispense with the myriad benefits they now bestow on their recruits, including lower admissions standards, early reads of applications, and financial aid packages that are unrelated to athletics in theory only. Instead of considering athletic ability a rarified talent that's more deserving of collegiate dollars and attention than flute-playing or acting, say, college admissions officers could treat sportiness the way they do other extracurricular skills. Under this scenario, high school athletes would be judged as a good fit for the college by the same standards as their fellow musicians, actors, journalists, and poets.

With little in the way of tangible perks to offer potential players, colleges might be able to pare down or eliminate recruiting. And if they did that, the showcase tournaments where college coaches now assess the assembled talent from elite teams would disintegrate as well. Most kids would have little incentive, then, to join and play for expensive, year-round clubs. Any teenagers who continued would be doing so for an actual love of the game, not as some means to another end. And college teams would consist of players who truly wanted to play, not just those from families who could afford the private teams that funnel kids to college. "Scaling back recruitment in nonrevenue sports (encompassing 90 percent of college athletes) would almost automatically tame a youth sports industry dependent on misrepresenting the opportunities for college athletic scholarships and admissions advantages," Eckstein wrote.

Might colleges ever suspend varsity sports, abandon sports scholarships, or do away with the admissions advantages that go to athletes? "I'm not optimistic," Eckstein wrote me when I asked about the likelihood of these ideas being actualized.

Indeed, if not for the pandemic, such proposed changes to intercollegiate sports would seem to resemble the 1928 Kellogg-Briand Pact that abolished war: a sweet idea, except for reality. But the abrupt halt of sports in 2020, including the unprecedented cancelation of March Madness and loss of its attendant millions, has compelled some universities to take action that would have been unthinkable any other time, including chopping some sports. Cutting teams would seem to make sense if you look at the budgets of NCAA athletic departments. According to a 2019 annual report released by the NCAA, of the 1,100 athletic departments that operate under NCAA rules, a mere twenty-five of them generated revenues that topped their expenses in 2018–2019. Among Division III colleges, not even one brought in more money than it spent. And these shortfalls took place *before* COVID slashed funding.

But athletic department budgets don't tell the whole story. Eckstein reminded me that small public universities and liberal arts colleges rely on their recruited athletes in part to pay more tuition for the privilege of attending; having applied early, these students give up the option of receiving financial aid packages that go to those admitted at the regular time. "These schools are literally addicted to the ever-expanding pipeline of athletes who clamor for a spot on the squad and are often willing to pay sticker price for the opportunity," Eckstein said. And stats on applicants who are accepted early (many of them athletes) are exempt from the data mining that dictates a college's selectivity.

Some colleges acted decisively during the COVID crisis. By late October 2020, seventy-eight colleges and universities in all three divisions dropped about three hundred teams. Among the hardest hit sports? Tennis, golf, and soccer. Though many former and current athletes protested the eliminations, arguing that the cuts would jeopardize American prospects in "Olympic" sports like rowing and gymnastics, which are cultivated in institutions of higher education, financial exigencies could make some of these cuts permanent.

And if you ask Tom Farrey, that might not be so bad. Varsity teams can transition to club or even intramural squads, with lower costs, fewer rules, and more student leadership. Some eleven million college kids already play on club and intramural programs, versus the roughly half a million who compete on varsity teams. What would be so wrong, he asks, about adding to the one and reducing the other? "Club athletes represent their colleges, wear the colors, but play more on their terms, not those of an athletic department groaning under the strain of an N.C.A.A. rule book and of a business model that turns many athletes into employees without paychecks," he wrote in *The New York Times*. And cutting some of the Olympic programs at colleges and universities might compel the governing bodies of those sports to get more creative about how they develop their athletes.

Upending collegiate sports like this would transform them at the youth level. Given the national obsession with athletics, adults will continue to fawn over athletically gifted kids and young adults. Status will still cling to their parents for having produced them. But without the hope of a gleaming reward at the end of the youth sports pipeline— being recruited, getting a scholarship, slipping past admissions officers with lower academic qualifications—the worst excesses of the current model would go away.

ESTABLISH A MINISTRY OF SPORTS.

Here's one compelling reason for more government oversight: most parents seem to believe it already exists. In studying Larry Nassar's grotesqueries, legal scholar Dionne Koller learned that parents don't realize how unregulated youth sports are. They couldn't believe that Nassar was "allowed" to move from one institution to another, that no one was monitoring him. "Everyone thinks someone is doing it," Koller said. They drop their kids off at practice and assume that the dad in charge has been vetted, monitored, and trained. "People have assumed too much, as if youth sports are regulated like a high chair," she told me. "They're not."

One grand way to do this would be to create a Ministry or Department of Sports, a sister to the Department of Commerce and other cabinet-level agencies, like some developed nations around the world. Alternatively, Washington could create a new office within an agency—an offshoot of Health and Human Services, say, or the Department of Education. What matters with youth sports is "baking it into the administrative state," Koller said. Under either setup, a federal department charged with overseeing youth sports would be subject to the same laws as any other agency. It would be obliged to report to Congress with accurate information on participation rates and trends, among other matters, and make formal requests for money. Bureaucrats in charge would have to monitor youth sports and their funding streams.

One of its most vital contributions would involve data collection. Absent such a central body, the Aspen Institute and various industry groups fill the void as best they can. But relying on sports manufacturing companies for accurate data on the products they sell doesn't make for wise public policy.

"If you think participation in sports is good for the country for lots of reasons, you better not rely on the people selling bats, mitts, and gloves to collect the data," Koller said.

A government entity could also set standards, register teams, offer best practices, and help states coordinate regional sports leagues. Farrey suggests that it could be modeled on the US Anti-Doping Agency, which is partially paid for by the government but not controlled by it. B. David Ridpath, a professor of sports business, brought up the Department of Homeland Security as a model. For all its flaws, that department pulled together under one umbrella all the disparate agencies involved in protecting the United States. A Ministry of Sports could do the same.

A federal body could also direct money where it's most needed, and Daniel Gould from the Institute for the Study of Youth Sports has ideas about where to start. The government could pay for coaching education, fund urban playgrounds and 4-H programs, underwrite services that allow children in unsafe areas to travel to local gyms without harm, he suggested. These could all have an impact without huge cost. Washington also could put some resources back into physical education, so that all kids develop the physical literacy they need. "Marines are saying that kids can't pass the physical fitness test because they have no physical literacy," Gould added. Hold gym teachers as accountable as math instructors. And don't expect unfunded mandates to do much. Title IX has been effective because the threat of losing government money coerced action, he said, and any youth sports reforms would have to have teeth.

"It would be really hard and messy, and we'd have twenty percent waste," Gould said. But as it stands now, things aren't working, and hope alone won't fix the various problems in play. Gould worries about the quality of people involved in youth sports, and their lack of training. He thinks coaches and parents need more education on how best to develop a child's athletic abilities. And he believes that the hodgepodge of youth sports outlets requires greater coordination and oversight, and that states and the federal government ought to be developing policies that address and correct the challenges. Take the impending shortage of youth sports officials: it's widely known that fewer kids and adults are opting to officiate, yet no national body has focused on it.

"We have to become involved as a government and fund some things," Gould concluded.

And organized leadership of youth sports could be strategic rather than reactive. Why not reevaluate the purpose of kids' athletics and how we provide them? It's not just about increasing participation in low-income areas, Dionne Koller suggested. If the US government has decided that widespread sports participation is vital to the health and well-being of the population, it could rethink some of the existing ways of doing things. Given what we know about concussions in football, for example, why do we encourage kids to play? Why separate boys' and girls' teams when they're children? What is the purpose of middle-school sports? The country should be able to step back and reconsider some of the assumptions that have guided sports for generations. A national entity could also establish standards for schools, propose more sports opportunities for boys and girls, and increase the options for disabled students.

Better still, it could even borrow from Norway, a small nation with a giant medal count in winter sports and an enormously active young population. When Tom Farrey—again—studied how Norway manages to succeed on both fronts, he found that much of its success stems from a top-down commitment to children's sports, which is embodied in a paper labeled *Children's Rights in Sport*. This extraordinary document puts children at the center by asserting, for example, that they have the right "to choose which sport, or how many sports, they would like to participate in—and decide for themselves how much they would like to train." It minimizes competition and insists that children have access to sports that "will facilitate development of friendship and solidarity"—a far cry from the fixation on winning in American youth sports. Clubs that break the rules may be denied the government grants that fund the facilities they need. What if the United States crafted and enforced its own bill of rights for children's sports?

DIVORCE SPORTS FROM SCHOOLS.

"The way we've organized sport in this country is so odd," Eckstein said. He was referring to the linking of sports to education, starting, often, in American middle schools, and lasting through high school and then college. "It brings out the worst in both endeavors," he added.

Suppose that this country divorced sports from schools entirely and returned athletics to communities. The United States could adopt the kind of club sport system that works in Western Europe, where competitive sports are absent from schools. There, clubs have a "Sports for All" mentality that emphasizes child development and public health. They are also mainly local, so that practices and games require minimal travel. Because European club teams are funded through some combination of state and local taxes, all interested kids can play.

B. David Ridpath spent years studying alternative models to the American sports system. He lived in Germany while he was at it and so had firsthand experience with European clubs. He identified one in particular, the Amsterdamsche Football Club Ajax in the Netherlands, as one worth emulating. Ajax is a wildly successful, first division club with about 250 "youth" players divided into three developmental slots, based on age. The youngest group, those aged seven to twelve, practice three times and play one game a week, always on a smaller field and against fewer players. There's no rush to develop technical abilities beyond the children's physical mental capacity; the focus is on motor skills, balance, agility, and basic soccer movements. Play other sports, the kids are told—it'll make you a better footballer. Only those children who can't stay even with their peers after two years are asked to join another club at a lower level.

The moderation continues with older kids, who are bused to their four weekly practices after school courtesy of the club. Before playing, children are required to study and finish their homework. "The view that most European clubs share is that education is a need, while playing sports is an additional opportunity," Ridpath wrote. "This philosophy is, arguably, exactly the opposite of what we too often find in America." The final level, for young adults aged seventeen to twenty-one, includes some of the older players on the professional team. They practice four days a week for no more than two hours at a time and compete twice a week—less than high school kids in America who often play for their school and private club teams.

Paying for it would be the tricky part. American tax dollars devoted to kids' sports at middle and high schools could be channeled to community clubs, but such a bold endeavor would require more tax revenue at every level. Ridpath suggested that clubs could impose modest membership fees, pull from lotteries, seek contributions from professional sports leagues and sports' national governing bodies, and develop partnerships with current clubs and schools. The greatest obstacle to such reform isn't the cost, necessarily, but the crushing forces of inertia, wishful thinking, and sway of those who benefit from how things stand. Still, he believes that the US structure that latches sports to education is a "thoroughly broken system" that will have to be blown up and replaced.

Models That Work

Despite the enthusiasm among experts for top-down reform, few of the ones I spoke to are sanguine about it happening. The greatest obstacle to change is the lack of an established and monied constituency to push for it. The parties who now "speak" for youth sports consist of trade lobbies, the NCAA, and the United States Olympic and Paralympic Committee, each equipped with varying degrees of money and players on the ground in Washington, DC. None of these groups is enthusiastic about government regulation or abolishing intercollegiate athletics or severing sports from schools. Opposite them are academics, think tanks, former professional athletes, and random others who would like to up-end the status quo. "There aren't groups that are well-funded or organized on the athletes' side who represent kids," Koller said.

But here's the good news: we don't need to wait for giant, impersonal institutions to make repairs in the youth sports ecosystem; dogged individuals can make a difference. "Bigger things have been done before," Ridpath told me via Zoom, optimism beaming through the screen. As more of us experience firsthand the deficiencies and distortions in the way our country provides sports to kids, some are taking action where they live or work. They offer practical models that can be applied elsewhere, and remind us that we needn't settle for what we have now.

RENEWING HIGH SCHOOL SPORTS.

"I don't think we'll ever get away from the school-sports tradition," Karissa Niehoff told me. Niehoff is the executive director of the National Federation of State High School Associations (NFHS), a loose body that serves as the de facto leader of American high school sports. Its members include fifty-one state associations (including Washington, DC), for a total of almost twenty thousand public high schools. Though NFHS doesn't govern or enforce national standards, it writes the rules for some sports, offers guidance, and provides educational materials that the state associations—its members—are free to adopt. Where I live, the New Jersey State Interscholastic Athletic Association, or NJSIAA, picks and chooses from what the national body recommends, and then mandates those rules locally. The state associations have enforcement power, but the national federation, which Niehoff runs, coordinates them all and provides national direction.

As well as being a trailblazer—Niehoff is the first woman to head the NFHS—she's also a fierce defender of school sports. She believes that school sports are ingrained, too central to American culture. We love the games and rivalries, the concessions stands and cheerleading, the varsity letters and team dinners. Sports are meant to be vehicles for learning, she added, and so are rightly bound to the school's educational mission. She doubts that the European club model, which separates sports from school, will ever take hold in the United States.

Niehoff herself first came to organized school sports in eighth grade, when her family moved to Marblehead, Massachusetts. Before then, her athletic interests consisted mainly of riding a horse on the family's self-sufficient farm in Nevada, where athletic opportunities were limited. She joined the track team in Marblehead and immediately blossomed, running the 440-yard sprint—the precursor to the 400-meter race, and a fraction longer than a quarter mile—in sixty seconds. She went on to compete in varsity volleyball and basketball, and finally, as a senior, in field hockey, after another coach told her to get to the gym and pick up a stick. Though she first dismissed the idea—"I thought it was a silly sport because girls wore skirts"—Niehoff later came to dominate the game and was recruited to Brown, where she played for one year before transferring to the University of Massachusetts on a sports scholarship.

"I was a product of my age," she told me. "A young person nowadays wouldn't have that journey."

High schools need to find ways to address emergent problems related to sports and exercise, she explained. Part of the answer lies in collaboration: between high schools, clubs, sports' national governing bodies, and local parks and recreation departments. As well, high schools can make up for the shrinking opportunities for average players and typically excluded kids by expanding and improving options in physical education classes—think ballroom dancing, Pilates, and weight training, for example—and by offering intramural and club programs.

Niehoff has found that school clubs are more appealing to kids who are squeamish about competition, because club programs revolve around a shared interest rather than a battle for supremacy. School clubs also can be simple and cheap: kids find a teacher to supervise, post a sign-up sheet, and meet at the park for a hike.

More athletic departments must also address the needs of physically and cognitively disabled kids, who have historically been left out of school athletics. As of 2019, twenty-seven states offered "adapted" sports on their menu of athletic options, in which kids with physical disabilities can participate in a modified version of a sport—like wheelchair basketball. A smaller number of states provide "unified" sports, where students with intellectual challenges and the general student body play together. Though sparse, these programs are growing. Administrators claim that unified sports foster inclusion among the student body and help build bonds among students who ordinarily wouldn't mix. An athletic official in Delaware described the unified sports in his state as "one of the purest examples of interscholastic athletics stressing education-based competition."

A model for the kind of school that others might emulate can be found at Tuscarora High School in Frederick, Maryland. The school is a little microcosm of America, ethnically and socioeconomically: though 41 percent of the student body of roughly sixteen hundred is white, the remaining population is comprised of mostly Black, Hispanic, and Asian students. One-fifth are disabled, and nearly a third of kids are eligible for free or reduced-price lunch, though the actual number of needy kids is likely higher. Howard Putterman is the athletic director there, and during the summer he runs a school for homeless children. Many of the teenagers who attend aren't included in the high school's accounting of low-income students. "Sometimes there's no parent to fill out the forms," he told me.

If you were wandering through the halls of this rambling suburban school at 10:35 in the morning, you might find students squaring off against each other in a game of volleyball or basketball, the two intramural sports Tuscarora offers. They'll play for a tidy thirty-five minutes, during the free period offered to all students—just enough time to clear kids' heads and get them moving. Elsewhere, you might encounter kids from the Learning for Life class, or those striving to master English playing soccer or walking the gym. After school, students might be tapping badminton birdies or lifting weights along with fellow members of their club. Around the corner, you might run into one of the school's three unified teams—in bocce, tennis, and track and field. All in, 53 percent of kids participate in school athletics.

What distinguishes Tuscarora High School and its athletic director from so many others is its commitment to getting more teenagers involved in sports, not simply those with the most athletic talent. This required toppling the typical school sports model—offering just varsity, junior varsity, and physical education classes—and providing intramural and club sports, and unified teams, as well. The school also allows teenagers who are academically ineligible to compete to continue practicing with their team, and some coaches integrate academic counseling into practice. Most important, the coaches and physical education teachers focus on building relationships with the students. "We have the time to talk to kids, and we use it," Putterman said.

Putterman is open and curious, anomalous traits for the stereotypical athletic director at a large school. "When I first started as a coach, I was full of vinegar, all X's and O's," he explained. But wise mentors and experience on the field helped steer him toward a broader, and more humble, view. He's made it a goal to never turn down a kid's request for a new club or team without first studying the possibility. The default response for such requests, Putterman said—we've never done it that way, we lack the resources and space and time in the day—doesn't cut it. Disciples of the idea that physical activity must live side by side with academic learning, the athletic staff brainstorms for solutions and compromises on the margins, all to keep kids engaged in sports.

Putterman has long since abandoned the notion that wins and losses are the measure of a school's athletic success. Tuscarora is in the middle of the pact in that regard, he said, ranked sixth out of ten schools in the district. But he's got the best coaches in the state. They share the worldview that their purpose is to help kids grow and learn and become productive members of society. Like him, they understand where they belong. "It's not about you, not about wins and losses, it's about the kids," Putterman said.

SECURING STATE FUNDING.

Monica Wallace was not an especially athletic child. Growing up on Long Island with her mother and two sisters, she wasn't able to play sports with any consistency. "There was always a problem getting there," she explained to me when we talked about her youth. The fees were burdensome, the travel was impossible, and there was no way for her single mother to navigate these time-consuming kids' activities.

After school, she and her sisters would trundle home to an empty house. "I was literally a latchkey kid," Wallace said.

Now a New York State Assembly member, Wallace understands that kids who play sports are afforded major advantages over those who don't. She also knows that opportunities to play are largely determined by family income and that many children in the district she represents lacked that opportunity. As a public servant well versed in budget negotiations, Wallace appreciates how challenging it is to lasso state funds for a new need.

In January 2021, an opportunity appeared when Governor Andrew Cuomo introduced a bill to legalize mobile sports betting in New York.

It was a new and popular, if morally dubious, way for states to acquire more revenue. Since 2018, when the Supreme Court legalized sports betting within states, some fourteen of them already had passed bills to allow residents to wager via their phones.

Wallace had a proposal. She would support Cuomo's bill if 5 percent of the state's tax revenues generated by mobile sports betting would be reserved for youth sports organizations that serve low-income kids. It wasn't an alien idea: Norway does this to fund its sports clubs. What distinguished Wallace's plan was that it would create a dedicated revenue stream for youth sports. "It would be a once-in-a-lifetime revenue stream," she said.

There wasn't much resistance. New York legalized mobile sports betting in April and set aside a portion of revenues to a fund for kids' sports—1 percent the first year, and five million dollars every year after. The Office of Children and Family Services will oversee the money and determine which youth sports organizations will receive the benefit. It's not for shiny new uniforms, Wallace told me. This money will fund groups with a clear mission to spur kids' development through sports, especially in low-income communities. Maybe in the years ahead, some of this money will extend to local municipalities to fund their parks and play spaces.

Wallace is excited about where this could go. New York's initiative is a model that other states can adopt. It might also activate the private sector. "If the state invests its own resources and gives an organization its stamp of approval, a lot of companies might give matching grants to those organizations," Wallace said.

She's hopeful, too, that the legislators who gathered to pass this bill will continue to search for ways to make sports more equitable around the state. And Wallace herself is toying with the idea of proposing a bill that would mandate a defined amount of recess time for kids in school.

"This was a good way of lifting all boats," she said.

RETURNING POWER TO COMMUNITIES.

This is ridiculous, Julie McCleery thought. She was driving across town in Seattle traffic at four on a Friday afternoon, having left work early to deliver one of her three sons to an irrelevant soccer match. In her kibbitzing with other parents, she heard the same unease with all the expectations on families and the pressure on kids. Eight soccer games in one week? A tournament in one-hundred-degree weather? "The parents had a deep, gut knowledge that this wasn't right, but we went along with it," she said.

It rankled. But what bothered her more was what she saw happening in youth sports throughout King County, the largest county in the state with more than two million people. The cost of sports was rising, and many kids were clearly unable to pay or play. McCleery has a PhD in education policy, as well as a lifelong interest in athletics. A three-sport high school athlete, and collegiate and US national team rower, she worked as a researcher at the Center for Leadership in Athletics at the University of Washington. The job involved studying youth sports and coaching as well as teaching undergraduate and graduate students. It was a natural fit for McCleery, as she'd spent years coaching elite rowers, as well as her own boys in Little League. She's long been an advocate for pulling more women into coaching. At the world championships for rowing in 2004, she flew to Spain with her six-month-old and spent the next several weeks coaching the team with the baby attached to her back.

In the wider Seattle area, McCleery learned, fewer and fewer low-income kids were playing sports. She wanted to understand why. So in the fall of 2017, McCleery began to organize. Together with King County Parks, she raised enough money to help fund an Aspen Institute State of Play report—an exhaustive study on the youth sports landscape in her area. Her thinking was, how can we fix the problems if we don't have a handle on them? McCleery also pulled together a coalition of leaders from local sports and outdoor recreation organizations that would serve as an advisory board to steer the research. She served as the principal investigator for the study.

The findings were alarming. Only 19 percent of kids in the county met the CDC recommendation to exercise sixty minutes a day. Among girls and non-English speaking kids, the rates were especially low: 16 and 11 percent, respectively. Play tracked to family income—the less money, the less physical activity among the kids. And fields and public parks were lacking, especially in the low-income southern part of the county, which also fell short on public transportation. Study after study confirms that what McCleery discovered in her own community is true in many low-income areas.

"I never thought sports couldn't be a part of someone's life," McCleery told me. Direct and serious when we spoke, she sounded angry when discussing the thousands of kids in her community left off the playing fields. "It's just obscene that access is based on income and race." She added, "It's a community problem."

Julie McCleery is not inclined to ignore crises she can work to repair. So, along with other community leaders who'd served on the advisory board, McCleery helped launch the King County Play Equity Coalition, a loose network of 115 member organizations, all determined to change the status quo with youth sports. "We're trying to shift power back to the communities, to increase access," McCleery said. "It takes a clear sense of the problem, deep and wide cross-sector community engagement, a vision for community-informed systemic solutions, and some funding/backbone organization to convene and support the work," she added.

They're doing this by petitioning to make sports equity a priority among state and regional policy makers. They want that reflected in the budget, so more public funds are available for parks and recreation facilities and other infrastructure that supports physical activity for all kids. The coalition provides grants, too, so that sports organizations serving mainly low-income families can collaborate with one another and build capacity. "We're trying to lift up BIPOC-led, BIPOC-serving community-based organizations, so they can build capacity and serve more kids," McCleery said. The Play Equity Coalition has received financial backing from King County Parks and Seattle's professional sports teams.

When COVID shut down the region, many well-off families simply scooted across state lines so their children could keep playing on private teams. Low-income children, meanwhile, languished. "It upsets me from a community health standpoint," McCleery said. Having launched the Play Equity Coalition, McCleery has now stepped back, acting as support staff to the coalition's leadership team, which is made up of its members; she resists taking credit for the initiative or acting as a spokeswoman.

Still, she's galvanized to keep pressing for system-wide change. "It galls me that something as important and protective as sports has become out of reach for so many kids," she said. "We need to find a better way forward to make sports and play accessible."

Other cities and regions have formed similar coalitions—the Philadelphia Youth Sports Collaborative, Project Play Western New York, and initiatives in a handful of cities that Laureus Sport for Good Foundation has sponsored. They're different in some ways, McCleery noted, but share the same goal: to change the system.

HARNESSING THE PRIVATE SECTOR.

Many in the youth sports industry are deeply troubled, it seems, about lower-income families being shut out of sports. They're also concerned about so many kids abandoning athletics entirely before hitting puberty. It's just so harmful for the kids, they insist. But it's also not great for profits when huge chunks of the population stop buying gear and yawn at the prospect of attending a game. It's hard not to feel slightly cynical about the sincerity of sports company and professional team executives when they fret about what's become of youth sports.

Jeremy Goldberg, the president of LeagueApps, a company that provides kids' teams with organizational software, believes that's an old way of thinking. There's no denying that the changes that have roiled youth sports have had negative (and positive!) consequences, he said. But we are where we are. The question is, how can we work together to repair some of the inequities and deficiencies?

Look at environmental advocacy as a proxy model. That movement found room for the Sierra Club and Greenpeace as well as Allbirds and Patagonia. Sports companies, too, if driven by authentic concern rather than mere public relations, can help correct gaps in the current model. "We can coexist together," he said.

Goldberg speaks at what sounds like twice the normal speed, his mouth apparently accelerating to keep up with his whirring brain. He was a champion debater during high school, and his knack for thinking quickly and coming up with complex policy-oriented solutions remains sharp. Being a middle school quarterback, despite his diminutive size, taught him about leadership: you don't have to be the best at something to lead a group. Sports also helped him discover his life's purpose, which is to act as a kind of social glue. His voice quickens again. "We're just scratching the surface of what we can do."

Goldberg's opinion is informed by his work for the peace organization Search for Common Ground. There, he learned that long-term, systemic shifts require action in three different spheres: government, social norms, and markets. It's the interplay of these forces, Goldberg said, that drives lasting change. "We live in a time when we don't have a lot of leadership emerging." It has fallen on business to step up where Washington won't.

LeagueApps has pushed for change in the markets, Goldberg said, by starting a designated fund drawn from company revenue that goes to nonprofit youth sports organizations. After COVID shut down most athletics around the country, he and others realized that kids' sports groups at all levels were toiling through the crisis in isolation. Goldberg helped establish the PLAY Sports Coalition, a collection of industry leaders, sports governing bodies, and grassroots organizations that share ideas and aim to speak for youth sports in one voice. It's a lobbying group, in effect, that makes the case in Washington and in state capitals for preserving youth sports organizations. The group pushed state legislators in New York to ensure that some proceeds from mobile sports betting go to nonprofit youth sports organizations, and they're gearing up to do the same in Ohio and Massachusetts. It's not about public relations, Goldberg insisted. "We want to drive change."

To shift social norms, Goldberg wants the PLAY Sports Coalition to unify around a clearer message: youth sports aren't just about having fun. Kids who play have a lifetime advantage over those who don't, and low-income kids are being systemically denied. "This is a form of privilege," he said. Everyone involved in youth sports needs to tell that story better if we hope to expand options for kids everywhere.

ENFORCING ACCOUNTABILITY.

Local bodies already possess the authority to impose conditions on organizations using public space. It's called "the power of the permit," and it allows agencies overseeing sports in city governments to insert their own restrictions on sports leagues that want to use publicly owned facilities. Through this permitting authority, local governments can also impose state mandates on organizations that are otherwise exempt (laws on treating concussions, for example, may only be enforced in schools) and step up coaching standards within their towns.

Doug Carlisle can tell you how it's done. While working as a senior manager at the Cincinnati Recreation Commission—the local version of a parks and recreation department—he was appalled when a news story went viral that featured a coach mistreating a player. In the footage, the coach was in his car making a child run home from a city park after a youth football practice. The boy was dressed in all his gear, slogging home on a sweltering day. Carlisle marched into his boss's office the next morning. We need to do something, he told his superior. That meeting marked the beginning of his monthslong campaign to hold sports leagues more accountable for their coaches' behavior.

Even before this incident, Carlisle had taken steps to improve the conduct of coaches who worked internally for the city's Recreation Commission. He demanded that if these coaches misbehaved while working with kids—yelling, berating, mistreating—they were to be reprimanded and possibly removed from their job. "I wanted to put some teeth in it," Carlisle said. But making these outside leagues answer for their coaches' behavior was something else entirely.

After video of the abusive football coach appeared, Carlisle went before every one of the twenty-eight youth sports organizations who required a permit from the city to agree to some minimal terms: one coach from each team would participate in a four-hour training session certified by the National Alliance for Youth Sports. Coaches would learn not only first aid and basic skills, but also how to run a practice, communicate with parents, and treat children responsibly. They also would have to sign a code of ethics. In exchange for the training and a $20 fee, the league would get $500,000 in liability insurance and a permit to use city facilities.

To be sure, many leagues resisted. "They feared I was coming in as Big Brother," Carlisle said—inspecting their accounting practices or poking around their team policies. Some objected that the $20 fee was too steep for their meager budgets. Another asserted that their coaches didn't need it, as the league did its own training. But Carlisle persisted, and by the end of the year his department had trained some twelve hundred coaches. They became partners when it was all over, he said, and the city and sports officials had a closer working relationship as a result.

Why don't more local cities and towns impose similar restrictions on the leagues who use their fields? It would seem like a painless way to impose some accountability on actors who work closely with children. It's likely politics that interfere, he explained. In many towns, elected members of the city council make these kinds of decisions about field and gym permits, and they are reluctant to impose burdens on local sports organizations. It's not popular to play the bureaucrat with people's kids. But it can be done if elected officials and mothers and fathers insist on it. "Parents should speak out to their youth league administrators and ask about certification for coaches," Carlisle added.

Saying No Thanks

COVID has forced this country to break with comforting routines and to adopt novel ways of living. Some of these new ways, we're learning, might stick. The pandemic also exposed the gross inequities between the haves and have-nots over access to health, education—and sports. These two realities might be all that's needed to invite national action.

The author Michael Lewis, for one, would like to see it. "I feel outraged," he told an audience assembled over Zoom about the state of youth sports. "You've taken this thing that has nothing to do with money and turned it into something that's all about money." What he valued most about his own sports experience growing up in New Orleans was the way it neutralized family backgrounds. Sports were a leveler, where the privileged and disadvantaged came together on the same turf. Now the travel teams and year-round play and abundance of commerce have altered their nature. "Sports are a regressive enterprise," he said.

Dream with me for a minute. Suppose the president, alarmed by what's happened to youth sports, and aware of the isolated reform efforts around the country, decides to wade in. Imagine he establishes a commission to study youth sports and offer tangible recommendations on how to fix them. Staffed with experts in the field, and pulling from the models discussed in this book, the commission identifies ways to address the big troubles in youth sports: the lack of athletic opportunities for all, insufficient accountability among coaches and private teams, inadequate coach training, unscrupulous for-profit entities, the epidemic of sports injuries among the young. *To start.*

Think what might happen if Michelle Obama, say, who has long been focused on childhood obesity and inactivity, were to lead the commission, and lobby Congress with her recommendations. The disparate efforts to reform youth sports would start to coalesce and gain speed. Then she could build a constituency and urge legislation that changes the landscape of youth sports.

There's another possibility, one that doesn't depend on buy-in from colleges, lawmakers, or private companies. Perhaps the kids who came of age during this period will want something different for their own children. The kids who grew up without enough—who never had a safe park to run around in; who never got a handle on the ball sports and couldn't make a team; who struggle to keep the weight off—might, when they're adults, demand more opportunities for their own children. Become a movement for them, willing to take on the establishment. On the other side, the kids who played too much—whose lives revolved around practices and games in a single sport; who now hobble upstairs after one too many meniscus tears; who struggle still to figure out who they are and what they want—might say "no thanks" to all that when it's time to make decisions for their own offspring.

I asked my son Paul, now out on his own in the world, how he thinks he'd approach it. "I want to think the play-all-the-time mentality will be different by then," he answered. "But if it isn't, I'll advocate against it."

CONCLUSION

The news clipping is old and yellow, a relic from the local paper, *The Madison Eagle*, circa 1976. "Whimsey Champs," the headline reads, and above it is a black-and-white photograph of my first softball team, Home Life. We're organized in three rows, probably on bleachers, and every one of the fourteen middle school girls in the picture is clutching a small trophy. The two coaches are also in the picture, at the very top—a mother of one of my teammates, and my mom, smiling and squinting into the sun. The article includes our record for the season. We were undefeated, 6–0, which explains the trophies.

I stumbled on this ancient article while picking through piles at my mother's house. She died in April 2021, right as we were beginning to emerge from what seemed like the worst of the pandemic. It hadn't affected her too much. She was already lost to Parkinson's disease when the world shut down; her social life, mobility, and mind were exhausted well before the annus horribilis of 2020. Now she was fully gone, and my siblings and I were tasked with going through her things. That's when I found the news story about my softball team. Mom had cut it out and put it in a drawer with other memorabilia. Those who have lost a parent and been involved in the grueling aftermath know what it's like. Between the horrifying old pictures—that hair! those clothes!—the tender correspondence, and the ephemera of ordinary life from a distant time, this journey into the past is haunting and melancholy, and also occasionally hilarious. It brings you up short.

I'd forgotten so much about that old team, but this photo of everyone brought them all back. There's Missy, before we played together in high school; and Lynn, a smarty-pants friend who went on to Princeton; and Suzy and Corinne and Jandy and Cindy. It was a blistering day when that picture was taken, after our last game. It appears we had no uniform pants, as some of us were wearing jeans and others shorts. Among the fourteen of us, we expressed the range of emotions you might expect from young teenagers at the time getting their pictures taken: indifference, delight, unease, annoyance, surprise, glee. Our mitts rested in our laps, and our trophies were propped on top of them: little batters coated in gold, standing on top of faux marble pedestals, about eight inches tall. I treasured mine, until I no longer did.

The same week I found this dated news clipping, the May 2021 issue of *SportsEvents*, "Great Stuff for Sports Event Planners," arrived in the mail. It's a "magazine" put out by the sports travel industry to grease the wheels of business. It's mostly advertisements, sponsored content, and thinly veiled pleas to come to Nebraska, say, to play your sport. A tourism person is quoted—"Nebraska has a lot of great sports venues that are located in lively parts of the city"—along with photos of young football players and gymnasts competing in two of the state's multiple sports facilities. (Lincoln alone has three major ones, including a sports complex that's 93,500 square feet.) In addition to all the pitches— "Dothan: the Sports Capital of Southeastern Alabama," "A True Diamond in the Rough: Howard County, Maryland"—the magazine is jammed with glossy pictures of kids playing every kind of sport: lacrosse, BMX, volleyball, beach volleyball, basketball, ice hockey, track, baseball, futsal, equestrian, rowing, gymnastics, tennis, soccer, skateboarding, wrestling, swimming, water polo, golf, and "fitness competitions." The photo of a roughly eight-year-old boy climbing over a barrier, his legs covered in mud and mouth open in a smile, made an impression. He was competing in a fast Spartan race, involving an "intense obstacle course" in Portland.

What I like about this publication is its lack of sentimentality. "The mission of *SportsEvents* Magazine," write its creators, "is to help planners of amateur sporting events and competitions be more effective, informed and successful with their events." It doesn't pretend to care about kids' personal growth, or the meaningful connections they glean through sports, or the health advantages that go with playing. It's about commerce, which has become the heart of youth sports in America.

Naturally, the magazine includes no pictures of kids getting their elbows and knees repaired at the Hospital for Special Surgery. Nor does it tell stories of children from low-income families trying to make the most of their sports-starved neighborhoods. There was nothing I could find about the psychic damage caused by relentless competition and high-stakes play—though a gauzy profile about a new aquatic center in Orlando with a fifty-meter pool gave me flashbacks to Caroline's infinite laps, and the emotional battering she endured. For all the shiny photo spreads of kids smacking balls and slicing through water, there's not one featuring a furious coach exploding at a child—or of an enraged father shaking his finger in the coach's face. (And not a woman coach in the bunch!) Absent too are the starry-eyed parents, the ones like me who made too much of it to quench our gasping egos.

These nasty things are also a part of youth sports today. They didn't make it into the magazine, but they're hovering there as well, right outside the frame.

It's tempting to gaze wistfully at the yellow photo of my old team and to long for what appears to be a simpler, better time. Insofar as we're discussing youth sports, I almost could: in the mid-1970s, big money hadn't yet weaseled its way into the system; kids' teams weren't all over the place, especially those for the very young; middle-class parents didn't depend so much on their children's achievements for their own self-worth; more women coached; obesity rates among children and adolescents were a mere 5 percent, a trifle compared to today.

But even then, there was much to improve. Coaches screamed at kids, and parents ripped into coaches (adults' egos are forever threatened). The disparities in what kids receive in our country based on race were just as entrenched. As important, female athletes weren't commonplace, because the reverberations from Title IX had yet to be felt among kids' teams. For some girls growing up at the time, daring to play sports meant getting heckled and humiliated. Indeed, when I was playing softball then, or running alone around my neighborhood, I was often on the receiving end of quizzical or hostile looks. My nostalgia only goes so far. And I am thankful that when my daughter goes out for a run today her presence on the road is no more novel than the sight of a squirrel hurrying up a tree.

We can't return to the past, nor should we aim to. But perhaps we can try a little harder to preserve what matters most about kids' sports, both then and now: the way they compel self-knowledge and discipline; the way they cement friendships among all types and tribes; the way they bolster habits of health and well-being that can persist into adulthood. Such virtues are attainable when athletics are carried out the right way. For these reasons, kids should play sports.

To procure these benefits, kids don't need to make the elite team, or travel many miles to play, or possess the sparkly new gear, or commit themselves to a decade of subjugation. These are the messages of the merchants who want parents to believe that they and their child will always need more to get to the next level. Or to simply measure up.

Forget the pageantry. Children need something much simpler. They need the opportunity to play—green parks and open fields, physical education classes, and community sports options. They need teams and outdoor spaces, irrespective of family income. They need humane coaches who know what they're doing and who can put the children's development over their own id. And they need parents who can cleave to what's important and keep their wits about them when all the rest around them have abandoned theirs.

Parents and coaches, what we have to do to make our kids' athletic experiences better is simple. Stifle our egos, put the child ahead of ourselves, and get out of the way. Then, maybe catch up with a friend over coffee, phone a sibling to check in, finish that book that's been collecting dust on the nightstand. It's time to resume our own lives.

As for me, I began to realize after so many years of coaching that it might be time to move on. The thought dawned on me one late afternoon, not long ago, when my team of teenagers gathered in a circle at a distance after their run. All the girls were prone on the fake grass, propped on their elbows and holding their bodies flat and straight in a plank. They'd been doing this exercise for weeks, and most could finally keep themselves steady without arching their backs or grimacing. (Most.) Afternoon sun still warmed the green turf they lay on, and light flickered through the tall trees that hung over the field. The captain, a green-eyed girl with a low voice and open heart, talked quietly to the team as they moved in sync to side planks and then push-ups. A few of them laughed at a shared joke, and even after they'd finished all their post-run work the girls lingered, sitting with their legs crossed.

I was off to the side, just watching. As a rookie coach, I had joined in, or led, the conversations with the girls, steering them this way or that. Had they seen *Shrek 2*? Or *The Incredibles*? My first year, I remember lying flat on my back with a winter-track runner, our legs up against a wall in the hall outside the gym to keep the lactic acid from settling in our calves. I'd done a hard workout with the team. We turned our heads toward each other and chatted, our ponytails mopping the floor, I playing the part of a kind and interested aunt. I loved knowing these girls and being included in their worlds.

"I keep getting older, and they stay the same," a veteran softball coach told me once, paraphrasing a line from *Dazed and Confused*. On that day, when my team carried out its maneuvers wholly and happily without my involvement, I had a similar feeling. Now, I was older than their parents. Were I to lie on the gym floor today as I had years before, I'd have to ease down slowly to protect my fragile knee and work my way up gradually so as not to induce back spasms. I'd moved away from being the coach who had a relationship with every individual girl to the one who set the tone for the team, allowing it to flourish without my ministrations. I'm not sure if this shift signified growth or stagnation. Still, the gap between our years, along with my body's rebellion, made me feel old, out-of-touch, and possibly ridiculous. It occurred to me that they might be better off with a coach closer to their age. A younger me, maybe, a fresh young woman with a passion for running who could take them places I no longer could.

When the girls finally hoisted themselves up off the ground and headed inside, they smiled and kept talking. It's exactly what I'd hoped they'd get from running together: friendship and peace of mind.

"Goodbye, girls!" I called out to them as they stumbled off together. Onward.

ACKNOWLEDGMENTS

Forgive me, but to thank everyone who got behind me while I toiled over this book demands a sports metaphor. And since I'm a runner, the best allegory for this intensive literary process is plotting, training for, and then completing a marathon. Make that a *first* marathon, where assistance from veterans is even more essential. For this one, a trio of fine literary women helped me cross the finish line, each of them guiding, prodding, and cheering me in her own distinctive way. My agent, Lauren Sharp, herself a runner and sagacious sort, inspired me to take on the challenge in the first place. She gave of her time and mind before there was anything to show for it and expertly guided me through the book's daunting early stages. Editor and magician Carrie Frye ran right alongside me during much of the training. Her generous spirit and intuitive grasp of the writer's mind made her a trusted partner and voice of reason. Trish Daly, editor supreme at Portfolio—and another runner—got me to the finish. She showed passion and perspective all the way through, and her brilliant editorial suggestions added precision and heft to my work. I am deeply grateful to all three of these sparkling women for applying their hearts and minds to this project. Though it's my name on the cover, their fingerprints are everywhere, right beneath the surface.

The book never would have come to press without backing from the team at Portfolio, starting with the publisher, Adrian Zackheim. Thank you for recognizing the value of the subject and supporting my work. As with any book (or marathon), there was a hidden army out of view who helped it come to be. At Portfolio, these included editorial assistant Megan McCormack; publicity director Tara Gilbride; managing editor Jessica Regione; cover designer Sarah Brody; marketer Regina Andreoni; and publicist Lillian Ball. I thank you for deploying your expertise on behalf of my book. That you soldiered on during a lonely and frightening pandemic rather than take to your beds is a minor miracle for which I am, again, profoundly grateful.

I wouldn't have managed without feedback from the many astute readers who gave up their time to evaluate and comment on various sections. Despite my frequent and annoying requests for her to "take a quick look at something," Sue Greenberg—friend, masterful writer, savvy sports mother—always obliged, offering sound editorial advice and her customary wit at every turn. Nora Wong slogged through early bits and pieces, and her counsel was always shrewd and direct. Edith Zimmerman graciously agreed to read an early chapter of some twenty thousand words; her enthusiasm during the grim summer of 2020 came at the best possible time. My friends Bobbi Moran, Kathy Castles, Tim and Elie Lear, and Kathy and Marcia Head (my sisters), also offered on-point advice, all of which made the book cleaner and sharper. Ki Sung, my beloved editor at the education site MindShift (have a look!), backed me at every turn; I never knew when I might receive a text from her in the middle of the night, just checking in.

But there were more: Fred Bowen at *The Washington Post*, a man of unusual warmth and rare wisdom; humane and hilarious Rick Eckstein, whose command of college sports and their discontents runs deep and wide. Mark Hyman, B. David Ridpath, Tom Farrey, Jon Solomon: your generosity was invaluable. And the legendary Jay Coakley, whose original work informed so much of my thinking—thank you. I am sincerely grateful to all of you for answering my emails, taking my calls, and communicating your ideas.

I have to offer a special thank-you to all the generous souls who shared their stories with me, some of them deeply personal: Danny O'Sullivan, Aly Carter, Jelani Taylor, David Archer, Mary Lou Carter, Katie McCafferty, Simone Ortega, Laura Gump, Sophie DeBode, Jacqui Young, Mike Millay, Don Schumacher, Brandon Whiting, Julie McCleery, Suzie Hoyt, Meredith Prior, Savannah Linhares, Charlene Crowell, Bruce Girdler, Howard Putterman, Monica Wallace, Karissa Niehoff, Jeremy Goldberg, Doug Carlisle, Maggie Lynch.

Thank you also to the legions of experts whose research and insight informed this book: Lenore Skenazy, Michaeleen Doucleff, Julie Lythcott-Haims, Madeline Levine, Rich Karlgaard, Travis Dorsch, Jack Bowen, Richard Weissbourd, Heather Bergeson, Charles Popkin, Andrew Solomon, Marshall Mintz, Victor Schwartz, Scott Goldman, Lonnie Sarnell, Tim Neal, Katherine Starr, Laurence Steinberg, Kody Moffatt, Celia Brackenridge, Nicole LaVoi, Lisa Damour, Jim Taylor, Richard Lapchick, Hendrie Weisinger, Garland Allen, Mary Helen Immordino-Yang, Dionne Koller, Daniel Gould, Susan Eustis, Ross Flowers, Luanne Peterpaul, Travis Vogan, and John Sullivan.

My friends, with whom I spent long hours commiserating on the subject, and whose voices and opinions are reflected here: Karen Eichler, Archie Gottesman, Lisa McGahan, Anne Britt, Monica Episcopo, Melissa Webber, Christine Galiardo, Ann Brodow, Kathleen Feeney, Sarah Sangree. Thank you all.

I would be remiss to overlook the indirect influence of three notable men in this project: Larry Smith, Denis Bovin, and Leo Hindery. Your longstanding interest in my work, to say nothing of your unswerving kindness, gave me the pluck to keep chugging along, pandemic or no pandemic. Don't ever think your big-heartedness was for nothing. I remain thankful.

And to all the girls I've coached over the years: our experiences together shaped my thinking about youth sports. Even on those days when the heat wouldn't let up, and our rivals kept beating us to the finish line, you made coaching worthwhile. Wherever you are, I hope you've stuck with running. You still don't know how good you can be.

Finally, I couldn't possibly have started this book, let alone completed it, without the wholehearted backing of my family. These include my daughter, Julie, our literary lion, who helped set the whole thing in motion; my son Jeff, our stubborn nonconformist, who illuminated the virtues of avoiding organized sports; and other son Paul, the family jock and my own little guinea pig, who not only permitted my use of his stories in the book but also tolerated his parents' involvement in his athletics. You all are troopers, kids. And finally, Bob. You kept me afloat and cheered me up and took loving care of our scrappy pre-pandemic pup, Margot, all so I could write. Your enduring faith in my ideas and ability—make that your uncompromising support for all my endeavors—sustain me. I am grateful every day.

Any mistakes in these pages are mine alone.

NOTES

INTRODUCTION

xvii **"Most people are oblivious"**: Jay Coakley, phone interview by the author, November 10, 2017.

xviii **"the market for addictive drugs"**: Michael Lewis, interview with Tom Farrey, "Michael Lewis: Youth Travel Sports Market Is 'Broken' without Easy Fixes," Project Play, Aspen Institute, October 16, 2020, https://www .aspenprojectplay.org/summit/2020/recap/day-4-michael-lewis-youth -travel-sports-market-is-broken-without-easy-fixes.

xviii **"Today it is the unimpeachable conviction"**: Jennifer Senior, *All Joy and No Fun: The Paradox of Modern Parenthood* (New York: Ecco, 2014), 123.

xviii **Indeed, according to Rick Eckstein:** Valerie Strauss, "Who Gets the Largest College Admissions Advantage? Let's Look at the Athletes," *Washington Post*, March 13, 2019, https://www.washingtonpost.com/education /2019/03/13/who-gets-largest-college-admissions-advantage-lets-look -athletes.

xxi **"The opportunity is now"**: "Call for Leadership," *Project Play: State of Play 2021*, Aspen Institute, https://www.aspenprojectplay.org/state-of-play -2021/call-for-leadership.

CHAPTER 1: MONEY

5 **an estimated $19.2 billion:** "Youth Team League, and Tournament Sports: Markets Reach $77.8 Billion by 2026," WinterGreen Research Press Release, November 26, 2019, https://wintergreenre search.com/youth-sports.

5 **"Who would have thought":** Susan Eustis, phone interview by the author, February 7, 2020.

5 **The ten most valuable sports brands:** Mike Ozanian,"The Forbes Fab 40: Puma Debuts on 2019 List of the World's Most Valuable Sports Brands," *Forbes*, October 16, 2019, https://www.forbes.com/sites/mikeozanian /2019/10/16/the-forbes-fab-40-puma-debuts-on-2019-list-of-the-worlds -most-valuable-sports-brands/?sh=3fb4d334d356.

5 **In 2016, visitors to sporting events:** Shelly Gigante, "Cost of Youth Sports: Dollars and Sense," Mass Mutual, June 24, 2018, https://blog .massmutual.com/post/cost-of-youth-sports-dollars-and-sense.

6 **"There has never been a better time":** Mark Hyman, *The Most Expensive Game in Town: The Rising Cost of Youth Sports and the Toll on Today's Families* (Boston: Beacon, 2012), ix.

6 **"Any time the livelihood of adults":** Hyman, *Most Expensive Game*, x.

6 **Danny is impossibly tall:** Danny O'Sullivan, in-person interview by the author, February 17, 2020. All the following quotes in this chapter from O'Sullivan were taken from interviews conducted on this day or on August 22, 2019.

10 **According to their findings:** "Survey: Kids Quit Most Sports by Age 11," Project Play, Aspen Institute, https://www.aspenprojectplay.org/national -youth-sport-survey/1. Researchers found that across the twenty-one sports they looked at, the average annual travel expense per child, per sport in each family was $196—though in some sports, the amount was much higher. Parents of field hockey players spend the most (an average of $934 per player), followed by ice hockey ($829) and then gymnastics ($763). The least costly youth sport, as far as travel expenses, was track and field.

10 **Parents are paying up:** "Cost of Youth Sports Delaying Retirement for Parents," Business Wire, May 15, 2019, https://www.businesswire.com /news/home/20190515005052/en/.

11 **"Communities didn't invest as much":** Daniel Gould, phone interview by author, March 4, 2020.

12 **"the business of sport in Walt Disney":** Mike Millay, "The Business Behind the Magic: Lessons from Disney and ESPN Wide World of Sports," Youth Sports Industry Conference, November 4, 2019.

12 **"We could use the expertise of Disney":** Mike Millay, phone interview by the author, November 8, 2019.

14 **Since Disney opened:** Millay, interview, November 8, 2019.

15 **Ratings for the Little League:** Mark Hyman, email exchange with the author, May 29, 2021.

16 **Pop Warner football players:** "Pop Warner Little Scholars," Pop Warner, accessed January 7, 2022, https://www.popwarner.com/Default.aspx?tabid =1579449.

16 **Some eighty newspapers:** Hyman, *Most Expensive Game*, 92.

16 **"There is a frighteningly strong relationship":** Rick Eckstein, *How College Athletics Are Hurting Girls' Sports: The Pay-to-Play Pipeline* (New York: Bowman & Littlefield, 2017), 40.

17 **"This likely speaks to lower-income kids'":** "Survey: Low-Income Kids Are 6 Times More Likely to Quit Sports Due to Costs," Project Play, Aspen Institute, January 14, 2020, https://www.aspenprojectplay.org /national-youth-sport-survey/low-income-kids-are-6-times-more-likely -to-quit-sports-due-to-costs.

17 **just 59 percent of kids did:** "Parenting in America," Pew Research Center, Washington, DC, December 17, 2015, https://www.pewsocialtrends.org /2015/12/17/parenting-in-america/.

17 **incomes of $100,000 and above:** "A New Scoreboard for Sports," Aspen Institute's Project Play Summit, Washington, DC, September 6–7, 2017, 5, https://www.aspeninstitute.org/wp-content/uploads/2017/12/FINAL -SOP2017-report.pdf.

17 **When the national economy:** "Survey: Kids Quit," Aspen Institute.

17 **offer no interscholastic sports at all:** *The State of High School Sports in America: An Evaluation of the Nation's Most Popular Extracurricular Activity*, Women's Sports Foundation, July 2019, https://www.womens sportsfoundation.org/wp-content/uploads/2019/10/state-of-high-school -sports-report-final.pdf.

17 **In schools that do:** "Sports Participation Gap Exists Between Youth from Lower-Income and Middle-Income Families," RAND Corporation, July 18, 2019, https://www.rand.org/news/press/2019/07/18.html.

17 **"may be linked to barriers":** Anamarie A. Whitaker et al., "Who Plays, Who Pays? Funding for and Access to Youth Sports," RAND Corporation, 2, https://www.rand.org/pubs/research_reports/RR2581.html.

19 **His research found that:** C. Ryan Dunn et al., "The Impact of Family Financial Investment on Perceived Parent Pressure and Child Enjoyment and Commitment in Organized Youth Sport," *Family Relations* 65, no. 2

(April 2016): 294, https://onlinelibrary.wiley.com/doi/abs/10.1111
/fare.12193.

19 **"Parents spend money to help":** Travis Dorsch, phone interview by the
author, February 12, 2020.

20 **"needed youth sports":** Jay Coakley, "The 'Logic' of Specialization: Using
Children for Adult Purposes," *Journal of Physical Education, Recreation &
Dance* 81, no. 8 (October 2010): 17, published online January 26, 2013, https://
www.tandfonline.com/doi/abs/10.1080/07303084.2010.10598520.

20 **"The most common question I'm asked":** Laura Gump, in-person
interview by the author, June 7, 2019.

23 **In 2021, virtually:** "The Circuit to the NBA: A Complete Breakdown of
AAU Alumni in the NBA," The Season Ticket, June 10, 2021, https://
www.theseasonticket.com/news_article/show/1168970.

24 **"growing up in a wealthier":** Seth Stephens-Davidowitz, "In the N.B.A.,
ZIP Code Matters," *New York Times*, November 2, 2013, https://www
.nytimes.com/2013/11/03/opinion/sunday/in-the-nba-zip-code-matters
.html?_r=1&pagewanted=all&.

26 **"The more experience you have":** Don Schumacher, phone interview by
the author, November 25, 2019.

CHAPTER 2: THE STAKES (AND STATUS)

31 **"independent consumers and participants":** Steven Mintz, *Huck's Raft:
A History of American Childhood* (Cambridge, MA: Harvard University
Press, 2004), 4.

31 **"combined to produce":** Mintz, *Huck's Raft*, 334.

31 **"existential fulfillment":** Senior, *All Joy and No Fun*, 7.

31 **"hyperparenting reflects a new sense":** Senior, *All Joy and No Fun*, 123.

32 **"Boomers tried to control and ensure outcomes":** Julie Lythcott-Haims,
*How to Raise an Adult: Break Free of the Overparenting Trap and Prepare
Your Kid for Success* (New York: Henry Holt, 2015), 5.

32 **"Time spent with the extended family":** Annette Lareau, *Unequal Childhoods:
Class, Race, and Family Life* (Berkeley: University of California Press, 2011), 58.

33 **"face-to-face interaction":** Lareau, *Unequal Childhoods*, 39.

33 **"Worried about how":** Lareau, *Unequal Childhoods*, 5.

33 **Here in Summit:** United States Census Bureau, *Income in the Past 12
Months (in 2019 Inflation-Adjusted Dollars)*, S1901, https://data.census.gov
/cedsci/table?q=Summit%20NJ%20Income%20.

34 **"Society became more individualistic":** David Brooks, "The Nuclear
Family Was a Mistake," *The Atlantic*, March 2020, 58.

34 **"A code of self-sufficiency prevails":** Brooks, "Nuclear Family," 60.

34 **"Due to this cultural shift":** Coakley, "'Logic,'" 17.

34 **"that the character and actions of children":** Coakley, "'Logic,'" 18.

34 **"from our employees to our bosses":** Senior, *All Joy and No Fun*, 9.

35 **thirty-four were professional athletes:** "The World's Highest Paid Celebrities 2020," *Forbes*, https://www.forbes.com/celebrities/.

35 **Three of the five:** Michael Schneider, "100 Most-Watched TV Shows of 2018–19: Winners and Losers," *Variety*, May 22, 2019, https://variety.com/2019/tv/news/most-watched-tv-shows-highest-rated-2018-2019-season-game-of-thrones-1203222287/.

35 **In the 2017–2018 academic year:** "Number of NCAA College Athletes Reaches All-Time High," NCAA, October 10, 2018, http://www.ncaa.org/about/resources/media-center/news/number-ncaa-college-athletes-reaches-all-time-high.

35 **NCAA earned more than one billion:** Ahiza Garcia, "NCAA Surpasses $1 Billion in Revenue for First Time," CNN Business, March 7, 2018, https://money.cnn.com/2018/03/07/news/companies/ncaa-revenue-billion/index.html.

35 **higher than teacher or astronaut:** "The 2017 Imagination Report: What Kids Want to Be When They Grow Up," *Fatherly*, December 22, 2017, https://www.fatherly.com/love-money/work-money/the-2017-imagination-report-what-kids-want-to-be-when-they-grow-up/.

36 **"The system builds":** Coakley, interview, November 10, 2017.

37 **"A desire to be observed":** John Adams, *Discourses on Davila* (Boston: Russell and Cutler, 1805), 308.

37 **"nowhere do citizens appear":** Alexis de Tocqueville, *Democracy in America*, trans. George Lawrence, edited by J. P. Mayer (Garden City, NY: Doubleday, 1969).

37 **"Where everybody is somebody":** Paul Fussell, *Class: A Guide Through the American Class System* (New York: Touchstone, 1983), 19.

38 **"official myth":** Fussell, *Class*, 20.

38 **"We are all steeped in it":** Sarah Bakewell, *How to Live, or, A Live of Montaigne in One Question and Twenty Attempts at an Answer* (London: Chatto & Windus, 2010), 43.

CHAPTER 3: COLLEGE

46 **The cost of attending:** Briana Boyington, Emma Kerr, and Sarah Wood, "20 Years of Tuition Growth at National Universities," *U.S. News & World Report*, September 17, 2021, https://www.usnews.com/education/best

-colleges/paying-for-college/articles/2017-09-20/see-20-years-of-tuition
-growth-at-national-universities.

46 **And the "student share":** "Net Tuition and Total Education Revenue,"
State Higher Education Finance (SHEF) Report, 2020, https://shef.sheeo
.org/report/.

46 **"This is the most complex":** Ron Lieber, *The Price You Pay for College: An
Entirely New Road Map for the Biggest Financial Decision Your Family Will
Ever Make* (New York: HarperCollins, 2021), 1.

46 **It can also damage:** Gillian B. White, "The Mental and Physical Toll of
Student Loans," *The Atlantic*, February 2, 2015, https://www.theatlantic
.com/business/archive/2015/02/the-mental-and-physical-toll-of-student
-loans/385032/.

46 **In 2019, national student loan debt:** Daniel M. Johnson, "What
Will It Take to Solve the Student Loan Crisis?" *Harvard Business Review*,
September 23, 2019, https://hbr.org/2019/09/what-will-it-take-to-solve-the
-student-loan-crisis.

47 **"The world, that great doofus":** Joseph Epstein, *Snobbery: The American
Version* (New York: Houghton Mifflin, 2001), 129.

47 **"So much of this is about parents'":** Tim Lear, phone interview by the
author, October 24, 2021.

48 **shares this and other enervating data:** Jeffrey Selingo, *Who Gets In and
Why: A Year Inside College Admissions* (New York: Scribner, 2020), 9.

48 **Selingo reports that the average student's:** Selingo, *Who Gets In*, 26.

49 **In 2021, after the pandemic:** Scott Jaschik, "A Great Admissions Year, for
Some," *Inside Higher Ed*, April 5, 2021, https://www.insidehighered.com
/admissions/article/2021/04/05/top-colleges-2021-great-year-admissions.

50 **Just over 800,000 girls:** Maya Riser-Kositsky and Holly Peele, "Statistics
on School Sports: How Many Students Play Sports? Which Sports Do
They Play?" *Education Week*, July 30, 2021, https://www.edweek.org
/leadership/statistics-on-school-sports-how-many-students-play-sports
-which-sports-do-they-play/2021/07.

50 **In college, about 33,000:** "Number of NCAA College Athletes Reaches
All-Time High," October 10, 2018, https://www.ncaa.org/about/resources
/media-center/news/number-ncaa-college-athletes-reaches-all-time-high.

50 **The surge in women's collegiate:** "More College Students Than Ever
Before Are Student-Athletes," NCAA, November 19, 2019, https://www
.ncaa.org/about/resources/media-center/news/more-college-students-ever
-are-student-athletes.

50 **Twenty years ago, researchers:** Edward B. Fiske, "Gaining Admissions: Athletes Win Preference," *New York Times*, January 7, 2001, 4, https://www.nytimes.com/2001/01/07/education/gaining-admission-athletes-win-preference.html.

51 **In keeping with this professionalization:** *Restoring the Balance: Dollars, Values, and the Future of College Sports,* Knight Commission on Intercollegiate Athletics, https://www.knightcommission.org/wp-content/uploads/2017/09/restoring-the-balance-0610-01.pdf.

53 **Scholars at the Mellon Foundation:** Eckstein, *How College Athletics,* 74.

53 **They discovered that:** William G. Bowen and Sarah A. Levin, *Reclaiming the Game: College Sports and Educational Values* (Princeton, NJ: Princeton University Press, 2003), 91.

54 **the academic discrepancy was even greater:** Thomas J. Espenshade et al., "Admissions Preferences for Minority Students, Athletes, and Legacies at Elite Universities," *Social Science Quarterly* 85, no. 5 (December 2004): 1444, https://scholar.princeton.edu/sites/default/files/tje/files/admission_preferences_espenshade_chung_walling_dec_2004_full.pdf.

54 **"14 times as likely":** Peter Arcidiacono, Josh Kinsler, and Tyler Ransom, "Legacy and Athlete Preference at Harvard," *IZA Institute of Labor Economics*, no. 12633 (September 2019), https://docs.iza.org/dp12633.pdf.

54 **"Although recruited athletes":** Arcidiacono et al., "Legacy and Athlete Preference," 16.

54 **"regardless of sport":** Eckstein, *How College Athletics,* 74.

54 **But at Trinity:** Paul Tough, *The Years That Matter Most: How College Makes or Breaks Us* (Boston: Houghton Mifflin Harcourt, 2019), 189.

54 **And at Amherst:** Selingo, *Who Gets In,* 155.

55 **"When you step back":** Selingo, *Who Gets In,* 148.

55 **Melissa Korn and Jennifer Levitz:** Melissa Korn and Jennifer Levitz, *Unacceptable: Privilege, Deceit & the Making of the College Admissions Scandal* (New York: Portfolio/Penguin, 2020), 93.

55 **Over the past few decades:** "Finances of Intercollegiate Athletics," NCAA, 2019, https://www.ncaa.org/about/resources/research/finances-intercollegiate-athletics.

56 **And many parents:** "Cost of Youth Sports Delaying Retirement for Parents," Business Wire, May 15, 2019, https://www.businesswire.com/news/home/20190515005052/en/.

56 **about one-third:** Eckstein, *How College Athletics,* 66.

56 **"(W)hite upper-class parents":** Selingo, *Who Gets In,* 156.

57 **The fifty-seven defendants implicated:** Sophie Kasakove, "Tracking Defendants in 'Varsity Blues' Admissions Scandal," *New York Times*, October 10, 2021, https://www.nytimes.com/2021/10/09/us/varsity-blues -scandal-verdict.html.

58 **These shots were photoshopped:** Korn and Levitz, *Unacceptable*, 145–46.

PART II: THE SIX PARADOXES OF YOUTH SPORTS TODAY

63 **"I think that we're going":** Heather Bergeson, phone interview by the author, June 1, 2019.

64 **"It's a model that's dysfunctional":** Tom Farrey, phone interview by the author, July 19, 2020.

CHAPTER 4: THE MYTH OF CHARACTER BUILDING

66 **"If my livelihood is really dependent":** Jack Bowen, phone interview by the author, August 20, 2020.

67 **"Sports can be a catalyst":** Bowen, phone interview, August 20, 2020.

68 **success goes to those who deserve it:** Interview with Jay Coakley by Brian J. Barth, "Stadiums and Other Sacred Cows: Why Questioning the Value of Sports is Seen as Blasphemy," *Nautilus* 39, August 11, 2016, http://nautil .us/issue/39/sport/stadiums-and-other-sacred-cows.

68 **"We assume sports build character":** Coakley, phone interview, November 10, 2017.

68 **"sports don't reveal a lot":** Richard Weissbourd, phone interview by the author, July 24, 2020.

74 **"Forty years of research":** S. K. Stoll and J. M. Beller, as quoted in *Ethics and College Sports: Ethics, Sports, and the University*, ed. Peter A. French (Lanham, MD: Rowman and Littlefield, 2004), 54.

74 **"I played sports":** Coakley, phone interview, November 10, 2017.

75 **"Sports can be harmful":** Weissbourd, phone interview, July 24, 2020.

75 **"My high school sports experiences":** Maggie Lynch, email correspondence with the author, November 18, 2018.

75 **"I learned to never quit":** Aidan Connly, phone interview by the author, February 19, 2019.

75 **"They made me feel":** Jacqui Young, in-person interview by the author, November 10, 2018.

76 **"It's hard to imagine":** Richard Weissbourd, *The Parents We Mean to Be: How Well-Intentioned Adults Undermine Children's Moral and Emotional Development* (Boston: Houghton Mifflin Harcourt, 2009), 145.

76 **"the experience of deep, passionate commitment":** Drew A. Hyland, "Paidia and Paideia: The Educational Power of Athletics," *Journal of Intercollegiate Sport 1*, no. 1 (2008): 66–71, https://journals.ku.edu/jis /article/view/9990.

77 **"I became a tougher, more daring person":** Mark Edmundson, "Do Sports Build Character or Damage It?" *The Chronicle of Higher Education*, January 15, 2012, https://www.chronicle.com/article/do-sports-build -character-or-damage-it.

77 **"Once the punch in the mouth":** Edmundson, "Do Sports Build Character?"

77 **"Players are encouraged to be":** Amitabh Avasthi, "Sport Machismo May be Cue to Male Teen Violence," *Penn State News*, January 23, 2008, https://www.psu.edu/news/research/story/sports-machismo-may-be-cue -male-teen-violence/.

77 **A study involving sixteen hundred:** Heather L. McCauley et al., "Differences in Adolescent Relationship Abuse Perpetration and Gender-Inequitable Attitudes by Sport Among Male High School Athletes," *Journal of Adolescent Health* 54, no. 6 (June 2014): 1–3, http://coachescorner.org/wp-content /uploads/2016/07/CBIM-Journal-of-Adolescent-Health-2014.pdf.

78 **one "causes" the other:** Matthew Kwan et al., "Sport Participation and Alcohol and Illicit Drug Use in Adolescents and Young Adults: A Systematic Review of Longitudinal Studies," *Addictive Behaviors* 39, no. 3 (March 2014): 497–506, https://pubmed.ncbi.nlm.nih.gov/24290876.

CHAPTER 5: THE PARENT TRAP

79 **While touting the benefits:** The majority of parents, school officials, and community sports administrators surveyed by the RAND Corporation in a study on youth sports believe that sports teach valuable life skills, including teamwork, self-confidence, and discipline. Whitaker et al., "Who Plays, Who Pays?"

80 **ramping each other up:** Weissbourd, *The Parents We Mean to Be*, 79.

83 **"It models a miserable":** Madeline Levine, phone interview by the author, July 5, 2018.

83 **And 60 percent of coaches:** Charlie Miller, "Syracuse.com survey: Parents, You're Driving High School Coaches Crazy," Syracuse.com, September 14, 2016, updated May 23, 2019, https://www.syracuse.com /sports/2016/09/syracusecom_survey_parents_youre_driving_high_school _coaches_crazy.html.

84 **"If only every one would do":** Edith Wharton, *The Custom of the Country* (New York: Vintage Books, 2012), 187.

88 **"Most people wouldn't know":** Kelly, interview by the author, December 6, 2017.

89 **"mentally and physically exhausted":** Corliss N. Bean et al., "Understanding How Organized Youth Sport May Be Harming Individual Players within the Family Unit: A Literature Review," *International Journal of Environmental Research and Public Health* 11, no. 10 (October 2014): 10226–68, https://www.ncbi.nlm.nih.gov/pmc/articles/PMC4210977/.

89 **"The middle-class children":** Lareau, *Unequal Childhoods*, 39.

90 **Lareau often heard:** Lareau, *Unequal Childhoods*, 57.

90 **"Any unathletic person":** Sarah Miller, "The Hockey Sister," *New Yorker*, July 7, 2021, https://www.newyorker.com/culture/personal-history/the-hockey-sister.

90 **After all, if the Harris Poll:** Deanie Wimmer, "The Cost to Compete: Solutions for Families Priced Out by Youth Sports," KSL TV, July 13, 2018, https://ksltv.com/398072/cost-compete-solutions-families-priced-youth-sports/.

CHAPTER 6: BODY SLAM

93 **more likely than their sedentary peers:** Xiaolin Yang et al., "Sustained Participation in Youth Sport Decreases Metabolic Syndrome in Adulthood," *International Journal of Obesity* 33, no. 11 (November 2009): 1219–26, https://pubmed.ncbi.nlm.nih.gov/19721447/.

93 **The rate of stress fractures:** Heather Bergeson, phone interview by the author, June 1, 2019.

93 **"an American public health disaster":** Samantha Pell, "As ACL Tears Pile Up, Doctors and Coaches Worry that Kids are Playing too Much Basketball," *Washington Post*, May 23, 2019, https://www.washingtonpost.com/sports/2019/05/23/acl-tears-pile-up-doctors-coaches-worry-that-kids-are-playing-too-much-basketball/.

98 **Just learning to kick, jump, and throw:** Kelsey Logan et al., "Organized Sports for Children, Preadolescents, and Adolescents," *Pediatrics* 143, no. 6 (June 2019), https://pediatrics.aappublications.org/content/143/6/e20190997.

98 **Playing outdoor sports:** Genevieve Dunton et al., "Organized Physical Activity in Young School Children and Subsequent 4-Year Change in Body Mass Index," *Archive of Pediatrics and Adolescent Medicine* 166, no. 8 (August 2012): 713–18, https://jamanetwork.com/journals/jamapediatrics/fullarticle/1263340.

98 **Exercise at any age:** Alycia N. Sullivan Bisson, Stephanie A. Robinson, and Margie E. Lachman, "Walk to a Better Night of Sleep: Testing the

Relationship Between Physical Activity and Sleep," *Sleep Health* 5, no. 5 (October 2019): 487–94, https://www.sciencedirect.com/science/article/abs/pii/S2352721819301056?via%3Dihub.

98 **"The single strongest predictor":** Simone Dohle and Brian Wansink, "Fit in 50 Years: Participation in High School Sports Best Predicts One's Physical Activity After Age 70," *BMC Public Health* 13, no. 1199 (December 2013): 13, https://link.springer.com/article/10.1186/1471-2458-13-1100.

98 **"fluid intelligence, cognitive flexibility":** Nils Opel et al., "White Matter Microstructure Mediates the Association Between Physical Fitness and Cognition in Healthy Young Adults," *Scientific Reports* 9 (September 2019), https://www.nature.com/articles/s41598-019-49301-y.

98 **It enhances executive function:** Charles H. Hillman et al., "Effects of the FITKids Randomized Controlled Trial on Executive Control and Brain Function," *Pediatrics* 134, no. 4 (October 2014): e1063–71, https://pubmed.ncbi.nlm.nih.gov/25266425/.

98 **Regular exercise also alters:** Jennifer Krizman et al., "Play Sports for a Quieter Brain: Evidence from Division I Collegiate Athletes," *Sports Health* 12, no. 2 (March/April 2020): 154–58, https://pubmed.ncbi.nlm.nih.gov/31813316/.

98 **exercise enhances the ability:** Megan Oaten and Ken Cheng, "Longitudinal Gains in Self-Regulation from Regular Physical Exercise," *British Journal of Health Psychology* 11, no. 4 (November 2006): 717–33, https://pubmed.ncbi.nlm.nih.gov/17032494/.

98 **exercise also improves word memory:** Junyeon Won et al., "Semantic Memory Activation After Acute Exercise in Healthy Children," *Journal of the International Neuropsychological Society* 25, no. 6 (April 2019), https://www.cambridge.org/core/journals/journal-of-the-international-neuropsychological-society/article/semantic-memory-activation-after-acute-exercise-in-healthy-older-adults/07DE0F919CEFBCE268A95474DFA1BC47.

98 **new neurons in parts of the brain:** Carmen Vivar et al., "Running Rewires the Neuronal Network of Adult-Born Dentate Granule Cells," *NeuroImage* 131 (May 1, 2016): 29–41, https://pubmed.ncbi.nlm.nih.gov/26589333/.

98 **Weight training has a similar effect:** Taylor J. Kelty et al., "Resistance-Exercise Training Ameliorates LPS-Induced Cognitive Impairment Concurrent with Molecular Signaling Changes in the Rat Dentate Gyrus," *Journal of Applied Physiology* 127, no. 1 (July 2019): 254–63, https://journals.physiology.org/doi/full/10.1152/japplphysiol.00249.2019.

98 **Because varied levels of movement:** Annie Murphy Paul, *The Extended Mind: The Power of Thinking Outside the Brain* (New York: Houghton Mifflin Harcourt, 2021).

99 **adult women who played sports:** A. M. Fehily et al., "Factors Affecting Bone Density in Young Adults," *American Journal of Clinical Nutrition* 56, no. 3 (September 1992): 579–86, https://pubmed.ncbi.nlm.nih.gov/1503072/.

99 **Women who exercise regularly:** C. M. Friedenreich and A. E. Cust, "Physical Activity and Breast Cancer Risk: Impact of Timing, Type and Dose of Activity and Population Subgroup Effects," *British Journal of Sports Medicine* 42 (August 2008): 636–47, https://pubmed.ncbi.nlm.nih.gov /18487249/.

99 **"Exercise can be a reprieve from confusion":** Damon Young, *How to Think About Exercise* (New York: Picador, 2014), 83.

102 **"I think I'd have been":** Katie McCafferty, in-person interview by the author, January 3, 2018.

102 **kids from poorer homes:** Jon Solomon, "7 Charts that Show Why We Need to Fix Youth Sports," Project Play, Aspen Institute, September 5, 2017, https://www.aspeninstitute.org/blog-posts/7-charts-show-fix-youth-sports/.

102 **suffer the highest obesity rates:** Kim Eagle, "Low-Income Communities More Likely to Face Childhood Obesity," Institute for Healthcare Policy and Innovation, University of Michigan, January 7, 2016, https://ihpi.umich .edu/news/low-income-communities-more-likely-face-childhood-obesity.

102 **overweight child is 70 percent:** Kim Eagle, "Low-Income Communities."

103 **have given up on sports entirely:** Julianna W. Miner, "Why 70 Percent of Kids Quit Sports by Age 13," *Washington Post*, June 1, 2016, https://www .washingtonpost.com/news/parenting/wp/2016/06/01/why-70-percent-of -kids-quit-sports-by-age-13/.

103 **between twelve and nineteen, were obese:** "Obesity and Overweight," National Center for Health Statistics, Centers for Disease Control and Prevention, https://www.cdc.gov/nchs/fastats/obesity-overweight.htm.

103 **Another 16.6 percent:** Cheryl D. Fryar, Margaret D. Carroll, and Cynthia L. Ogden, "Prevalence of Overweight, Obesity, and Severe Obesity Among Children and Adolescents Aged 2–19 Years: United States, 1963–1965 Through 2015–2016," National Center for Health Statistics, Centers for Disease Control and Prevention, https://www.cdc.gov/nchs/data/hestat /obesity_child_15_16/obesity_child_15_16.htm.

103 **Since the start of the pandemic:** Scott Neuman, "Children and Teens Gained Weight at an Alarming Rate During the Pandemic, the CDC Says," NPR, September 17, 2021, https://www.npr.org/sections/coronavi

rus-live-updates/2021/09/17/1038211236/weight-gain-obesity-children
-teens-pandemic#:~:text=More%20Podcasts%20%26%20Shows-
,Children%20And%20Teens%20Saw%20Significant%20Weight
%20Gain%20During%20The%20Pandemic,from%205%20to%2015
%20pounds.

103 **accumulated wear and tear:** David R. Bell et al., "Sport Specialization and Risk of Overuse Injuries: A Systematic Review with Meta-Analysis," *Pediatrics* 142, no. 3 (September 2018), https://pediatrics.aappublications.org/content/142/3/e20180657.

103 **Nearly half the sports:** "Youth Sports Injury Statistics That Will Surprise You," NorthEast Spine and Sports Medicine, June 16, 2014, https://www.northeastspineandsports.com/youth-sports-injury-statistics-that-will-surprise-you/.

103 **"There's an epidemic":** Charles A. Popkin, phone interview by the author, May 17, 2019.

103 **Other typical overuse injuries:** Mary L. Solomon et al., "The Pediatric Endurance Athlete," *Current Sports Medicine Reports* 16, no. 6 (November/December 2017): 428–34, https://pubmed.ncbi.nlm.nih.gov/29135641/.

104 **women are more susceptible:** Erik Lief, "Arthritis Follows 50% of Knee Surgeries Performed on Teens, Young Adults," American Council on Science and Health, November 7, 2017, https://www.acsh.org/news/2017/11/07/arthritis-follows-50-knee-surgeries-performed-teens-young-adults-12102.

104 **Endurance athletes, especially::** Solomon, "The Pediatric Endurance Athlete," 429.

104 **They're also likely to develop:** Solomon, "The Pediatric Endurance Athlete," 431.

104 **Head injuries are another:** "All About Concussions," Northwestern Medicine, accessed January 3, 2022, https://www.nm.org/healthbeat/healthy-tips/all-about-concussions.

105 **Girls' volleyball:** "Ongoing Study Shows Continued Increase in Concussions Among High School Athletes," American Academy of Orthopaedic Surgeons, May 20, 2020, https://www.prnewswire.com/news-releases/ongoing-study-shows-continued-increase-in-concussions-among-high-school-athletes-301062589.html.

105 **Even those who had played:** Jesse Mez, Daniel H. Daneshvar, and Patrick T. Kiernan, "Clinicopathological Evaluation of Chronic Traumatic Encephalopathy in Players of American Football," *Journal of the American Medical Association* 318, no. 4 (July 25, 2017): 360–70, https://jamanetwork.com/journals/jama/fullarticle/2645104.

105 **"The data suggest that":** Barbara Moran, "CTE Found in 99 Percent of Former NFL Players Studied," *The Brink*, July 26, 2017, http://www.bu .edu/articles/2017/cte-former-nfl-players/.

105 **Dislocated shoulders, too:** Gina Kolata, "If You Tear a Knee Ligament, Arthritis Is Likely to Follow in 10 Years," *New York Times*, November 6, 2017, https://www.nytimes.com/2017/11/06/health/arthritis-risk-acl.html.

106 **"development of knee":** Britt Elin Øiestad and Constance R. Chu, "Early Clinical Findings May Predict Long-Term Development of Radiographic Knee Osteoarthritis in Patients with Anterior Cruciate Ligament Reconstruction," *Annals of Joint* 3, no. 72 (September 2018), http://aoj.amegroups .com/article/view/4560/5140.

106 **"The stairs are always painful":** Callie, phone interview by the author, April 3, 2018.

106 **Of the seven factors studied:** Janet Simon and Carrie Docherty, "Current Health-Related Quality of Life Is Lower in Former Division I Collegiate Athletes Than in Non-Collegiate Athletes," *American Journal of Sports Medicine* 42, no. 2 (February 2014): 423–29, https://www.researchgate.net /publication/259248859_Current_Health-Related_Quality_of_Life_Is _Lower_in_Former_Division_I_Collegiate_Athletes_Than_in_Non -Collegiate_Athletes.

CHAPTER 7: LONELY AT THE TOP

107 **"You're supposed to push":** Caroline, phone interview by the author. All quotations included here were drawn from a series of phone interviews and email exchanges carried out in 2020 and 2021.

110 **"The professional consensus":** Marshall Mintz, phone interview by the author, March 28, 2019.

110 **"higher levels of negative emotional states":** Timothy L. Neal et al., "Interassociation Recommendations for Developing a Plan to Recognize and Refer Student-Athletes with Psychological Concerns at the Secondary School Level: A Consensus Statement," *Journal of Athletic Training* 50, no. 3 (2015): 231–49, https://www.nata.org/sites/default/files/developing_a _plan_to_recognize_and_refer_student_athletes_with_psychological _concerns_at_the_college_level.pdf.

111 **"based on decades":** Tim Neal, phone interview by the author, March 19, 2019.

111 **Between 2007 and 2017:** Kate Julian, "The Anxious Child, and the Crisis of Modern Parenting," *The Atlantic*, May 2020, 30, https://www.theatlantic

.com/press-releases/archive/2020/04/the-anxious-child-and-the-crisis-of
-modern-parenting/609901/.

111 **"There's both an escalation":** Andrew Solomon, phone interview by the author, March 11, 2015.

111 **"ghost peer pressure":** Scott Goldman, phone interview by the author, March 2019.

112 **"Nearly 30% of female":** "GOALS Study: Understanding the Student-Athlete Experience," NCAA Convention, January 2020, https://ncaaorg
.s3.amazonaws.com/research/goals/2020AWRES_GOALS2020con.pdf.

112 **"high percentages of study participants":** *NCAA GOALS Study of the Student-Athlete Experience,* Initial Summary of Findings, January 2016, 2.

112 **"Kids have come to feel":** Victor Schwartz, phone interview by the author, November 7, 2018.

112 **"High-stakes sports take":** Lonnie Sarnell, phone interview by the author, March 27, 2019.

113 **athletic identity foreclosure is especially:** Britton W. Brewer and Albert J. Petitpas, "Athletic Identity Foreclosure," *Current Opinion in Psychology* 16 (August 2017): 118–22, https://pubmed.ncbi.nlm.nih.gov/28813333/.

113 **"Your personal dream and desire":** Katherine Starr, phone interview by the author, March 2015.

113 **"I'd grown up playing lacrosse":** Isabelle, in-person interview by the author, December 6, 2017.

113 **A study carried out:** Ajay Shridar Padaki et al., "The Psychosocial Trauma of ACL Ruptures in Young Athletes," *Orthopedic Journal of Sports Medicine* 5, no. 7, suppl. 6 (July 2017), https://www.ncbi.nlm.nih.gov/pmc/articles
/PMC5542139/.

115 **And some fear ostracism:** Luanne Peterpaul, phone interview by the author, April 7, 2016.

115 **Even low levels of exercise:** George Mammen and Guy Faulkner, "Physical Activity and the Prevention of Depression: A Systematic Review of Prospective Studies," *American Journal of Preventive Medicine* 45, no. 5 (November 2013): 649–57, https://www.sciencedirect.com/science/article
/abs/pii/S0749379713004510.

115 **Just fifteen minutes of daily jogging:** Fabien D. Legrand et al., "Brief Aerobic Exercise Immediately Enhances Visual Attentional Control and Perceptual Speed. Testing the Mediating Role of Feelings of Energy," *Acta Psychologica* 191 (November 2018): 25–31, https://www.sciencedirect.com
/science/article/abs/pii/S0001691817301336?dgcid=raven_sd_via_email.

115 **Most athletes of both genders:** *Teen Sport in America: Why Participation Matters*, Women's Sports Foundation, January 2018, https://www .womenssportsfoundation.org/wp-content/uploads/2018/01/teen-sport-in -america-full-report-web.pdf.

115 **higher self- and body image:** *Go Out and Play: Youth Sports in America*, Women's Sports Foundation, October 2008, http://www.womenssports foundation.org/wp-content/uploads/2016/08/go_out_and_play_exec.pdf.

115 **hold on to their confidence:** "Female Athletes Fare Better in Nearly Every Aspect of Adolescence Compared to Non-Sport Playing Peers," The Girls' Index: Girls in Sports, April 1, 2018, https://rulingourexperiences.com /girls-and-sports.

115 **less apt to get pregnant:** *Benefits—Why Sports Participation for Girls and Women: The Foundation Position*, Women's Sports Foundation, October 15, 2016, https://www.womenssportsfoundation.org/advocacy/benefits-sports -participation-girls-women/.

115 **"We do know that girls":** Nicole LaVoi, phone interview by the author, June 23, 2017.

115 **And girls who play competitively:** Alexandra Starr, "For Women, Being a Jock May Also Signal Political Ambition," *All Things Considered*, NPR, March 29, 2014, https://www.npr.org/2014/03/29 /292475438/for-women-being-a-jock-may-also-signal-political-ambition.

115 **Boys who play sports:** "Youth Sports Facts: Benefits," Project Play, Aspen Institute, https://www.aspenprojectplay.org/youth-sports/facts/benefits.

115 **Researchers have pointed out:** Daniel I. Rees and Joseph J. Sabia, "Sports Participation and Academic Performance: Evidence from the National Longitudinal Study of Adolescent Health," *Economics of Education Review* 29 (2010): 751–59, https://www.csus.edu/faculty/m/fred.molitor/docs /sports%20and%20academic%20performance.pdf.

116 **"It appears as if sports participation":** "After the Buzzer: How Time on the Field Helps Women in the Workforce," Knowledge@Wharton, Wharton School, University of Pennsylvania, June 9, 2010, https:// knowledge.wharton.upenn.edu/article/after-the-buzzer-how-time-on-the -field-helps-women-in-the-workforce/.

116 **In premodern society:** Bruce D. Perry and Oprah Winfrey, *What Happened to You? Conversations on Trauma, Resilience, and Healing* (New York: Flatiron Books, 2021), 200.

116 **Structured movements help:** Perry, *What Happened*, 227.

116 **"Team sports participation during adolescence":** Molly C. Easterlin et al., "Association of Team Sports Participation with Long-Term Mental

Health Outcomes Among Individuals Exposed to Adverse Childhood Experiences," *Journal of American Medical Association Pediatrics* 173, no. 7 (July 1, 2019): 681–88, https://pubmed.ncbi.nlm.nih.gov/31135890/.

117 **"came into my life":** Jelani Taylor, phone interview by the author, September 1, 2020. All the quotations and information from Jelani Taylor were drawn from interviews on September 1, 2020, September 28, 2020, and November 5, 2020, as well as frequent email exchanges.

118 **One 2020 review:** Samuel Stebbins and Evan Comen, "These Are the Worst Cities to Live in Based on Quality of Life," *USA Today*, June 13, 2018, https://www.usatoday.com/story/money/economy/2018/06/13/50-worst-cities-to-live-in/35909271/.

119 **After Cornell head coach:** David Archer, phone interview by the author, September 29, 2020.

CHAPTER 8: THE TROUBLE WITH COACHES

129 **In April 2020, two former runners:** "Sex Abuse Lawsuit Filed by 2 Former South Pasadena High School Students Continues," *Pasadena Star-News*, April 9, 2020, https://www.pasadenastarnews.com/2020/04/09/sex-abuse-lawsuit-filed-by-2-former-south-pasadena-high-students-continues/.

129 **High school baseball players:** "Under Fire From Parents & Players, Columbia HS Baseball Coach Is Reappointed," *Village Green*, February 25, 2015, https://villagegreennj.com/schools-kids/fire-parents-players-columbia-hs-baseball-coach-reappointed/.

129 **Parents of football players:** Liz Teitz, "Parents File Suit Against Former Hamshire-Fannett Coaches," *Beaumont Enterprise*, September 14, 2017, https://www.beaumontenterprise.com/news/article/Parents-file-suit-against-former-Hamshire-Fannett-12198078.php.

129 **"To prepare an athlete for abuse":** Celia Brackenridge, Skype interview by the author, July 15, 2015.

129 **Of the roughly 7.5 million:** Jennifer Etnier, "Your Kids' Coach Is Probably Doing It Wrong," *New York Times*, March 11, 2020, https://www.nytimes.com/2020/03/11/opinion/youth-sports-coaches.html.

130 **The interscholastic level isn't much better:** Etnier, "Your Kids' Coach."

130 **Recognizing the deficit:** "Announcing SCE's Million Coaches Challenge Partners," Susan Crown Exchange, June 15, 2021, https://scefdn.org/announcing-sces-million-coaches-challenge-partners/.

130 **"youth always reported":** David Shields et al., "The Sport Behavior of Youth, Parents, and Coaches: The Good, the Bad, and the Ugly," *Journal of Research in Character Education* 3, no. 1 (2005): 43–59, https://www

.semanticscholar.org/paper/THE-SPORT-BEHAVIOR-OF-YOUTH%2C
-PARENTS%2C-AND-COACHES%3A-Shields-Bredemeier/
1a372d21a0390e880872d5ba6e8a79468277aa02.

130 **A study of nearly twenty thousand:** Mariya A. Yukhymenko-Lescroart, Michael E. Brown, and Thomas S. Paskus, "The Relationship Between Ethical and Abusive Coaching Behaviors and Student-Athlete Well-Being," *Sport, Exercise, and Performance Psychology* 4, no. 1 (2015): 36–49, https://www.apa.org/pubs/journals/releases/spy-0000023.pdf.

130 **both victims of bullies:** William E. Copeland et al., "Adult Psychiatric Outcomes of Bullying and Being Bullied by Peers in Childhood and Adolescence," *Journal of the American Medical Association* 70, no. 4 (2013): 419–26, https://jamanetwork.com/journals/jamapsychiatry/fullarticle/1654916.

130 **"I'm starting to view bullying":** Emily Bazelon, "Childhood Bullying Linked to Adult Psychological Disorders," *Pioneer Press*, February 24, 2013, https://www.twincities.com/2013/02/24/emily-bazelon-childhood bullying-linked-to-adult-psychological-disorders/.

131 **"It can't be good for them":** Laurence Steinberg, phone interview by the author, February 9, 2015.

131 **"can shake kids to the core":** Kody Moffatt, phone interview by the author, February 17, 2015.

131 **"Yelling doesn't work":** John Sullivan, phone interview by the author, October 4, 2016.

131 **"Nothing taught by force":** Plato, *Republic*, trans. G. M. A. Grube (Indianapolis: Hackett Publishing, 1992).

133 **In 1972, 90 percent:** *The Women's Sports Foundation Report Brief: Her Life Depends On It III & Collegiate Coaching and Athletic Administration,* Women's Sports Foundation, October 17, 2016, https://www.womenssportsfoundation.org/wp-content/uploads/2016/11/her-life-depends-on-it-coaching-administration-brief-final.pdf.

133 **Data on high school coaches:** Nicole M. LaVoi, *Minnesota High School Coaches Report 2013–14, Tucker Center for Research on Girls & Women in Sport,* August 2014, https://www.cehd.umn.edu/tuckercenter/library/docs/research/MSHSCA-2013-14-MN-High-School-Coaches-Report.pdf.

133 **A 2015 study conducted:** *State of Play 2016: Trends and Developments,* Project Play, Aspen Institute, 2016, 14, https://www.aspeninstitute.org/wp-content/uploads/2016/06/StateofPlay_2016_FINAL.pdf.

133 **One is that Title IX:** Laura Burton and Nicole M. LaVoi, "The War on

Women Coaches," *The Conversation*, June 4, 2019, https://theconversation.com/the-war-on-women-coaches-116643.

133 **These athletic directors:** Rachel Stark, "Where Are the Women?" *NCAA Champion Magazine*, Winter 2017, http://s3.amazonaws.com/static.ncaa.org/static/champion/where-are-the-women/index.html.

133 **Powerful norms about gender:** Michael A. Messner and Suzel Bozada-Deas, "Separating the Men from the Moms: the Making of Adult Gender Segregation in Youth Sports," *Gender & Society* 23, no. 1 (February 2009): 49–71, https://journals.sagepub.com/doi/abs/10.1177/0891243208327363?journalCode=gasa.

134 **"don't see women as capable":** Nicole LaVoi, phone interview by the author, June 23, 2017.

134 **"She was definitely a role model":** Leland Jones, phone interview by the author, July 11, 2017.

134 **Their example transformed:** William Ebben, email with the author, September 14, 2021.

CHAPTER 9: THE CONNECTION CONUNDRUM

137 **Putnam found multiple culprits:** Robert Putnam, *Bowling Alone: The Collapse and Revival of American Community* (Simon & Schuster, New York: 2000).

137 **"America has continued":** Putnam, *Bowling Alone*, 10.

137 **Since then, we've seen upticks:** Matthew Yglesias, "All Kinds of Bad Behavior Is on the Rise," *Slow Boring*, January 10, 2022, https://www.slowboring.com/p/all-kinds-of-bad-behavior-is-on-the.

139 **"Social connections are really good for us":** Robert Waldinger, "What Makes a Good Life? Lessons from the Longest Study on Happiness," filmed November 15 at 2015 TEDx Beacon Street, Brookline, MA, video 6:28, https://www.ted.com/talks/robert_waldinger_what_makes_a_good_life_lessons_from_the_longest_study_on_happiness/transcript?language=en.

139 **"Family and school connectedness":** Riley J. Steiner et al., "Adolescent Connectedness and Adult Health Outcomes," *Pediatrics* 144, no. 1 (July 2019): e20183766, https://doi.org/10.1542/peds.2018-3766.

139 **Earlier, narrower studies:** Christine M. Markham et al., "Connectedness as a Predictor of Sexual and Reproductive Health Outcomes for Youth," *Journal of Adolescent Health* 46, suppl. 3 (2010): S23–S41, https://www.researchgate.net/publication/51442181_Connectedness_as_a_Predictor_of_Sexual_and_Reproductive_Health_Outcomes_for_Youth; Marisa E. Marraccini and Zoe M.F. Brier, "School Connectedness and Suicidal

Thoughts and Behaviors: A Systematic Meta-Analysis," *School Psychology Quarterly* 32, no. 1 (2017): 5–21, https://www.ncbi.nlm.nih.gov/pmc /articles/PMC5359058/; Maryam Ghobadzadeh, Renee E. Sieving, and Kari Gloppen, "Positive Youth Development and Contraceptive Use Consistency," *Journal of Pediatric Health Care* 30, no. 4 (July–August 2016): 308–16, https://pubmed.ncbi.nlm.nih.gov/26481270/.

139 **The authors assert:** Renee E. Sieving et al., "Youth-Adult Connectedness: A Key Protective Factor for Adolescent Health," *American Journal of Preventive Medicine* 52, no. 3, suppl. 3 (March 2017): S275–78, https:// pubmed.ncbi.nlm.nih.gov/28215380/.

140 **"Loving relationships with adults":** Lisa Damour, phone interview by the author, January 18, 2019.

140 **"offline friends matter a lot for our happiness":** Putnam, *Bowling Alone*, 431.

143 **"I realized how happy":** Aly Carter, interviews with the author, September 22, 2013; December 17, 2017; November 15, 2018; and several email exchanges.

145 **"She brought this strength":** Mary Lou Carter, in-person interview with the author, March 26, 2018.

147 **"There's shared passion":** Jim Taylor, phone interview by the author, December 22, 2020.

147 **We had achieved:** Paul Bloom, *The Sweet Spot: The Pleasures of Suffering and the Search for Meaning* (New York: HarperCollins, 2021).

147 **"muggy, monolithic comfort":** Young, *How to Think*, 142.

148 **"We know that during adolescence":** Laurence Steinberg, phone interview by the author, February 9, 2015.

149 **Doing life together:** David Brooks, "2020 Taught Us How to Fix This," *New York Times*, December 31, 2020, https://www.nytimes .com/2020/12/31/opinion/social-change-bias-training.html.

150 **"I don't know of any place":** Richard Lapchick, phone interview by the author, January 27, 2021.

150 **This is the "miracle of sports":** Richard Lapchick, "Generation W: A Message from Dr. Richard Lapchick," filmed January 4, 2021, posted by Generation W, 24:30, https://www.youtube.com/watch?v=cVjFkr-VfKU.

150 **Research suggests that hazing:** Alex B. Diamond et al., "Qualitative Review of Hazing in Collegiate and School Sports: Consequences from a Lack of Culture, Knowledge and Responsiveness," *British Journal of Sports Medicine* 50, no. 3 (February 2016): 149–53, https://pubmed.ncbi.nlm.nih .gov/26675087/#affiliation-1.

150 **One study found:** Aaron Slone Jeckell, Elizabeth Anne Copenhaver, and Alex Benjamin Diamond, "The Spectrum of Hazing and Peer Sexual

Abuse in Sports: A Current Perspective," *Sports Health* 10, no. 6 (November–December 2018): 558–64, https://www.ncbi.nlm.nih.gov/pmc/articles/PMC6204631/.

151 **A few years ago, the girls':** Tina Kelley, "A Rite of Hazing, Now Out in the Open," *New York Times*, September 18, 2009, https://archive.nytimes.com/www.nytimes.com/2009/09/19/nyregion/19hazing.html.

151 **This was small potatoes:** Matthew Stanmyre, "Wall HS Football Hazing, Assault Investigation: What We Know After Another Tumultuous Week," NJ.com, November 20, 2021, https://www.nj.com/news/2021/11/wall-hs-football-hazing-investigation-what-we-know-so-far-after-another-tumultuous-week.html.

151 **the basketball players in San Diego:** Pauline Villegas, "High School Basketball Team Is Stripped of Title after Tortillas Were Thrown at Opposing Latino Players," *Washington Post*, July 1, 2021, https://www.washingtonpost.com/sports/2021/07/01/california-highschool-stripped-of-basketball-title-over-tortillas-incident/.

151 **"But what they see is":** Brandon Whiting, phone interview by the author, May 21, 2021.

153 **Because he had no prior exposure:** Jelani Taylor, phone interview by the author, September 21, 2020.

CHAPTER 10: WHAT PARENTS CAN DO

161 **"In retrospect, it was a mania":** David Brooks, Aspen Institute Forum on Sports as Social Fabric, September 17, 2019.

162 **"frittered away frightening sums":** Hyman, *Most Expensive Game*, xii–xiii.

162 **"It didn't occur to me that it was weird":** Michael Lewis, interview by Tom Farrey, Project Play, Aspen Institute, October 16, 2020.

163 **"They don't know who the kid is":** Marshall Mintz, phone interview by the author, March 28, 2019.

165 **"Let the kids direct the action":** Ross Flowers, phone interview by the author, December 18, 2020.

165 **"careerist approach to childhood":** Peter Gray, *Free to Learn: Why Unleashing the Instinct to Play Will Make Our Children Happier, More Self-Reliant, and Better Students for Life* (New York: Basic Books, 2013), 12.

165 **"Real life is an informal sport":** Peter Gray, "Some Lessons Taught by Informal Sports, Not by Formal Sports," *Psychology Today*, November 11, 2009, https://www.psychologytoday.com/us/blog/freedom-learn/200911/some-lessons-taught-informal-sports-not-formal-sports.

166 **In 2020, the leading cause:** Jason E. Goldstick, "Current Causes of Death in Children and Adolescents in the United States," *New England Journal of Medicine* 386 (May 19, 2022): 1,955–56, https://www.nejm.org/doi/full/10.1056/NEJMc2201761.

166 **"Americans today are safer":** Ames Grawert, Matthew Friedman, and James Cullen, "Crime Trends: 1990–2016," Brennan Center for Justice at New York University School of Law, April 18, 2017, https://www.brennancenter.org/our-work/research-reports/crime-trends-1990-2016.

166 **Of the hundreds of thousands:** "Kidnapped Children Make Headlines, but Abduction Is Rare in U.S," Reuters, January 11, 2019, https://www.reuters.com/article/us-wisconsin-missinggirl-data/kidnapped-children-make-headlines-but-abduction-is-rare-in-u-s-idUSKCN1P52BJ.

166 **"If it was safe enough":** Christopher Ingraham, "There's Never Been a Safer Time to Be a Kid in America," *Washington Post*, April 14, 2015, https://www.washingtonpost.com/news/wonk/wp/2015/04/14/theres-never-been-a-safer-time-to-be-a-kid-in-america.

168 **"choose early, focus narrowly, never waver":** David Epstein, *Range: Why Generalists Triumph in a Specialized World* (New York: Riverhead Books, 2019), 64.

168 **kids should drive these decisions:** Jim Taylor, phone interview, December 22, 2020.

168 **"to experience what it feels":** Jim Taylor, email correspondence with the author, February 19, 2021.

170 **"In the wider world of work":** Epstein, *Range*, 143.

170 **I need to add that the word:** Nick Haslam, "Concept Creep: Psychology's Expanding Concepts of Harm and Pathology," *Psychological Inquiry* 27, no. 1 (2016): 1–17, https://psycnet.apa.org/record/2016-08154-001.

172 **The "magical kiddie worlds":** Michaeleen Doucleff, phone interview by the author, February 10, 2021.

176 **"look for coaches who are not":** Hendrie Weisinger, phone interview by the author, May 10, 2019.

177 **"We lose our own compass":** Madeline Levine, phone interview by the author, July 5, 2018.

177 **"We're stunting their development":** Rich Karlgaard, *Late Bloomers: The Power of Patience in a World Obsessed with Early Achievement* (New York: Currency, 2019), 29.

179 **A study comparing international Olympic *medalists*:** Arne Güllich, "International Medallists' and Non-Medallists' Developmental Sports

Activities—a Matched-Pairs Analysis," *Journal of Sports Sciences* 35, no. 23 (December 2017): 2281–88, https://pubmed.ncbi.nlm.nih.gov/27923322.

179 **"The majority of Division I athletes":** Eric G. Post et al., "High School Sport Specialization Patterns of Current Division I Athletes," *Sports Health: A Multidisciplinary Approach* 9, no. 2 (March–April 2017): 148–53, https://journals.sagepub.com/doi/abs/10.1177/1941738116675455.

179 **They look for healthy kids:** "Sports Specialization May Lead to More Lower Extremity Injuries," American Orthopaedic Society for Sports Medicine, news release, July 23, 2017, https://www.sportsmed.org//aossmimis/Members/About/Press_Releases/AM2017SundayB.aspx.

180 **"There's just not that much room":** Karen Crouse, "Want to Play Football at Ohio State or Clemson? Try Playing Other Sports, Too," *New York Times*, December 30, 2016, https://www.nytimes.com/2016/12/30/sports/ncaafootball/ohio-state-clemson-multisport-athletes-fiesta-bowl.html.

180 **"It's beneficial to start later":** Garland Allen, phone interview by the author, March 31, 2021.

181 ***This mental exercise can:*** Ethan Kross, *Chatter: The Voice in Our Head, Why It Matters, and How to Harness It* (New York: Crown, 2021): 48–55.

182 ***Responsible* is the attribute:** "And the Quality Most Parents Want to Teach Their Children Is . . . ," *Time*, September 18, 2014, https://time.com/3393652/pew-research-parenting-american-trends.

183 **friction among the grown-ups:** Damour, phone interview.

CHAPTER 11: HOW COACHES CAN HELP

188 **"Coaches have a privileged view":** Mary Helen Immordino-Yang, phone interview by the author, November 29, 2018.

189 **"That one decision":** Bobbi Moran, email correspondence with the author, March 10, 2021.

189 **"Warmth is the sense that":** John Neffinger and Matthew Kohut, *Compelling People: The Hidden Qualities That Make Us Influential* (New York: Hudson Street Press, 2013), xi–xii.

192 ***"the most important things":*** Suzie Hoyt, email exchange with the author, February 15, 2021.

193 **16.1 percent of Americans:** United States Census Bureau, *Income and Poverty in the United States: 2020*, Report P60-273, September 14, 2021, https://www.census.gov/library/publications/2021/demo/p60-273.html.

193 **less than 10 percent of coaches:** "Youth Sports Facts: Challenges," Project Play, Aspen Institute, accessed January 17, 2022, https://www.aspenprojectplay.org/youth-sports-facts/challenges.

196 **"I'm not going to coach them"**: Marianne, phone interview by the author, March 11, 2021.

197 **She cautions mothers and fathers**: Madeline Levine, *The Price of Privilege: How Parental Pressure and Material Advantage Are Creating a Generation of Disconnected and Unhappy Kids* (New York: HarperCollins, 2006), 224.

199 **"rude, argumentative, arrogant, and sucky"**: Bruce Girdler, email correspondence with the author, March 27, 2021.

209 ***"The discipline which makes"***: "Schofield's Definition of Discipline," Bugle Notes: Learn This!, West Point, accessed January 3, 2022, https://www.west-point.org/academy/malo-wa/inspirations/buglenotes.html.

CHAPTER 12: REFORM OPPORTUNITIES POST-PANDEMIC: BOLD MODELS AND IDEAS THAT WORK

211 **"We could hold on to"**: Oliver Burkeman, *4,000 Weeks: Time Management for Mortals* (New York: Farrar, Straus and Giroux, 2021), 207.

212 **Suddenly it's not clear**: "Pandemic Trends," *Project Play: State of Play 2021*, Aspen Institute, accessed January 3, 2022, https://www.aspenprojectplay.org/state-of-play-2021/pandemic-trends.

212 **This trend was most pronounced**: "Pandemic Trends," Project Play.

212 **A majority of mothers and fathers**: Travis E. Dorsch and Jordan A. Blazo, *COVID-19 Parenting Survey*, Project Play, Aspen Institute, September 2020, 29, https://static1.squarespace.com/static/595ea7d6e58c62dce01d1625/t/5fa984fb066f8a0264beb4f2/1604945148149/COVID-19+Parenting+Survey+FINAL+REPORT.pdf.

213 **"Any attempts to make youth sports"**: Eckstein, *How College Athletics*, 200.

214 **"without the quid pro quo"**: Eckstein, *How College Athletics*, 176.

214 **"the largest increases have been"**: Eckstein, *How College Athletics*, 56.

216 **"Scaling back recruitment"**: Rick Eckstein, email exchange with the author, May 10, 2021.

216 **According to a 2019 annual report**: "Finances of Intercollegiate Athletics," NCAA, accessed January 2022, https://www.ncaa.org/about/resources/research/finances-intercollegiate-athletics.

217 **Among the hardest hit**: Molly Ott and Janet Lawrence, "Colleges Are Eliminating Sports Teams—and Runners and Golfers Are Paying More of a Price Than Football or Basketball Players," *The Conversation*, March 3, 2021, https://theconversation.com/colleges-are-eliminating-sports-teams-and-runners-and-golfers-are-paying-more-of-a-price-than-football-or-basketball-players-148965.

217 **"Club athletes represent their colleges"**: Tom Farrey, "Colleges Are Cutting Varsity Sports. That Could Be a Good Thing," *New York Times*,

October 13, 2020, updated October 16, 2020, https://www.nytimes.com
/2020/10/13/sports/college-sports-cuts.html.

218 **"People have assumed too much":** Dionne Koller, phone interview by the
author, May 3, 2021.

219 **Farrey suggests that it could be:** Tom Farrey, "How Sports Can Help
Rebuild America," Aspen Institute, June 1, 2020, https://www.aspeninsti
tute.org/blog-posts/how-sports-can-help-rebuild-america.

220 **When Tom Farrey:** Tom Farrey, "Does Norway Have the Answer to
Excess in Youth Sports?" *New York Times*, April 28, 2019, https://www
.nytimes.com/2019/04/28/sports/norway-youth-sports-model.html.

220 **It minimizes competition:** *Children's Rights in Sport: Provisions on
Children's Sport*, Considered by the General Assembly on May 11–13, 2007,
Norwegian Olympic and Paralympic Committee and Confederation of
Sports. Adopted changes incorporated and approved by the Executive
Board on August 28, 2007, https://www.aspeninstitute.org/wp-content
/uploads/2019/04/Childrens-Right-to-Sport-in-Norway.pdf.

221 **"It brings out":** Rick Eckstein, phone interview by the author, April 6, 2021.

222 **"The view that most European clubs":** B. David Ridpath, *Alternative
Models of Sports Development in America: Solutions to a Crisis in Education
and Public Health* (Athens: Ohio University Press, 2018), 151.

222 **"thoroughly broken system":** Ridpath, *Alternative Models*, 174.

223 **"Bigger things have been done before":** B. David Ridpath, Zoom
interview by the author, May 5, 2021.

224 **"I thought it was a silly sport":** Karissa Niehoff, phone interview by the
author, April 28, 2021.

225 **"one of the purest":** Andrea Mortimer, "Making the Move from the
Sidelines to Game Time: 2019 Winter Unified Sports Highlights," NFHS,
April 12, 2019, https://nfhs.org/articles/making-the-move-from-sidelines
-to-game-time-2019-winter-unified-sports-highlights/.

226 **"Sometimes there's no parent":** Howard Putterman, phone interview by
the author, July 2, 2021.

226 **All in, 53 percent:** "Reimaging School Sports: Large Suburban Public
High Schools," Project Play, Aspen Institute, Sports & Society Program,
June 29, 2021, https://www.aspeninstitute.org/publications/reimagining
-school-sports-large-suburban-public-high-schools.

227 **"There was always a problem":** Monica Wallace, phone interview by the
author, July 7, 2021.

228 **Since 2018, when the Supreme Court:** Jared Joyce, "Governor Cuomo
Proposes the Legalization of Online and Mobile Sports Betting in New
York," *Syracuse Law Review*, February 4, 2021, https://lawreview.syr.edu

/governor-cuomo-proposes-the-legalization-of-online-and-mobile-sports
-betting-in-new-york/.

228 **The Office of Children and Family Services will oversee:** Scott Scanlon,
"New York to Steer $5 Million a Year in New Mobile Sports Betting to
Youth Sports," *Buffalo News*, April 17, 2021, https://buffalonews.com
/news/local/new-york-to-steer-5-million-a-year-in-new-mobile-sports
-betting-to-youth/article_99773e28-9efc-11eb-b821-bbe07011fd90.html.

229 **"The parents had a deep":** Julie McCleery, phone interview by the author,
June 25, 2021.

230 **And fields and public parks:** State of Play: Seattle–King County, Analysis
and Recommendations, Project Play, Aspen Institute, accessed January 8,
2022, https://www.aspeninstitute.org/wp-content/uploads/2019/08/2019
-SOP-Seattle-KingCounty-Web-FINAL.pdf.

232 **"We can coexist together":** Jeremy Goldberg, phone interview by the
author, July 2, 2021.

234 **We need to do something:** Doug Carlisle, phone interview by the author,
July 13, 2021.

235 **"I feel outraged":** Michael Lewis, interview by Tom Farrey, Project Play,
Aspen Institute, October 16, 2020.

CONCLUSION

238 **Lincoln alone has three major ones:** "Nebraska," *SportsEvents*, May 2021,
43–44, https://lsc-pagepro.mydigitalpublication.com/publication/?m
=58498&i=705843&p=1&ver=html5.

239 **He was competing in:** John Torsiello, "Pushing the Limits: Fitness
Competitions Pit Athletes Against Themselves & Others," *SportsEvents*,
May 2021, 37. https://lsc-pagepro.mydigitalpublication.com/publication
/?m=58498&i=705843&p=1&ver=html5.

239 **"The mission of *SportsEvents* Magazine":** SportsEvents Media Group,
accessed January 8, 2022, https://sportseventsmediagroup.com/about.

240 **obesity rates among children:** "Too Many Kids Are Too Heavy, Too
Young," Obesity Prevention Source, Harvard T.H. Chan School of Public
Health, accessed January 8, 2022, https://www.hsph.harvard.edu/obesity
-prevention-source/obesity-trends/global-obesity-trends-in-children.

240 **a trifle compared to today:** "Childhood Obesity Facts," Centers for
Disease Control and Prevention, April 5, 2021, https://www.cdc.gov
/obesity/data/childhood.html.

INDEX

ABC-TV, 15
abuse. *See* bullying; coaching abuse
academic discrepancies in college recruitment,
    53–54
accountability, 233–35
ACL tears, 104, 105–6, 113
Adams, John, 37
Adidas, 5, 23
Age of Opportunity (Steinberg), 148
aggression, 75–76, 77, 90
alcohol use, 77–78
Allbirds, 232
Allen, Garland, 180
All Joy and No Fun (Senior), xviii, 31, 34–35
Amateur Athletic Union (AAU), 13, 23–24,
    41–43, 177
AmperVue, 6
Amsterdamsche Football Club, 221
Anti-Doping Agency, U.S., 219
anxiety, xix, 48, 74, 99, 110–12, 120,
    130–31, 183
apps, 6, 232
Archer, David, 119–20, 153–56, 180
Aspen Institute, 218
    Project Play, 17, 133–34, 164, 167
    Sports & Society, xxi, 9–10, 64, 213
    State of Play report, 9–10, 229–30

athletic ability, 28–30, 215
    allure of athleticism, 34–36
    author's experience with son, xiii–xiv, xv,
        28–29, 30, 39–43, 79–83
athletic identity, 112–13, 114
"athletic identity foreclosure," 113
authority figure and control, 195–96

baby boomers, 32
baseball, 11, 13
    author's experience, 29, 70–74, 134, 237–38
basketball, 76, 117, 134
    author's experience with son, xiii–xiv, 39–43
    Danny's experience, 7–9, 11, 22–25
    Girdler and life lessons, 199–200
belonging, sense of, 147–48
Bergeson, Heather, 63–64, 93
"bergy bit," 194–95
Berlin, Isaiah, 19
bigotry, 150–52
Bloom, Paul, 147
body slam, 92–106
    author's experience becoming a runner,
        94–97
    physical costs, 102–6
    trinity of wellness, 99–102
bone density, 99

Boston College, 165
Boston University's CTE Center, 105
Bowen, Jack, 67
Bowling Alone (Putnam), 136–37, 138, 140
Boys & Girls Clubs, 11
Bozada-Deas, Suzel, 133
Brackenridge, Celia, 129
brain
    emotional experiences and social
        relationships, 148–49, 187–88
    exercise's role, 98–99, 100
    head injuries, 104–5
Brandeis University, 39
breast cancer, 99
Brennan Center for Justice, 166
Brooks, David, 34, 149, 161
Buehrle, Mark, 178
bullying, 108–9, 130–31, 170–71
    hazing, 150–51
bullying coaches, 115, 128–32
    Caroline's experience, 108–9, 131–32, 170–71
Burkeman, Oliver, 211–12
business of youth sports, xvii–xviii, 3–26,
        239–40
    author's experience, 3–4
    class and disparity issues, 16–18
    contributing factors to, 11–16
    cost for families, 9–11
    Danny's experience, 6–9, 11, 22–25
    money's effect on families, 18–22
    reform opportunities. *See* reform
        opportunities
    unorganized sports, 6–7

Carlisle, Doug, 233–35
Carter, Aly, 141–46, 157
Center for Leadership in Athletics, 229–30
chaotic home environment, Jelani's experience,
        117–20
character building, 65–78
    author's experience, 65–66, 70–74
    myths and values about sports, 67–69
    research data on, 74–78
Chatter (Kross), 181, 182
chess, 167, 205
child abductions, 166
child-directed play, 165–66
child safety, 166
chronic traumatic encephalopathy (CTE), 105
Cincinnati Recreation Commission, 233–34

Class (Fussell), 37–38
Clemson University, 180
club sport system, 221–22
coaches, taking back the game, 187–210
    academic counseling, 226
    author's experience, 83–85, 187, 193–98,
        201–4, 205, 207–9
    being positive, 191–92
    communicating with parents, 204–5
    connecting with child, 190–91
    focusing on process, not outcomes, 194–95
    fostering an inclusive culture, 192–94
    guiding through disappointment, 201–4
    meeting them where they are, 196–97
    myth of character building, 66–67
    never giving up on players, 197–98
    parents and. *See* coaches and parents
    relinquishing some control, 195–96
    showing strength and warmth, 188–90
    teaching larger life lessons, 199–200
coaches, trouble with, 122–35. *See also*
        coaching abuse
    author's experience, 123–28, 132–35, 135
    lack of women coaches, 132–34
    untrained, 128–32
coaches and parents
    just saying no, 174–75
    knowing the, 175–76
    letting child quit, 169–70
    objecting every now and then, 173–74
    respecting, 182–83
    role of communication, 204–5, 207–9
    role of empathy, 204–7
coaching abuse, 122, 128–30, 170–71, 218
    Caroline's experience, 108–9, 131–32,
        170–71
    enforcing accountability, 233–34
Coakley, Jay, xvii, 6, 20, 21, 33–34, 35–36,
        67–68, 74, 78, 168
Coddling of the American Mind, The (Lukianoff
        and Haidt), 170
cognitively disabled children, 225
College Board, 48–49
college rankings, 47, 48–49, 51
college sports and recruitment, xviii–xix,
        44–60
    advantages for recruited athletes, 52–57
    author's experience, 44–46, 52–53, 59–60
    changes in admissions, 48–50
    costs of college, 46–48

Operation Varsity Blues, 57–59
playing for a purpose, 59–60
professionalization of, 50–51
reform ideas, 213–17, 221–22
scholarships, 46–47, 55–56, 215–17
commercialism, xvii–xviii. *See also* business of youth sports
Common App, 49
Compelling People (Neffinger and Kohut), 189–90
"concept creep," 170
"concerted cultivation," 32–33
concussions, 104–5
connections. *See* social connections
Connly, Aidan, 75
Continental Basketball Association (CBA), 23
Cornell University, 119–20, 152–56, 180
COVID-19 pandemic, 50, 103
    evisceration of youth sports, 211–13
    loss of connections, 137–38
    reform opportunities post-pandemic, xx–xxi. *See also* reform opportunities
cross-country
    author's experience, xv, 44–46, 52–53, 59–60, 63, 67, 83–85, 94–97, 123–28, 132–35, 140–41, 187, 193–98, 201–4, 205, 207–9
    Katie's experience, 101–2
Crowell, Charlene, 191
Cuomo, Andrew, 227–28
Custom of the Country, The (Wharton), 84

Damour, Lisa, 140, 183
Democracy in America (Tocqueville), 37
depression, 104, 105, 106, 110–11, 113, 115, 130
diabetes, 98, 103
disappointments, coach's role, 201–4
Discourses on Davila (Adams), 37
Disney's Wide World of Sports, 5, 11–12, 15–16, 25
disrupted families, 88–91
"distancing," 181
Division I college athletes, 7, 51, 106
    author's experience, 29
    Danny's experience, 22–25
    GOALS study, 112
    high school specialization and, 179
    Jelani's experience, 117–20
    Kathryn's experience, 127

Katie's experience, 101
    scholarships and admissions, 55–56, 215–17
Division II college athletes, 56, 106, 112, 119–20, 215
Division III college athletes, 51, 53, 55, 102, 106, 215, 216
dopamine, xv
Dorsch, Travis, 19, 89, 90–91
Doucleff, Michaeleen, 171–72
Drew University, 95

Ebben, Will, 134
Eckstein, Rick, xviii–xix, 16–17, 54, 59, 213–14, 216–17, 221
economic anxiety, 33
Edmundson, Mark, 76–77
Edwards, Harry, 152
emotional abuse of coaches, 122, 128–30
emotional costs, 110–15. *See also* bullying; coaching abuse
    Caroline's experience, 107–10, 120–21, 170–71
    Jelani's experience, 117–20
empathy, 69, 75, 76, 185
    coaches and parents, 204–7
Epstein, David, 167–68, 170
Epstein, Joseph, 47
equipment expenses, 10
ESPN, 5, 15–16
European club sports system, 221–22
Eustis, Susan, 5
exercise, 92–103
    author's experience becoming a runner, 94–97
    brain and, 98–99, 100
    health benefits of, 18, 92–94, 98–99
    as mood booster, 115–16
    physical costs of lack of, 102–3
    trinity of wellness, 99–102
Extended Mind, The (Paul), 99

families, keeping whole. *See* whole family
family dinners, 90–91
family expenses, 9–11
family income disparities. *See* income disparities
Farrey, Tom, 64, 133–34, 213, 217, 219, 220–21
Federer, Roger, 179

"female athlete triad," 104
field hockey, 189
financial aid, 46, 96, 214–17
financial crisis of 2007–2008, 11, 14
Flowers, Ross, 165
Floyd, George, 151
football, 35, 66, 76–78
    Jelani's experience, 117–20, 152–56
Fordham University, 9, 22–25
4,000 Weeks (Burkeman), 211–12
fox and the hedgehog, 19
framework for parents, 162–84
    keeping your family whole, 171–76
    looking at your child, 163–71
    modeling the behavior, 182–84
    striving to keep perspective, 176–82
Free-Range Kids, 166
Free to Learn (Gray), 165
Friday Night Lights (TV show), 208
fun, xxi, 4, 8, 39, 42, 69, 82, 165–66, 192
Fussell, Paul, 37–38

Gatorade, 5
gender differences, 115–16, 240. *See also*
        women's collegiate sports
    dearth of women coaches, 133–34
Georgetown University, 54, 58
"ghost peer pressure," 111–12
Gilead (Robinson), xx
Girdler, Bruce, 199–200
Gladwell, Malcolm, 20
GOALS study, 111–12
Goldberg, Jeremy, 232–33
Goldman, Scott, 111, 112
golf, 66, 142, 167, 217
GotSoccer, 16
Gould, Daniel, 11, 219–20
Go4-Ellis, 6
grade-based model for youth sports, 199–200
Graf, Steffi, 179
Gray, Peter, 165
Great Sports Myth, 67–68
Greenpeace, 232
group identity, 147–48
Gump, Laura, 20–22

Haidt, Jonathan, 170
Hamshire-Fannett High School, 129
Harris Poll, 10, 90
Harvard Medical School, 104

Harvard Study of Adult Development, 138–39
Harvard University, 54, 68, 138–39
Haslam, Nick, 170
hazing, 150–51
head injuries, 104–5
health benefits, 92–94, 98–99
heart disease, 98, 166
Hernandez, Pierre-Jonas, 129
HitCheck, 6
Hodge, Douglas, 58
honesty with kids and parents, 208
Hospital for Special Surgery, 239
How College Athletics Are Hurting Girls' Sports
        (Eckstein), xviii–xix
How to Think About Exercise (Young), 99
Hoyt, Suzie, 188, 191–92, 199
Huck's Raft (Mintz), 30–31
Huffman, Felicity, 58
Hunt, Gather, Parent (Doucleff), 171–72
Hyland, Drew, 76
Hyman, Mark, 6, 16, 161–62, 162

Immordino-Yang, Mary Helen, 187–88
inclusive sports culture, 192–94
income disparities
    coaches and, 193
    college admissions, 54–55
    Danny's experience, 23–24
    Jelani's experience, 117–20
    returning power to communities, 229–31
    social norms and, 32–33
    youth sports participation, 16–18, 64
individualism, 34, 137, 138
injuries, 103–6, 113–14
Institute for Diversity and Ethics in Sport, 150
Institute for the Study of Youth Sports, 11, 219

JAMA Pediatrics, 116
James, LeBron, 35
Jed Foundation, 112
jock sniffers, 30
Johns Hopkins University, 47
Jones, Leland, 134
Jordan, Michael, 178

Karlgaard, Rich, 177–78
Kellogg-Briand Pact, 216
King County Play Equity Coalition, 230–31
Kocher, Mininder, 104, 105
Kohut, Matthew, 189–90

Koller, Dionne, 218–19, 220, 223
Korn, Melissa, 55
Kreager, Derek, 77
Kross, Ethan, 181, 182

lacrosse, 20–22, 26
    advantages for recruited athletes,
        52–53, 55, 87
    Aly's experience, 141–46, 157
    author's experience with son, 81–83
    Callie's experience, 106
    Kelly's experience with son, 88–89
    Louisa's experience coaching, 196–97
    Rosemary's experience with
        daughter, 205–6
Lapchick, Richard, 150, 151
Lareau, Annette, 32–33, 89–90
Late Bloomers (Karlgaard), 177–78
Laureus Sport for Good Foundation, 231
LaVoi, Nicole, 115, 134
LeagueApps, 232–33
Lear, Tim, 47
Levine, Madeline, 83, 177, 184, 197
Levitz, Jennifer, 55
Lewis, Michael, xvii–xviii, 162, 235
Liar's Poker (Lewis), xvii–xviii
Lieber, Ron, 46
"life lessons," 199–200
limping along, 184–86
Linhares, Savannah, 191
Little League Baseball, 11, 13, 15
local sports leagues, 173
loneliness, 137–38, 140
looking at the child, 163–71
    encouraging variety of sports, 167–68
    following child's lead, 164–65
    letting them play, 165–66
    letting them quit, 169–70
    providing off-ramps., 168–69
    tolerating no actual abuse, 170–71
"lost causes," 198–99
Lukianoff, Greg, 170
Lynch, Maggie, 75
Lythcott-Haims, Julie, 31–32

McCafferty, Katie, 101–2
McCleery, Julie, 229–31
Madison Eagle, 237–38
Mahomes, Patrick, 179
Massachusetts General Hospital, 139

Mass Mutual, 5
Mayo Clinic College of Medicine and
    Science, 93
media, 5, 15–16, 140–41
Mellon Foundation, 50–51, 53
mental clarity, 98–99, 100
mental health problems. See emotional costs
Messi, Lionel, 35, 178
Messner, Michael, 133
metabolic syndrome, 98
Mez, Jesse, 105
Military Academy, U.S. (West Point),
    209–10
Millay, Mike, 12–13, 25, 26
Miller, Sarah, 90
Ministry of Sports, 218–21
Mintz, Marshall, 110–11, 113, 114,
    163–64
Mintz, Steven, 30–31
missing games, 183–84
modeling behavior, 80–83, 182–84
    author's experience, 80–83
    getting a life, 184
    missing some games, 183–84
    respecting coaches and referees, 182–83
Moffatt, Kody, 131
money, 239–40. See also business of youth
    sports; income disparities
    effect on families, 18–22
    costs of college, 46–48
    securing state funding, 227–28
Montaigne, Michel de, 38
mood and exercise, 115–16
Moran, Bobbi, 189
Most Expensive Game in Town, The
    (Hyman), 16
Murphy, Shane, 148
Murray, Mary, 8, 24, 35
myths and values about sports, 67–69

Nassar, Larry, 128, 218
National Alliance for Youth Sports, 234
National Association of Sports Commissions
    (NASC), 13–14
National Athletic Trainers' Association
    (NATA), 110–11
National Committee for Accreditation of
    Coaching Education, 130
National Federation of State High School
    Associations (NFHS), 194, 223–24

NBA (National Basketball Association), 7, 22–25
NCAA (National Collegiate Athletic Association), 13, 15, 35, 50, 55–56, 111–12, 216, 223
Neal, Tim, 111
Neffinger, John, 189–90
New Jersey State Interscholastic Athletic Association (NJSIAA), 223–24
New York Times, 24, 149, 217
NFL (National Football League), 151, 153, 155
NHL (National Hockey League), 15
Niehoff, Karissa, 223–25
Nike, 5, 9, 23
Noonday Demon, The (Solomon), 111
Norway, 220, 228
nutrition and snacks, 86

Obama, Michelle, 103, 236
obesity, 102–3, 236, 240
Office, The (TV show), 41–42
Oiestad, Britt Elin, 105–6
Olympic Trials (1992), 97
Operation Varsity Blues, 57–59
osteoporosis, 99
O'Sullivan, Danny, 6–9, 11, 22–25
Outliers (Gladwell), 20
overbearing parents, 83–85
overparenting, 31–32
overtraining, 93, 111–12
"overtraining syndrome," 104
overuse injuries, 103–4
Oxford University, 95–97, 214

paradoxes of youth sports, 63–157
    body slam, 92–106
    connection conundrum, 136–57
    lonely at the top, 107–21
    myth of character building, 65–78
    the parent trap, 79–91
    trouble with coaches, 122–35
parents, framework for staying grounded, 162–84
    keeping your family whole, 171–76
    looking at your child, 163–71
    modeling behavior, 80–83, 182–84
    striving to keep perspective, 176–82
parents and coaches. See coaches and parents
Parents We Mean to Be, The (Weissbourd), 68

parent trap, 79–91
    author's experience, 79–83
    body slam, 92–106
    disrupted families, 88–91
    overbearing parents, 83–85
    snack creep, 86–88
participation trophies, 69
Patagonia, 232
Paul, Annie Murphy, 99
Pediatrics, 139
Pell Grants, 9
permitting and enforcing accountability, 233–35
Perry, Bruce D., 116
perspective, 176–82
    on specialization, 176–80
Peterpaul, Luanne, 115
Pew Research Center, 17
Philadelphia Youth Sports Collaborative, 231
phones and social media, 140–41
physical activity. See exercise
physically disabled children, 225–27
play, 165–66, 192
    Aspen Institute's State of Play report, 9–10, 229–30
PLAY Sports Coalition, 233
Popkin, Charles A., 103
Pop Warner, 11, 16, 117
positive attitude, 191–92
Positive Coaching Alliance (PCA), 151–52, 191, 194
prefrontal cortex, 149
prejudice, 149–52
Price of Privilege, The (Levine), 197
Prior, Meredith, 191
private sector, 231–33
processes vs. outcomes, 194–95
professionalization of college sports, 50–51
Project Play Western New York, 231
propinquity theory on relationships, 201
psychological costs. See emotional costs
Puma, 5
punishment, 131
Putnam, Robert, 136–37, 138, 140
Putterman, Howard, 225–27

quitting, 169–70, 181

racial disparities in college admissions, 54–55
racism, 151–52
Range (Epstein), 167–68, 170

ranking system, 16
Rapinoe, Megan, 179
Raukar, Neha, 93
recruitment. *See* college sports and recruitment
Reebok, 5
referees and umpires
    respecting, 76, 182–83
    Silbo app, 6
reform opportunities, 179, 211–36
    divorcing sports from schools, 221–22
    enforcing accountability, 233–35
    establishing Ministry of Sports, 218–21
    harnessing the private sector, 231–33
    renewing high school sports, 223–27
    returning power to communities, 229–31
    saying no thanks, 235–36
    securing state funding, 227–28
    transforming intercollegiate sports, 213–17
registration fees, 10
renewing high school sports, 223–27
respect, 209–10
Ridpath, B. David, 219, 221–22, 223
Robinson, Marilynne, xx
"runner's knee," 114
running, 18–19. *See also* cross-country
    author's experience, xv–xviii, 63, 94–97,
        99–101, 146–47
    injuries, 103–4, 113–14

same-sex teams and trans athletes, 193–94
Sarnell, Lonnie, 112
SAT test, 48, 53–54, 58
saying no, 174–75
Schofield, John M., 209–10
scholarships, 46–47, 55–56, 215–17
Schumacher, Don, 13–14, 15
Schwartz, Victor, 112
Search for Common Ground, 232–33
sedentary lifestyle, 93, 102–3
self-confidence, 74, 84, 98, 101, 111, 115, 134,
        177–78
self-esteem, 32, 69, 115, 116
self-knowledge, 66, 67, 76–77
self-possession, 100
Selingo, Jeffrey, 47–49, 55, 56
Senior, Jennifer, xviii, 31, 34–35
September 11 attacks (2001), 12
sexual abuse of coaches, 122, 128–30, 218
shin splints, 114
Shirley Povich Center for Sports Journalism, 6

siblings of child athletes, 29, 32–33, 89–90,
    109, 172
Sierra Club, 232
SignUpGenius, 86
Silbo, 6
Singer, Rick, 57–59
Skenazy, Lenore, 166
Sky Sports, 5
sleep disturbances, 111
Sloane, Devin, 58
"slut list," 151
snack creep, 86–88
Snobbery (Epstein), 47
soccer, 134, 151, 213–14, 217
    author's experience with son, 3–4, 27–28,
        36–37, 80–83
    head injuries, 104–5
    Kelly's experience with daughter, 88–89
    returning power to communities,
        229–31
social class, 16–18, 23–24. *See also* income
    disparities
social connections, 136–57
    Aly's experience, 141–46, 157
    coaches and children, 190–91
    Jelani's experience, 152–56
    role of sports in, 146–52
    as root of human thriving, 138–41
social media, 49, 140–41
social norms, 32
social status, 30–34
    allure of athleticism, 34–36
    promise of, 36–43
social trust, 136–37
Solomon, Andrew, 111
specialization, 20–21
    athletic identity and, 112–13
    encouraging variety of sports vs.,
        167–68
    injuries due to, 104
    proper perspective on, 179–80
    providing off-ramps., 168–69
Sports and Fitness Industry
        Association, 5, 133
sports betting, 227–28, 233
sports brands, 5, 232
sports camps, 20–21, 39–41
SportsEvents, 238–39
sports facilities, 11–15
sports injuries, 103–6, 113–14

sports specialization. *See* specialization
sports tourism, 5–6, 11–15
　Disney's Wide World of Sports, 5, 11–12,
　　15–16, 25
stakes, 27–43
　allure of athleticism, 34–36
　larger landscape of children, status, and
　　sports, 30–34
　promise of status, 36–43
Stanford University, 21, 31, 58, 186
Starr, Katherine, 113
state funding, 227–28
steeplechase, 96–97
Steinberg, Laurence, 131, 148
Stevenson, Betsey, 116
strength, 188–90
stress fractures, 103–4
suicide and bullying, 130
suicide rate, 111
Sullivan, John, 131
Susan Crown Exchange, 130
swimming, Caroline's experience, 107–10,
　170–71
Swinney, Dabo, 180

Taylor, Jelani, 117–20, 152–56
Taylor, Jim, 147–48, 168–69
TD Ameritrade, 10, 56
team culture, fostering an inclusive culture,
　192–94
team dinners, 87–88
team identity, 147–48, 165
teamwork, 68, 69, 73–75, 82
tennis, 65–66, 73–74, 99, 179, 217
time outlays, 10–11
Title IX, 50, 70, 116, 122, 133–34, 219, 240
Tocqueville, Alexis de, 37
tourism. *See* sports tourism
trans child athletes, 193–94
transparency with kids and parents, 207–9
travel expenses, 10, 248*n*
travel leagues, 4, 173
Tucker Center for Research on Girls & Women
　in Sport, 115, 134
Tuscarora High School, 225–27
Twitter, 137, 140

UFC (Ultimate Fighting Championship), 5
Under Armour, 5

Unequal Childhoods (Lareau), 32–33, 89–90
United States Specialty Sports Association, 16
University of California, Los Angeles (UCLA),
　187–88
University of Colorado, 67
University of Pennsylvania, 47
university sports. *See* college sports and
　recruitment
"unorganized sports," 8
U.S. News & World Report college rankings,
　47, 48, 51
USA Today, 16
US Gymnastics Championship, 13
Utah Jazz, 23
Utah State University, 10, 19, 89

vacation time, 90
variety of sports., 167–68

Waldinger, Robert, 139
Waldron, Patty, 191
Wallace, Monica, 227–28
Wall Street Journal, 55
warmth, 188–90
weight training, 98–99
Weisinger, Hendrie, 176
Weissbourd, Richard, 68, 69, 75, 76, 80, 82
Western State Connecticut University, 148
Wharton, Edith, 84
Whiting, Brandon, 151–52
Who Gets In and Why (Selingo), 48–49
whole family, 171–76
　delaying start of sports, 172
　just saying no, 174–75
　knowing the coach, 175–76
　objecting every now and then, 173–74
　staying local, 173
Wilde, Oscar, 161
WinterGreen Research, 5
women coaches, 132–34
women's collegiate sports, 50–51
　role of Title IX, 50, 70, 116, 122, 133–34,
　　219, 240
Woods, Tiger, 20

YES Network, 5
YMCA, 8, 11, 117, 146
Young, Damon, 99, 147
Young, Jacqui, 75